THE SNATCH RACKET

The Snatch Racket

The Kidnapping Epidemic That Terrorized 1930s America

CAROLYN COX

Potomac Books

AN IMPRINT OF THE UNIVERSITY OF NEBRASKA PRESS

All rights reserved. Potomac Books is an imprint of the University
of Nebraska Press.
Manufactured in the United States of America.

∞

Library of Congress Cataloging-in-Publication Data
Names: Cox, Carolyn, 1949– author.
Title: The snatch racket: the kidnapping epidemic that terrorized 1930s
America / Carolyn Cox.
Description: [Lincoln, Nebraska]: Potomac Books, an imprint of the
University of Nebraska Press, [2021] | Includes bibliographical references
and index.
Identifiers: LCCN 2020022808
ISBN 9781640122031 (hardback)
ISBN 9781640124325 (epub)
ISBN 9781640124332 (mobi)
ISBN 9781640124349 (pdf)
Subjects: LCSH: Kidnapping—United States—History—20th century.
Classification: LCC HV6598 .C69 2021 | DDC 364.15/4097309033—dc23
LC record available at https://lccn.loc.gov/2020022808

Set in Arno Pro by Laura Buis.

For Sam

CONTENTS

ILLUSTRATIONS

Following page 156

THE SNATCH RACKET

....

Prologue

Detroit, July 1929

"Give them what they want. For God's sake don't go to the police."

Those were the words, in his son's handwriting, that persuaded Gerson Cass to drive through the dark streets of Detroit's west side, stand on the corner of Chicago Boulevard and Lawton Street, and hand a package containing $4,000 in $20 bills to a stranger who walked by and whispered the word "eight."

As the man walked away with the package, another stranger stepped from the shadows, pointed his gun at the man, and ordered him to freeze. He ran instead, as three other detectives, tipped off by an informant, opened fire. Cass watched in despair as Joseph "Legs" Laman, his only link to his son's kidnappers, went down with a police bullet in his spine. Two hundred $20 bills spilled onto the ground.

Gerson Cass was a wealthy Detroit real estate developer and friend of Henry Ford. Three days before delivering the money to Laman, he had answered the telephone at his home at 4:00 a.m. The voice on the other end said the dreaded words, "We have your son." It would cost $25,000 to get him back. Twenty-three-year-old David Cass worked for his father. He also gambled heavily, which brought him into contact with the wrong kinds of people. A pitiful note from David convinced Gerson he had no choice but to do as the kidnappers demanded. "Dear Dad," wrote David. "The boys got me. They are touching me and I am sick. Give them what they want. For God's sake don't go to the police."[1] Gerson bargained the ransom down to $4,000 (about $60,000 in 2020).

The hospital doctors misled Laman into believing he wouldn't survive his wounds; the detectives sat at his bedside for weeks. They were finally rewarded for their patience when he gave them the names of seven members of his kidnap gang, including those hiding David. The police arrested them, though not before they had panicked, murdered David, and dumped his body into the Flint River. Laman survived after all and went to prison for extortion. The police pronounced his kidnap gang "smashed to bits."[2]

At twenty-eight, Legs Laman, known for his long legs and fleet feet, was the leader of a gang of young thugs, mostly Irish, who specialized in kidnapping bootleggers, gamblers, and other well-to-do lawbreakers in Prohibition-era Detroit. In their previous lives they had been pickpockets, rumrunners, armed robbers, and murderers. While the Laman Gang was hardly the only kidnap gang in the Motor City, it was one of the first to use kidnapping as something other than a nasty way to punish underworld enemies. They envisioned the "snatch racket" as a lucrative, stand-alone business of snatching vulnerable men or family members with access to money.

They were right about the money: the ordinary bootlegger or gambler—even many law-abiding husbands stepping out on their wives—would readily pay $5,000 or even $25,000 (between $75,000 and $375,000 in 2020) for his life. They were also right that the shady characters and rich men with dark secrets they had in their sights (they called them "wiseguys") wouldn't want to report their kidnappings to the police or cooperate with them in catching their kidnappers.

No matter how lucrative it might be, though, there had always been a particular stench about kidnapping for ransom—most criminals drew the line at kidnapping. That was why the snatch racket seemed like such a good opportunity to Laman and the criminals he met in prison. Five of them managed to get released on parole around the same time in May 1928, and they all headed for Detroit to launch their business. In little over a year, the gang had twenty members and claimed credit for kidnapping thirty wiseguys and collecting more than half a million dollars in ransom money (almost $7.5 million in 2020)—without a single arrest or conviction.[3] Then it all began to unravel with the ill-fated snatch of the blue-blooded gambler David Cass.

The secret to the Laman Gang's remarkable success was their reliance on what came to be known as "the System." They divided every kidnapping job into the same basic tasks and assigned specific individuals to each one. The "finger man" identified a potential target and investigated to make sure he could pay the ransom in cash. (The gang learned the hard way that promissory notes never worked out.) The finger man also observed the target (the "package") going about his daily routines to help plan the when, where, and how of the snatch.

At least two, and no more than four, masked "pickup men" abducted the package, ideally when he was driving or walking alone, and either hijacked his car or forced him at gunpoint into theirs. As soon as they could manage it without being seen, they strapped goggles with adhesive-taped lenses over his eyes, bound his hands, shoved him face down onto the floorboards, and started out for the hideout where they planned to keep him until they collected the ransom (the "castle").

"Keepers" guarded the package and provided food and drink. They made sure the package remained blindfolded except when he sat in the corner with his back to the room to eat or write notes urging his family or business associates to pay the ransom. The notes were typically dictated by the "voice," whose job was to communicate with the package without the package ever seeing him. If the package didn't cooperate in writing the notes, the keepers were expected to use torture. They might "toast" the victim's skin with lighted matches, cigars, or cigarettes; pluck his eyelashes out; or "play poker" by singeing his eyes or skin with hot pokers. Some keepers tied their packages up and stood them against a wall or a tree for "fancy shooters" to fire bullets that grazed their skin.[4]

Communicating with the victim's representatives to make the necessary arrangements for the ransom posed the greatest risk of apprehension for the kidnappers. They had to fix the amount of money and the denominations of the bills, as well as specify the time, place, and manner of the delivery—all without revealing their identity or providing an opportunity for the police or private detectives to disrupt the payoff. Since communications by mail, telephone, and in person were too easy to monitor or intercept, the kidnappers often proposed an intermediary acceptable to both parties, often a racketeer or other borderline character known to both parties; sometimes the go-between was a clergyman. The intermediary would pass messages back and forth to finalize the deal; in some cases he would also deliver the ransom money.

Finally, there was often a "front man," someone who wasn't a member of the gang but stood ready to assist the gang, if necessary, by hiring lawyers or bribing police, judges, witnesses or jurors. When the System functioned properly, the victim's representatives never saw the kidnappers, and the police never knew who to watch or wiretap to lead them to the kidnappers.

Two months after he was convicted for his role in David Cass's kidnapping, Legs Laman was convicted of another, previous kidnapping and sentenced to forty more years in prison. The police tricked him into believing his fellow gang members had reneged on their promise to take care of his family while he was incarcerated. Laman decided to strike back at them and chop years off his sentence at the same time by turning state's evidence. He gave the police the names of additional Laman Gang members and revealed their plans to kidnap other children of wealthy Detroit families, including an alleged plot to gun down the bodyguards protecting the children of Henry Ford's son, Edsel, and kidnap them.[5] He explained how the System worked and testified in court against the members of his gang.

Once again, the police announced they had destroyed Laman's gang and with it the kidnap threat in Detroit. Other kidnap gangs, however, were now operating their own versions of the System not only in Detroit but also in St. Louis, Kansas City, Chicago, Peoria, and other large cities. The snatch racket was fanning out through the Midwest and heading for the East and West Coasts.

Legs Laman and his long-forgotten gang pioneered the System that made ransom kidnapping a profitable business and triggered a kidnap epidemic in America in the last days of Prohibition. Stretching federal powers to the limit and then expanding those powers, President Franklin D. Roosevelt and his new administration launched a war against kidnappers that changed law enforcement in America forever. This is the story of that epidemic and that war.

One

....

The Snatch Racket

1

....

The Good Samaritans

St. Louis, April–August 1931

Dr. Dee Kelley's every instinct told him not to leave his comfortable chair by the fireplace and venture out into the heavy downpour to meet a stranger with a peculiar request.

The telephone rang in his library about 9:15 p.m., and he got up to answer it. A man identifying himself as "Mr. Holmes" asked Kelley to make a house call to treat his young nephew's earache. He said he was making the call because the boy's family had recently moved to St. Louis and didn't have a telephone yet. A Dr. Ballenger, who had treated the boy in Chicago, recommended his parents contact Dr. Kelley if he needed a doctor after the move. Holmes offered to pick him up and drive him to the boy's house, but Kelley said that wouldn't be necessary and asked for directions. Holmes paused, then said he would have to contact the parents to get them. Taken aback, Kelley began to wonder who this man Holmes was. He asked him to find out from the parents whether the boy really needed a doctor that night. "If he really is suffering, I will be very glad to come," he said. Holmes promised to call back.[1]

As he hung up, Kelley told his wife, Kathleen, there was something odd about the call: why didn't Holmes know the way to the child's house? What bothered him even more, he realized, was that earaches normally aren't late night emergencies. Kathleen agreed there was something not quite right about this Mr. Holmes and told Dee she didn't want him going out on this call. He sat back down and reached for his book, hoping he had heard the last from Holmes.

Forty-five minutes later, the telephone rang again. It was Holmes, reporting that the boy was in pain and the parents wanted him to come right away. As he gave the address and directions, Kelley repeated them aloud and jotted them down. He recognized the name of the street, Oleta Drive, and began to relax. It was located in the Davis Place subdivision in St. Louis County. The large, English-style Tudors and brick colonials there were the kinds of homes where many of his patients lived. Holmes promised to be waiting at the house.

Kelley grabbed his raincoat and medical bag. He backed his black Lincoln out of the garage and into wide, tree-lined Portland Place. Rain poured as he drove past the stone guard tower and through the iron gates that protected the exclusive enclave where forty-three of St. Louis's wealthiest and most prominent families lived.

Dr. Isaac Dee Kelley Jr. was from one of St. Louis's oldest families. He was descended from the French pioneer Jean Lajoie, one of the founders of the city in 1764. At six feet two inches tall and just over two hundred pounds, Kelley had been known as a scrapper from back when he played football for St. Louis University. While serving as a medical officer for British and American forces in France during World War I, he was the only officer in his battalion to survive a German attack. Now, at age forty-five, he was St. Louis's leading ear, nose, and throat specialist. He would have had a busy, prestigious practice even if he made no house calls, but he took pride in never shirking an emergency call no matter the hour.

Kathleen was wealthy and socially prominent in her own right: her father, the late William Cullen McBride, had been one of the nation's largest independent oil producers before selling his holdings to Standard Oil. She and Dee had a son off at boarding school and two young daughters at home.

Heavy rain pounded Kelley's windscreen, but even in the pitch black of the unlit county road, he easily located 835 Oleta Drive, one of only two houses on the street. Turning into the driveway, he realized right away that neither the outside lights nor the indoor lights on the ground floor were on. There was no sign of Holmes either. He took a moment to look around and spotted a car parked around the corner that appeared to be occupied. Probably just spooners, he thought. Just the same, he decided to remain in his car and honk the horn.

As he waited, Kelley could make out a man in suspenders looking down from an upstairs window. Was he Holmes? Why didn't he go down and open the front door? Before he could make up his mind whether to follow his instincts and drive away or ignore them and ring the doorbell, a Ford quietly rolled in behind his Lincoln and blocked the driveway. A man with a handkerchief over his face got out and opened Kelley's passenger door.[2]

"Don't look at me," warned the gunman, as he stuck a pistol into Kelley's ribs. He ordered him to drive out the other end of the circular driveway and follow his directions from there. Though angry that he had allowed himself to become such an easy target for a holdup, Kelley remained calm and even managed to slide the platinum and diamond ring from his finger and hide it in the seat cushion as he steered. After a short drive, the gunman ordered him to stop the car, and a second man climbed into the back seat. When the two men didn't then take his wallet and tell him he could go, Kelley finally realized he'd been kidnapped.[3]

Back at the house on Oleta Drive, the man in the upstairs window, Preston Sultan, had thought no more about the unfamiliar car driving through the driveway. Sultan was a minor St. Louis celebrity: a World War I flying ace and now a business partner of aviation hero Charles Lindbergh. He was staying that night at the home of his sister Ethel while her husband, Estes Pershall, was away on business. The year before, gangsters had snatched Estes's brother Charles Pershall, who owned a bank and a chain of grocery stores in the St. Louis area. His family had paid $40,000 for his release (about $614,000 in 2020 dollars), and Charles was still fighting with the Internal Revenue Bureau about deducting the ransom payment from his income tax as a business expense. Ever since the kidnapping, Ethel had felt uncomfortable staying alone when her husband was away.[4]

Until he picked up a newspaper two days later and read about the Kelley kidnapping, Preston Sultan had no idea what it was he had witnessed from Ethel's upstairs window on the night of April 20, 1931.[5]

After a short drive, the kidnappers ordered Kelley out of his car, blindfolded him, pulled a hood down over his head, and forced him into another car and down onto the floor. After several more stops, they reached their destination: a rundown farmhouse with creaky stairs and missing treads leading up to a musty attic. Kelley was still wearing his rain-soaked clothes and waterlogged shoes when the kidnappers shoved him down onto an iron cot. They took his wristwatch, wallet, keys, pipe, and tobacco pouch, then demanded he hand over his pearl tie pin.

Kelley shivered as the cold wind penetrated the flimsy attic walls. He asked for covers and for water. The kidnappers brought him a cup and lifted his hood long enough for him to take a drink. In the dim lantern light, he caught a glimpse of a man in a mask— like a pirate, he thought. The rough bed clothing reminded him of France during the war when the soldiers would go to the stables and borrow blankets from the horses. Cold, alone, and in the dark, Kelley thought of his family and how anxious they must be. He resented how the kidnappers had taken advantage of his willingness to go out alone at night to help a sick child he didn't even know.[6]

The following morning the kidnappers drove Kelley to a second hideout. The familiar sound of a toll gate told him they were crossing a bridge over the Mississippi River and into East St. Louis in Illinois. Once settled in the new hideout, the kidnappers demanded he give them the name of a criminal lawyer they could deal with to arrange his ransom payment. Kelley bristled; he told them he was a doctor and didn't know any lawyers except as patients. But by day's end he had given them the names of a dozen lawyers, refusing to put another innocent person at risk by singling out anyone in particular. He had also followed orders and written two notes the kidnappers dictated urging Kathleen to pay the ransom of $250,000 (over $4.2 million in 2020).

The preliminaries were now completed, and Kelley's wait began. When he wasn't eating or being shuttled among five shabby hideouts, he had nothing to do but read detective stories the kidnappers brought. They hardly spoke to him; when they did, it was usually to raise false hopes that he was about to be released or to warn him not to tell the police anything. "You know, there's a lot of doorsteps dirtied up on account of telling too much," his keepers told him several times. "If you do some talking, some of these days you'll be hearing about doorsteps on Portland Place getting smeared up."[7] To relieve their own boredom, the kidnappers clicked the safety catches on their automatic pistols, over and over.

Kelley refused to let himself become rattled, but as the days dragged on, he kept coming back to the question, "Why me?"

For twenty years Nellie Tipton Muench had owned one of the most exclusive dress shops in St. Louis. The Mitzi Shop sold dresses to society ladies and delivered them to their homes in a white Cadillac limousine. The shop also did a good business selling lingerie to the ladies' husbands, though not always for their wives.

Nellie and her husband, Dr. Ludwig O. Muench, were well known quite apart from her shop. Ludwig was the chief of staff at St. Louis's prestigious Barnes Hospital and a cellist of local renown; Nellie herself was an accomplished pianist. The Muenches were active in St. Louis music circles and often opened their comfortable Westminster Place home to perform duets and host chamber music events. The couple had "many warm friends in St. Louis," occupying "an enviable social position," according to the *Centennial History of Missouri*.[8] Nellie came from a prominent and respected Missouri family. Her father, the Reverend William M. Tipton, had been a Baptist minister for more than forty years; her brother Ernest, a college football coach turned lawyer, would soon be elected to the Missouri Supreme Court.[9]

Though Nellie moved among St. Louis's socially prominent, she was "in trade" and not a member of the social elite herself. One of her favorite pastimes was observing and exploiting the foibles of St. Louis's high and mighty. She wrote contemptuously of the "sheltered and protected wives and daughters of the so-called socially and semi-socially prominent":

> I wonder if the idea ever occurs to them of some of the Bacchanalian orgies that take place behind closed doors in well protected spots in the city. [My shop] was in close proximity and within plain view of several of the fashionable establishments of ill repute. It was a continual source of amusement both to myself and my employees to recognize some of the socially and semi-socially prominent faces coming and going. The "Mesdames" and the subjects who held themselves on call were patrons of my shop, as were many of the wives and daughters of their customers.[10]

One of Nellie's favorite scams was sending bills to recent widows for intimate apparel she claimed their husbands had purchased before they passed away. She also filed false insurance claims for allegedly lost or stolen jewelry, but it all collapsed in 1928 when unpaid creditors forced the Mitzi Shop into bankruptcy, and Nellie went to work at another shop.[11]

Once her shop closed, the ordinariness of her life with Ludwig became intolerable. Nellie began frequenting "recreation establishments" in and around St. Louis where a variety of illegal entertainments, especially drinking and gambling, were freely available without interference from law enforcement. Though she remained true to her Baptist upbringing and didn't drink or smoke, Nellie loved the excitement of mixing with the kinds of people she met at places like Adolph Fiedler's pool hall, otherwise known as the "Arcade Country Club." The most interesting people she met there were gangsters. One in particular, Angelo Rosegrant, was handsome and dressed like a well-to-do businessman, yet he had an air of going places and doing things Ludwig Muench could never have imagined. Chatting with Angelo and his drinking buddies about ways to make big money in a hurry was how Nellie Muench, the preacher's daughter and doctor's wife, became the finger person who identified the well-connected Dr. Dee Kelley, with access to the McBride fortune, as a good kidnap prospect.

Kelley wasn't Nellie's first choice. That was Oscar Johnson II, known as Jack, whose late father was a founder of the International Shoe Company, the largest shoe manufacturer in the world. Jack still lived in the house he grew up in, two doors down on Portland Place from Dee and Kathleen Kelley. The twenty-six-year-old bachelor didn't have a regular job, but he devoted much of his time to playing the piano, and he was about to become president of the St. Louis Symphony Society. Jack was traveling, however, and wasn't in town when Nellie tried to gather information about his daily routines to plan his snatch. So she scratched Jack Johnson off her list, at least for now.

Nellie also considered sixteen-year-old Jacqueline Busch Jones, the granddaughter of August Anheuser Busch Sr., head of the Anheuser-Busch Brewing Company. Jacqueline lived with her parents at Grant's Farm, her grandfather's 281-acre estate in St. Louis County. The problem with Jacqueline was that her cousin, thirteen-year-old Adolphus Busch "Buppie" Orthwein, had been kidnapped recently from his parents' country estate in St. Louis County. Nellie suspected that security surrounding the Busch family would be too tight.

That left Dee Kelley as the best prospect for quick money without unnecessary complications. Nellie turned her attention to figuring out how to get him alone in a place where he could be snatched without any witnesses. Being a doctor's wife herself, Nellie thought of grabbing him when he was making a house call late at night. But would a prominent ear, nose, and throat specialist even make house calls?

Leaving nothing to conjecture, Nellie arranged for a colleague at her new dress shop to sell an expensive evening gown—in the wrong size—to Kathleen Kelley. When the gown was delivered and Kathleen called the shop to return it, Nellie kindly offered to go to her home to see whether it could be altered to fit. Invited into Kathleen's bedroom for the fitting, Nellie took a good look around. She commented on the photograph of Dee on Kathleen's dressing table and commiserated with her about the annoyances of being a doctor's wife, especially late-night house calls. Kathleen admitted she didn't like it when her husband went out at night, but she said she knew it was important to him to be available when his patients needed him.[12]

When it got to be past midnight on that rainy night and Kathleen still hadn't heard from Dee, she knew something must be terribly wrong: he always telephoned when he didn't expect to make it home by midnight. She worried that he might have had an accident in the downpour and called one of the family's lawyers, R. D. Fitzgibbon. He reported the disappearance to the police and then headed to the Kelley home, where he began calling hospitals. Then he called every "Holmes" in the St. Louis telephone directory, but no one had called Dr. Kelley that night. Kathleen recalled that Dee had said the sick child lived in the Davis Place subdivision. Fitzgibbon rode with sheriff's deputies through every street in Davis Place, but they found no trace of Kelley.

Incredulous family members, friends, and lawyers gathered during the night and early morning hours at the Kelleys' Beaux

Arts mansion on Portland Place. Many of the same people had waited with Percy and Clara Orthwein four months before, on New Year's Eve, when a lone gunman kidnapped their son (and August Anheuser Busch's grandson) Buppie. (Kathleen Kelley's sister Dorothy was married to Buppie's cousin Bill Orthwein.) They wanted to believe that Buppie's safe return was reason to be optimistic about Dee, but those who knew Kelley best worried he might take chances or suffer abuse rather than cooperate with his captors. He was feisty and determined, and he never shied away from a fight or forgave an injury. He had even been known to sue acquaintances who wronged him over very small sums.[13]

Early the next morning, a St. Louis County deputy sheriff located Kelley's abandoned Lincoln, with his medical bag and diamond ring, near one of the bridges crossing the Mississippi between St. Louis and East St. Louis. Detectives began picking up members of the most active kidnap gangs—the Cuckoos, Hogans, Sheltons, and East Siders—on trumped up vagrancy charges, but after grilling them without result about the Kelley snatch, they released them all before noon.

Kathleen's brother-in-law Bill Orthwein cut short his business trip to Memphis and returned to St. Louis to take charge of what he called the "executive committee" of lawyers, friends, and family enlisted by Kathleen to do whatever it took to secure Kelley's release. He quietly passed the word to the reporters camped out on Portland Place that there was no limit to the amount Mrs. Kelley was prepared to pay for her husband's safe return, but she would need proof he was still alive.

Several days went by without the kidnappers establishing contact. Orthwein received several telephone calls; each time the voice on the other end of the line—always the same voice—would say, "Mr. Orthwein, Mr. Orthwein." Then there would be a click, and he would hang up, suspecting, correctly, that the police had tapped the lines. Finally, one of the kidnappers called the wife of one of the family's lawyers and told her that there was a message for Mrs. Kelley in a particular mailbox in rural St. Louis County.

The lawyers sped to the mailbox and retrieved an envelope containing Kelley's pearl tie pin and a note in his handwriting asking Kathleen to get in touch with a criminal lawyer in St. Louis named Sigmund Bass. The tie pin and the note weren't proof Kelley was alive, but they were evidence, at least, that the family was finally in contact with the real kidnappers and not opportunistic extortionists seeking to capitalize on the real kidnappers' crime.

In the meantime a well-known St. Louis lawyer suggested to Bill Orthwein that he contact John Rogers, the veteran crime reporter for the *St. Louis Post-Dispatch*. Rogers had investigated organized crime in the St. Louis area for years and had already won a Pulitzer Prize for his reporting. If anyone could help get Dr. Kelley back, the lawyer said, it would be Rogers.[14]

Events moved quickly after that. Rogers advised Orthwein to retain an Illinois lawyer who practiced in East St. Louis, for two reasons: first, the widely held belief at that time that retaining a licensed lawyer to advise a kidnap victim's family protected them from possible criminal charges for paying the ransom and helping the kidnappers escape; second, an East St. Louis criminal lawyer's contacts could be useful in making contact with the East St. Louis gangs that had been snatching St. Louisans recently. Rogers recommended Charles A. Karch for the job: he sometimes represented East St. Louis gangsters in criminal matters and was now East St. Louis's representative in Congress.

Karch agreed to do what he could, with two caveats: he would not "barter with the underworld," and his representation would cost at least $7,500 (over $126,000 in 2020).[15] In other words he wouldn't jeopardize his law license by assisting a criminal act or compounding the kidnappers' felony, but he wanted authority and latitude to do what he had to do without having to report his specific activities to his clients.[16] Orthwein authorized Karch to pay whatever he had to pay.[17] Rogers then confirmed with Karch one additional aspect of the three-way arrangement: "Charlie, if you find Dr. Kelley, I want to see him ahead of any other newspaper man." "Don't worry," replied Karch, "I've never failed you yet, have I?"[18] In other words, for his part in the arrangement, whatever that might be, Rogers would get the first crack at interviewing Kelley after his release.

The following morning, Monday, Karch called on Sigmund Bass, the lawyer Dee's note directed Kathleen to contact. Bass was a well-known criminal lawyer who frequently represented St. Louis–area gangsters. That afternoon Karch met with another lawyer, Anthony Canzoneri, who often represented Italian gangsters in criminal matters. Both Bass and Canzoneri later claimed they told Karch they didn't want to have anything to do with the kidnapping of Dr. Kelley. Nonetheless Karch was satisfied he had made contact with lawyers he had reason to believe could get negotiations going.[19]

All day Monday and late into the night, Orthwein, Rogers, and other members of the executive committee continued trying to make contact with the kidnappers while doing their best to elude the police and reporters. One of their greatest fears was that the police would learn of an attempt to pay the ransom and either sabotage it or take the kidnappers into custody, or even kill them, before Kelley was released.

At 1:15 Tuesday morning, Rogers received a call at his home from a man who didn't identify himself. "A friend of yours wants to see you," the man said. "You'll be glad to meet him." He told Rogers to drive to the intersection of Grand and Finney Boulevards in central St. Louis, then flash his headlights a couple of times.

Rogers did as he was told. When he flashed his headlights, a man with a cover over his face got into the car and told him to head toward East St. Louis.[20] They crossed the Mississippi and continued eastward. After they exchanged flashing headlight signals with another car on a dark country road, he told Rogers to stop at an abandoned filling station nearby, where he said Dr. Kelley would be standing with his back to the road. "Take him home," he said, as if Kelley had had too much to drink after a night of carousing. He handed Rogers a package containing Kelley's wallet, wristwatch, keys, and lighter. Then he slammed the car door and dashed across the road to a waiting car.

Rogers rolled slowly into the filling station and pulled up alongside a broad-shouldered man in a filthy raincoat. "Is this Dr. Kelley?" he asked. The man turned around. A pair of cheap goggles with adhesive-taped lenses perched on top of his head; a cigarette dangled between his fingers.

"Yes. Is this Mr. Rogers? The man who let me out here said, 'John Rogers of the *Post-Dispatch* will take you home. Do what he tells you. He was the only person in St. Louis who helped you.'"

"Get in here quick and let's get out of here," said Rogers.[21]

It took a few moments for Kelley to realize his seven-day ordeal was finally over. "My poor family," he said. "I suppose they had to pay a large sum of money."

"I didn't pay anything, doctor," replied Rogers.[22]

As they drove away, Rogers told Kelley that instead of taking him home to Portland Place, he was taking him to his own home, where he could call his family. Then Kelley was to give Rogers and his *Post-Dispatch* colleagues a detailed account of everything he had been through. Kelley was confused: he had assumed, naturally, that he would go straight home and that he would heed the kidnappers' warnings to say nothing to the police or anyone else about his experience. But he also remembered that his kidnappers had told him, not once but twice, to do exactly what Rogers told him to do. So Kelley spent the first three hours after his release giving John Rogers one of the biggest scoops of his stellar career.

Once he got started, the voluble Kelley could hardly stop. "It seemed like the events of a dime novel," he said, with machine guns, diamond rings, and gangsters with the faces of pirates outlined in lantern light. "Those fellows mean business," he said, describing them as well-educated, "scientific operators." "You haven't got a chance with them. And don't think they don't work hard in their occupation. Kidnapping is a twenty-four-hour-day job. Those fellows had as hard a time as I had."[23]

Kelley's exclusive accounts of his kidnapping and release ran on the front pages of the *Post-Dispatch* and newspapers around the country. Soon after they appeared, Rogers received another telephone call. He recognized the voice as that of the man who had given him the directions for picking up Kelley. "Tell those people," the voice said, "that everything is all right, nothing to be afraid of—nobody is going to get hurt." Rogers delivered the message to Kelley, who understood it immediately: the doorsteps of his Portland Place neighbors would not be "smeared up" because he had told his story to Rogers.[24]

Congressman Karch issued a statement saying that he had no idea Kelley was going to be released or how it had come about.[25] Bill Orthwein insisted that "not a dime" had been paid in ransom.[26] The police were frustrated. They didn't believe for a minute that the kidnappers had released Kelley without collecting a ransom. They expected a lack of cooperation when underworld figures and other borderline victims were kidnapped, but Dr. Kelley was professionally and socially prominent as well as wealthy. If victims like Kelley and their families didn't trust the police enough to cooperate with them, how were the police going to stop kidnappings?

The *Post-Dispatch*'s archrival, the *St. Louis Star and Times*, lambasted Rogers for failing to notify the police that he was going to meet a stranger connected with Kelley's kidnappers, arguing that the police might have captured the kidnappers if they had known of the rendezvous.[27] The paper harshly criticized the Kelleys, too. They have a "solemn duty to the public, to their neighbors, to every person now living under the shadow of the kidnapping menace to tell the whole truth about the return of Dr. Kelley," they wrote. "Kidnapping can't be fought in the dark."[28] The Kelleys, their lawyers, Orthwein, Karch, and Rogers would say only that they had nothing more to say.

In the coming years, however, it would come to light that eyebrow-raising sums of money had indeed changed hands. Rogers's boss at the *Post-Dispatch*, Joseph Pulitzer II, had paid him a bonus equal to a year's pay for about five days' work on the case,[29] while Kathleen Kelley's family coffers had paid Congressman Karch a legal fee of $1,500 (over $25,000 in 2020) for two days' work,[30] plus an additional $11,000 (over $185,000 in 2020) for expenses he was not expected to explain.[31] (Despite their public denials of involvement in securing Kelley's release, it is worth noting that Karch and Rogers would team up at least once more to arrange a St. Louis kidnap victim's release and would offer to provide similar assistance when Charles A. Lindbergh Jr. was kidnapped the following year.)

Three months later, on a Sunday afternoon in August, Kelley's neighbor Jack Johnson, the International Shoe heir, was driving back to town in his sixteen-cylinder Cadillac roadster after spending the weekend at his mother's summer home west of St. Louis. As he neared a bend in the road and slowed down, two big, muscular men got out of a Ford coupe and flagged him down on the pretext they were out of gasoline. Jack stopped, and the men drew handkerchiefs up over their faces. One pulled out a sawed-off shotgun, and the other flashed a pistol. They opened the doors of the roadster and slid in, wedging Jack between them. As the driver took off, Jack handed over his wallet and told the men they could have the car, too, but when the two thugs ordered him to put on a pair of smoked glasses and stick his head under the dashboard, the 130-pound musician decided he would rather fight back than be kidnapped. He thrashed around, kicked, and banged the car key until it broke off in the ignition, disabling the car.

The thugs then dragged Jack to a nearby cornfield, where they beat him in the head with their guns. "You are the toughest guy we ever got hold of," one muttered. When they'd had enough, they fled on foot with Jack's wallet and $70. Jack ended up in Barnes Hospital (where Dr. Ludwig Muench, coincidentally, was chief of staff) with fractured ribs, broken teeth, and severe lacerations.[32]

An hour later the police picked up two men in torn clothes walking along a road near the cornfield who fit the descriptions of eyewitnesses who had seen the fight. From his hospital bed Jack identified Felix McDonald as one of his attackers, but he couldn't be sure about the other, Bart Davit. McDonald and Davit were "alky cookers," known to the police for making moonshine whiskey and working as muscle men for a big-time St. Louis gangster named Tommy Hayes, of the East Side Gang. Hayes and his gang had always been leading suspects in the Kelley kidnapping, but the police had no evidence. Now they had a possible basis for linking McDonald and Davit's attempted kidnapping of Jack Johnson with the unsolved kidnapping of Dee Kelley: both victims had been snatched while trying to be Good Samaritans and help strangers in need.

The police still had no reason to suspect Nellie Muench, the bored doctor's wife turned finger person. It would be another three years before Nellie's friend Adolph Fiedler, proprietor of the Arcade Country Club, would sell his story to John Rogers's *Post-Dispatch* and tell how Nellie, Angelo Rosegrant, and their accomplices, including McDonald and Davit, had plotted the kidnappings of Kelley and Johnson in his pool hall and had used his telephone to place the two calls that brought Dee Kelley out that night to help the child with the earache.[33]

By the time those revelations were made, Tommy Hayes and two other Kelley kidnappers had been murdered by rival gangsters. The poor farmer who let the kidnappers hide Kelley in his drafty attic confessed and turned state's evidence. Hit men murdered him before he could tell his story of the Kelley kidnapping in court.[34]

2

"This . . . Is Not Manchuria or China or Russia"

St. Louis, Kansas City, and Washington, December 1931–February 1932

The kidnapping of Dr. Dee Kelley thoroughly roiled St. Louis. The snatch of a rich, prominent family man willing to tell the story of his abduction and captivity was rare; the newspapers covered it unsparingly. The consensus was that the kidnappers were experienced professionals: they expertly lured Kelley from the gated and guarded confines of Portland Place to a dark county road in a sparsely populated suburb and managed to hide him for seven days and nights in five different places in two states. And yet Kelley seemed an unusual target for professionals: he had no apparent ties to the underworld, nor any secret life to shield from the police that would have made him vulnerable in the eyes of kidnap gangs. Were all wealthy St. Louisans now potential kidnap targets?

Coming less than four months after the armed kidnapping of August Anheuser Busch's grandson Buppie Orthwein, the Kelley kidnapping again brought unflattering media attention to St. Louis. In a dispatch titled "Kidnappers Have Taken Heavy Toll in Middlewest in Recent Months," the United Press thematically linked the kidnapping to more than twenty recent kidnappings of wealthy men that have "so alarmed midwestern citizens that [vigilante] movements are under way in many cities for an organized offensive against what police say has become one of the most lucrative of all 'rackets.'"[1] The *Chicago Tribune* needled its rival city by calling organized kidnapping "St. Louis' contribution to contemporary crime."[2]

As long as kidnapping had been a crime gangsters perpetrated against other gangsters, it had remained largely invisible outside the underworld and of little public concern, even in St. Louis, but when "legitimate" citizens like Buppie Orthwein, Dee Kelley, and Jack Johnson were snatched, many of St. Louis's wealthy and prominent began to see themselves as potential targets. Some started leaving their limousines in the garage and going about in their less conspicuous sedans and coupes with the doors locked, their chauffeurs armed, and loaded handguns and sawed-off shotguns on the seat beside them.[3] Kelley's brother-in-law Bill Orthwein, as well as several of Kelley's Portland Place neighbors, obtained firearm permits.[4] Since his grandson's kidnapping, Busch had carried a pair of loaded revolvers wherever he went and tucked a double-barreled derringer inside his fedora.[5] The sixty-six-year-old, who blamed bootleggers and gangsters for all kidnapping, refused to be intimidated: "I can shoot as straight as they can," he said.[6]

The Kelley kidnapping also galvanized St. Louis's business community into action. As chambers of commerce across the country were slowly awakening to the growth of organized crime and beginning to launch antiracketeering campaigns in their cities, members of the St. Louis Chamber of Commerce recognized that nothing would be more detrimental to the city's aspirations to become a major industrial and commercial center than a reputation for the kidnapping of its citizens and visitors.

The St. Louis Chamber was always looking for ways to market St. Louis as a major city to outsiders. In the 1920s it began promoting the idea of a "spirit of St. Louis" that "seemed to explain and guarantee progress."[7] In their desire to promote St. Louis and its promising future, members of the Chamber in 1927 provided financial backing for an unknown, young pilot flying the U.S. Mail between St. Louis and Chicago who believed he could become the first person to fly nonstop between New York and Paris. Charles A. Lindbergh named his plane the *Spirit of St. Louis*; St. Louis had basked in the luster of its special relationship with him ever since. Now, just four years later, St. Louis was called the kidnap capital of America.

After the Kelley kidnapping, the president of the St. Louis Chamber, Walter B. Weisenburger, convened a group of prominent St. Louisans to come up with a plan for attacking the kidnap problem. One after another, leading citizens, in an outpouring of emotion, admitted living in fear that they or their families or friends would be the next to be kidnapped.[8] They were fed up with carrying guns and locking themselves inside their cars, and they were convinced the situation would only get worse when Prohibition came to an end, which was expected soon. With gangsters and bootleggers already looking for alternate sources of revenue to replace the proceeds of illegal alcohol, the demand for wealthy kidnap targets could easily skyrocket.

Weisenburger's group wanted to act quickly to send a message both to kidnap gangs and to elite citizens that St. Louis was punching back. Following the examples of businessmen in Chicago and Kansas City, they set up a private organization called the Crime Investigating Bureau to assist the police by investigating kidnappings in secret, using paid informants.[9] They hired as the Bureau's investigator the retired postal inspector A. D. Bunsen, seventy, whose detective career dated back to the 1870s, when he rode stagecoaches to protect the mail from Jesse James and his gang.[10]

The model for the Crime Investigating Bureau was Chicago's Citizens' Committee for the Prevention and Punishment of Crime, a private group of six anonymous businessmen formed in 1930 to investigate crime by Chicago gangs. Better known as the "Secret Six," its ultimate goal was to destroy organized crime in Chicago.

Its greatest accomplishment was assisting (and helping finance) federal efforts to obtain the evidence to convict Al Capone of income tax evasion, but the Secret Six also claimed credit for solving twenty-five kidnapping and extortion cases.[11] By interviewing witnesses and informants in secret, away from police stations and courtrooms, the Secret Six circumvented, to a degree, the codes of silence and methods of intimidating witnesses and jurors that organized crime successfully employed in many major cities to sabotage the prosecutions of gangsters.

The backers of St. Louis's Crime Investigating Bureau hoped it might help bring at least some kidnappers to justice, but they were under no illusion that the gumshoe Bunsen would put a dent in kidnapping in America's kidnap capital. Already home to some of the Midwest's most violent gangs of Sicilian and Neapolitan immigrants, St. Louis had attracted a steady stream of veteran kidnappers experienced in the Laman Gang's System who began heading south in 1929 after the Detroit police moved against the Laman Gang and other Detroit kidnap gangs. The trend was alarming.

The business and civic leaders behind the Crime Investigating Bureau understood they were dealing with organized crime and with a patchwork of multiple state and local law enforcement jurisdictions that had so far proved impotent and even complicit in the face of the rapidly growing menace. Realizing they needed a different law enforcement approach to defeat kidnapping, they decided to concentrate on the ultimate goal of persuading Congress to make kidnapping for ransom a federal crime.

One obvious problem with their strategy was that the U.S. Constitution does not give the federal government any general law enforcement power or any broad authority to enact federal criminal laws. Those powers, under the Constitution, are reserved to the states. But despite the absence of any direct delegation of such authority to the federal government, Congress and the Supreme Court had interpreted the federal government's power, under the

Interstate Commerce Clause, to regulate commerce "among the several states" to include the power to regulate (and thus to criminalize) activities affecting commerce that involve more than one state or transportation across state lines.

By 1931 Congress had already used the Interstate Commerce Clause as authority to pass laws making it a federal crime to transport such items as contraceptives, obscene books, prizefight films, poached wildlife, prostitutes, and stolen automobiles across state lines. Still, many "states' righters," including President Herbert Hoover, were opposed to using the Interstate Commerce Clause to expand federal criminal jurisdiction. For more than a year, Michigan congressman Roy O. Woodruff had been trying unsuccessfully to use the Interstate Commerce Clause to make it a federal crime for an organized criminal gang to cross a state line to commit a crime. So far, though, Congress had shown no appetite for empowering the federal government to attack organized crime directly, regardless of a gang's interstate activities.[12]

While Woodruff's experience didn't bode well for antikidnapping legislation, there were other signs that growing doubts about the states' ability to crack down on organized criminal conduct might be creating an opening for expanded federal intervention. In October 1931 a federal jury in Chicago convicted Al Capone of income tax evasion; a federal judge sentenced him to eleven years in prison, the longest sentence that had ever been handed out in an income tax case. For over a decade Capone had committed armed robbery, murder, extortion, and other violent and corrupt acts as he rose to the top of Chicago's largest criminal enterprise, but neither state and local law enforcement agencies nor federal Prohibition authorities had brought charges against him that stuck. With the Capone example, momentum began to build for the idea that federal law enforcement might also be effective in addressing other types of crimes that the states had not been effective in curbing.

Weisenburger's group decided to take advantage of that momentum and try to persuade Congress that kidnapping in the automobile age had become an interstate crime that required federal law enforcement. As an example, they argued that kidnappers were taking advantage of St. Louis's proximity to the Illinois border and East St. Louis's proximity to the Missouri border to deliberately cross from one state to the other to make it harder for the police to pursue them and for prosecutors to get witnesses to come to court and testify against them. If kidnapping were made a federal crime, they argued, boundary lines between states would effectively disappear and, with them, kidnappers' advantage over state and local law enforcement.

There was merit to the argument. The boundary between Missouri and Illinois is the Mississippi River. The three bridges spanning the Mississippi at St. Louis had made travel between the two states so fast and so convenient that perpetrators of crimes on either side knew they had an excellent chance of escaping apprehension if they could make it across the river without getting caught. They were exploiting the situation wherein the police of one state pursuing an investigation into the other state needed the consent and assistance of the local authorities in each jurisdiction they entered. "In many instances these peace officers are either stupid or are unwilling to assist local police in tracking down the criminals," complained former St. Louis police commissioner Arthur Freund. "In some instances, information given to peace officers in other states is tantamount to communicating the same facts to the criminals."[13]

The Kelley kidnapping illustrated the interstate problem perfectly, but it was only one example—until December 16, 1931, when kidnappers snatched the vivacious and much-loved Nell Donnelly and her chauffeur, George Blair, in Kansas City.

It was almost 6:00 p.m. when Nell Donnelly finished work and headed for home in the fashionable Countryside neighborhood of Kansas City's South Side. When George Blair steered her lizard-green Lincoln convertible into the driveway, a carload of men waiting by the road quietly pulled in behind and boxed in the Lincoln. Three men got out, guns drawn, swung open the doors of the convertible, and slid inside. As Nell leaned out the window to scream for help, one of the gunmen pulled a muslin sack down over her head and forced her, face down, against the floorboard, kicking and punching. An hour later, after ditching the convertible and switching to another car, the kidnappers pulled up to a rundown bungalow in the country. They led Nell and George, blindfolded, down some stairs to a foul-smelling cellar, tied their hands and feet with rope, and shoved them down onto cots. Then they turned the lights off, climbed the stairs, and left Nell and George alone in the dark.

Forty-year-old Nell Quinlan Donnelly was the head of the Donnelly Garment Company, the largest manufacturer of women's clothing in the country. With more than a thousand employees and over $3.5 million in annual sales, her company was one of Kansas City's largest employers. *Fortune* magazine in 1935 would call her "possibly the most successful businesswoman in the country."[14] She built her manufacturing empire upon the novel notion that American housewives didn't necessarily have to look the part. Millions of them cheerfully discarded their drab, shapeless housedresses in favor of "Nelly Don's" slim-fitting "Handy Dandy" aprons and shapely day dresses in bright fabrics with saucy ruffles and bows. She was a widely admired Kansas City celebrity and an emerging power in Missouri's Democratic Party.

The kidnappers dictated a note, handwritten by Nell, to her husband, Paul Donnelly, demanding a $75,000 ransom (over $1.2 million in 2020) in unmarked $50, $20, and $10 bills with unrecorded serial numbers. They threatened to blind Nell and murder George if he contacted the police. The Donnellys' next-door neighbor, attorney James A. Reed, stepped in and took charge of getting them back.

Jim Reed—"Our Jim" to high and low alike in Missouri— was the most famous person in Kansas City. When he was first starting out as a lawyer, he had accepted a helping hand from the young Pendergast brothers who were beginning to build a political empire, and he had found himself ever after a key part of their powerful Kansas City political machine. Described as an "example of the Pendergast machine's sometimes selecting capable and appealing candidates rather than simply men who would work with the machine,"[15] Reed ascended steadily from Jackson County prosecutor (winning 285 of the 287 cases he prosecuted) to mayor of Kansas City to three-term U.S. senator. He also ran three times for the Democratic Party's nomination for president, but never made it. At seventy, Reed was vigorous, handsome though unpolished, and widely admired for his stentorian oratory. "Like [Daniel] Webster it is impossible for Mr. Reed 'to be as great as he looks or sounds,'" wrote journalist Oswald Garrison Villard in 1928.[16] He was also Nell's lover and the father of her only child, seventeen-week-old David, though that fact would not emerge for years to come.

After huddling with Paul and the Kansas City police chief, Senator Reed called in the press to make a statement to the kidnappers. "If these men release or deliver Mrs. Donnelly unharmed, they can get their $75,000," he announced. "They can get it in any form they desire and under any conditions they name. In this I am speaking for Mr. Donnelly and I add my personal guarantee. On the other hand," continued the former prosecutor, "if a single hair of Mrs. Donnelly's head is harmed, I will, and Mr. Donnelly will, spend the rest of our lives running the culprits to earth and securing for them the extreme penalty of law, which in Missouri is death by hanging."[17]

Reed then dismissed the reporters and called Johnny Lazia at his desk in Kansas City Police headquarters. "Brother John," known for his fine three-piece suits and gold-rimmed spectacles with thick, Coke-bottle lenses (he had glaucoma), was the boss of Kansas City's Mafia. In return for delivering the North Side ballot boxes every election day for the Pendergast machine and keeping Al Capone and his Chicago Outfit out of Kansas City, Lazia had the run of police headquarters, a free hand in hiring police officers, and exclusive control over bootlegging and gambling in Kansas City.[18]

Reed was brief and blunt: he expected Mrs. Donnelly home, unharmed, within twenty-four hours or he would buy radio time to reveal some of the more damning details of Lazia's crimes and corruption. Lazia knew instantly that the kidnappers weren't Kansas City gangsters. Only out-of-towners could be so clueless as to think they could slip into Kansas City, under the noses of the Kansas City mob, and kidnap Nell Donnelly. Clearly they had no idea what she meant to Kansas City or of her political connections. Lazia marshaled twenty-five carloads of armed gangsters and known criminals and ordered them to canvass underworld hangouts until they discovered who had kidnapped Nell and George and where they were holding them.[19]

Before dawn the next morning, three of Lazia's men donned masks and muscled their way inside a nasty little bungalow in Bonner Springs, Kansas, fifteen miles from Kansas City across the Missouri-Kansas border. There they found Nell and George on their cots, seemingly more terrified of the masked intruders than the kidnappers themselves, who quickly fled. One of the rescuers helped Nell to her feet and gently removed her blindfold.

"Mrs. Donnelly, there has been a mistake," he said. "These men were from out of town. You have a lot of friends. We have come to rescue you."[20]

Without ever removing their own masks or identifying themselves, Lazia's men drove Nell and George to a spot a mile from town and put them out on the side of the road. Then they called the Kansas City police chief and told him where to find them.[21] Senator Reed denied payment of any ransom. "We did not arrange the matter," he said. "It happened. That is all. It's wonderful. Now all we need to crown this is a hanging."[22]

In the confusion of the rescue, Nell accidentally took with her from the hideout a towel the kidnappers had used to blindfold her. The police later discovered that it contained a small laundry

mark, which led them to the dairyman who rented the bungalow. Under questioning he confessed that he had made the place
available for the use of the kidnappers: two hoodlums and their
accomplices, including a home nurse who had recently taken care
of the ailing Paul Donnelly.[23]

Weisenburger's group now had another good example of kidnappers transporting their victims across state lines. They were ready
to take their antikidnapping proposals to Washington.

On December 31 Missouri senator Roscoe Patterson and St.
Louis congressman John Cochran submitted two pieces of legislation to Congress: one to make it a federal crime punishable
by death to transport a ransom kidnap victim across a state line
and the other to make it a crime punishable by up to five years
in prison to demand ransom by mail. President Hoover opposed
the bills for the same reason he consistently opposed other pieces
of legislation designed to expand the role of the federal government: he didn't believe the federal government should do the
work of the states. Kidnapping was already illegal in every state.
He believed existing laws were adequate to suppress kidnapping if
they were enforced, and he was against creating a national police
force to do the job. His attorney general, William D. Mitchell, also
opposed the legislation. The Justice Department was already laying off employees due to Depression-induced budget cuts; there
was no money in the budget to hire the additional investigators
and prosecutors that would be needed to enforce the proposed
laws. The press mostly ignored the proposals.

In late January there were unconfirmed reports that the Secret
Six had foiled a plot by Chicago gangsters to kidnap the former
vice president of the United States, Charles G. Dawes, who had
served under President Calvin Coolidge.[24] The underworld had
particular animosity for Dawes, a Chicago native and outspoken
enemy of organized crime. As vice president he had persuaded

President Coolidge in 1928 to issue an order to the Internal Revenue Bureau to pull out all the stops to get Capone. Dawes had been in the news recently as the president's choice to head the federal government's Reconstruction Finance Corporation and was an overnight guest at the White House the day the story of the plot broke.[25] Dawes played down the report and denied concern, but Senator Patterson, one of the bills' sponsors, said it was further proof that kidnap gangs were getting bolder about going after the "most prominent people in the nation."[26]

In late February the chairmen of the House Post Office and Judiciary Committees held short hearings on the bills. Instead of kidnap victims telling their stories, it was the proponents of the legislation who testified. Chamber of Commerce president Walter Weisenburger told of riding in an automobile with a wealthy St. Louisan whose life had become "virtual hell." Convinced he would be the next to be kidnapped, he had removed the outside door handles from his car, armed his chauffeur, and tucked a submachine gun away in the back seat.[27]

The head of the Secret Six, Colonel Robert Isham Randolph, read examples of threatening letters from kidnappers and extortionists. One letter to a Chicago businessman demanding $25,000 warned, "It will cost you $50,000 if we have to come and get you."[28] Another letter to the mother of a child named Dorothy threatened that if she did not "come through," the writer would strangle Dorothy. As he read the letter, Randolph pulled an ominous loop of rope from the envelope addressed to the mother.

Chicago police detective Leroy Steffens described how some kidnap gangs tortured their victims to obtain cooperation in arranging ransom payments: baths in lime vats, imprisonment in gasoline-saturated rooms, and submersion in underwater diving bells with the air cut off.[29]

"This, gentlemen, is not Manchuria or China or Russia. It is the United States," Weisenburger reminded the committee.[30] But in the United States, as President Hoover liked to point out, kidnapping was already a crime in all forty-eight states. Even the bills' supporters had to admit it was fair to ask why, in that case, there was a need for federal intervention.

Part of the answer was that some kidnappers were crossing state lines to evade capture and prosecution. "A state boundary is merely an imaginary line to the criminals, but it presents an almost insurmountable barrier to police officers seeking to apprehend them," said Weisenburger. "The fact is, oxen laws are trying to keep up with automobile criminals."[31]

The frequency of kidnappings despite state criminal laws was logically another part of the argument, but kidnapping statistics had never been collected in any systematic way. To fill that gap, St. Louis police chief Joseph Gerk had sent questionnaires to police departments in selected cities across the country asking how many kidnappings had been reported to them in 1931. Of the 948 police departments he surveyed, 501 departments in twenty-eight states responded. Their responses indicated that a total of 282 kidnappings had been reported to them in 1931.[32] (By comparison, apples to oranges, there were approximately thirteen thousand homicides in the United States in 1931.)[33]

Chief Gerk's flawed data-gathering procedure produced numbers that fell far short of demonstrating a compelling need for federal intervention. When he testified, he tried to put the numbers in context by explaining that most kidnappings were never reported to the police. In his opinion the actual number of kidnappings was at least ten times the number of those reported, resulting in an estimate of nearly three thousand kidnappings in 1931 alone. The newspapers seized the number three thousand for their reports. No one challenged it.

The House Post Office and Judiciary Committees completed their hearings in a day. No one testified in opposition; no votes were scheduled. On the Senate side, the chairman of the Judiciary Committee didn't consider the bills an urgent matter. February came to an end without anyone scheduling a hearing.[34]

Two

The Crime of the Century

3

The Snatch of the Eaglet

Hopewell, March 1, 1932

It was a Tuesday. Charles and Anne Lindbergh hadn't even planned to be in Hopewell, New Jersey, that night. On any other Tuesday they would have been at Anne's mother's home in Englewood, where they were staying until their dream house in the country was completed—on a hilltop deep in the woods with room for dogs, horses, and chickens. For now, missing curtains and furnishings, the Hopewell house was where they spent weekends with their firstborn, twenty-month-old Charlie.

Charlie was getting over a cold, and Anne decided not to take him out for the drive back to Englewood on Monday or on Tuesday either, when the rain was cold and the winds blustery. Instead she stayed another night with Charlie and called his nurse, Betty Gow, to join her at Hopewell to help with the toddler.

Lindbergh had driven himself to work in Manhattan on Monday morning. In addition to his aviation activities and related business interests, he was collaborating with the French surgeon and biologist Dr. Alexis Carrel at the Rockefeller Institute for Medical Research to develop a perfusion pump capable of keeping human organs functioning during transplant surgery.[1] After spending Monday night in Englewood and working in Manhattan again on Tuesday, he drove back to Hopewell, arriving around 8:30.

After his supper Betty readied Charlie for bed. She rubbed his chest with Vicks VapoRub and wrapped him in a flannel shirt she had made for him to wear under his sleeping suit. Then Betty and Anne tucked him into his crib, pinned his blanket to the mattress so he wouldn't kick it off during the night, and checked to make sure the nursery windows and shutters were closed. One of the shutters attached to the corner window was warped; Betty couldn't fasten it. Neither could Anne, though she tried. Charlie was asleep by about 7:30.

At 10:00, Betty tiptoed into the nursery to check on Charlie, as she always did, but the crib was empty. She hurried to the master bedroom on the other side of the bath connecting with the nursery to see whether Anne had Charlie and then downstairs to the library, where Lindbergh was reading. There was no sign of Charlie. Lindbergh bounded up the stairs to check the empty crib himself, then grabbed his rifle from a closet and sent Betty to the other side of the house to get Olly Whateley, the butler. Lindbergh and Whateley went outside to look around while Anne, Betty, and Olly's wife, Elsie, the housekeeper, searched inside. They checked behind doors and in closets, praying the toddler had climbed out of his crib and was playing hide-and-seek.

The men returned empty-handed. Lindbergh told Whateley to call the Hopewell police. Then Lindbergh rang the switchboard operator himself, shortly after 10:20 p.m., and asked to be connected with the New Jersey State Police (NJSP) training school headquarters at Wilburtha, near Trenton. Lieutenant Daniel J. Dunn answered right away.

"This is Charles Lindbergh," the caller said. "My son has just been kidnapped."

After a brief conversation, Dunn hung up, shaking his head, and commented to the detective on duty, "Some guy said he was

Lindbergh—said the baby was kidnapped. Jesus! Now what am
I supposed to do? I mean, he's probably a nut. We get this shit
all the time."[2]

Hopewell's chief of police Harry Wolf and his constable, Charles
Williamson, were the first to arrive at the Lindbergh home. Word
now traveled fast, and local police, sheriffs, and state troopers from
every nearby jurisdiction headed for Hopewell. Soon the superintendent of the NJSP, Colonel H. Norman Schwarzkopf Sr., and
his second-in-command, Major Charles Schoeffel, arrived from
Trenton, sixteen miles away.

At 10:46 p.m., the Teletype machine at NJSP headquarters
began relaying an alert to all law enforcement agencies in New
Jersey and every state east of the Mississippi: "COLONEL LIND-
BERGHS BABY WAS KIDNAPPED FROM LINDBERGH HOME
IN HOPEWELL NJ SOMETIME BETWEEN 7-30 PM AND 10-
00 PM THIS DATE. BABY IS 19 MONTHS OLD AND A BOY. IS
DRESSED IN SLEEPING SUIT. REQUEST THAT ALL CARS BE
INVESTIGATED BY POLICE PATROLS. AUTHORITY STATE
POLICE TRENTON NJ. NS."

Within the hour police and sheriffs' departments all over New
Jersey had set up roadblocks on state roads and highways. The
commissioner of the New York City Police Department ordered
patrolmen and motorcycle officers to search every vehicle entering Manhattan from New Jersey; checkpoints were put in place at
the Holland Tunnel, the George Washington Bridge, and every
ferry terminal on the Hudson River.

At the headquarters of the Bureau of Investigation in Washington DC, the night dispatcher called the young director, J. Edgar
Hoover, at his Capitol Hill home, waking him to report the news
that the Lindbergh baby was missing.[3] Not long after he called
with an update: a note demanding a $50,000 ransom had been
found in the nursery of the Lindbergh home. By 1:00 a.m. Hoover
was at his desk at FBI headquarters trying to figure out how to

get the FBI involved in what could be the most important law enforcement event in the country since he had become its director seven years earlier.

Hoover's first move was to order FBI special agents in California to begin guarding President Hoover's two adult sons and three grandchildren around the clock. It was a bone of contention with him that the Secret Service, not the FBI, was responsible for protecting the president and his family. Under the circumstances he decided it was worth the risk of irritating the Secret Service and the president.

"No conceivable event, unless it were an invasion of the White House itself, could have so dramatized the crime of kidnapping," wrote the *New York Times*.[4] If anything, that was an understatement. To most of America and large parts of the world, Charles Lindbergh was a hero with no equal.

Lindbergh's public story had begun five years before, in May 1927, when a lanky, boyish, and offhandedly handsome twenty-five-year-old called "Slim" flew nonstop and solo from Roosevelt Field on Long Island to Le Bourget Aerodrome in Paris, some 3,600 miles and over thirty-three hours away. The flight earned Lindbergh (whom the press quickly dubbed "the Lone Eagle" and "Lucky Lindy") the $25,000 Orteig Prize for the first nonstop flight between New York and Paris. (Others had previously flown nonstop across the Atlantic between Newfoundland and Ireland, only half as far as the New York to Paris route.) For eight years the prestigious prize had eluded teams of experienced, well-financed aviation pioneers, including the famous polar explorer and aviator, Commander Richard E. Byrd; six fliers had lost their lives attempting it. Lindbergh made the perilous flight through darkness, sleet, and snow without a copilot. When he left the United States on May 20, he was a shy, unknown airmail pilot; when he returned twenty-two days later, he was the most revered man in the world, the honored guest of kings and presidents, the role model for untold millions of boys and girls and adventurers alike.

Charles Augustus Lindbergh was born in Detroit in 1902, the only son of lawyer Charles August Lindbergh and Evangeline Land Lindbergh, a high school science teacher. He lived on a farm in Little Falls, Minnesota, until the age of five, when his father was elected to Congress in 1907. Always a bit of a loner, Charles displayed an early aptitude for taking mechanical things apart and putting them back together again, but he didn't do well in school or in his engineering courses at the University of Wisconsin-Madison, where he dropped out in his sophomore year. To support himself, he took up barnstorming and became an excellent stunt pilot and wing-walker.

Aviation had interested Lindbergh long before his barnstorming days. Flying convinced him he wanted to be a serious pilot—an aviator, not an exhibitionist; he had a keen interest in navigation and the mechanics of flying machines. To obtain serious pilot training, he enlisted in the army and attended its Air Service Advanced Flying School near San Antonio, finishing first in his class in 1925. Though commissioned a second lieutenant in the Air Service Reserve Corps, there were no hostilities at the time and no jobs for active duty pilots, so he became instead one of the first pilots to fly the airmail, in rebuilt army salvage planes, between St. Louis and Chicago.

When Lindbergh heard about the Orteig Prize—$25,000 offered to the first Allied aviator(s) to fly nonstop between New York and Paris—he was confident he could win it with the right airplane. The head of the St. Louis Chamber of Commerce, banker Harold M. Bixby, a World War I army balloon pilot, thought so too. One of a growing number of businessmen envisioning America's aviation future, Bixby joined with Major Albert Bond Lambert, an Orville Wright–trained pilot, and seven other St. Louis businessmen to lend Lindbergh $13,000. Along with another $2,000 of Lindbergh's own money, this was enough to commission a stripped-down airplane from the Ryan Aeronautical Company. Unlike the larger, more sophisticated airplanes his competitors had flown, Lindbergh decided on a single-engine monoplane with canvas-covered wings, a linen-covered fuselage (fortified), no brakes, no forward vision—and no radio, sextant, or parachute either.[5] By eliminating every nonessential item, he figured, the plane would be able to carry enough fuel to fly nonstop to Paris and still lift off from the ground.

Lindbergh's bold undertaking fit perfectly with the aspirations of his backers, who actively promoted "the spirit of St. Louis" and the city's potential as a leading center of industry and commerce. Harold Bixby could not have imagined a better symbol for St. Louis and its bright future than Slim Lindbergh. He suggested Lindbergh name his plane the "Spirit of St. Louis" and "just leave the finances to us, and we'll leave the flying to you."[6]

While Lindbergh was on his quest, still in the air far from Paris, Will Rogers, arguably America's most widely read columnist,[7] expressed the emotions of many around the world: "A slim, tall, bashful, smiling American boy is somewhere out over the middle of the Atlantic Ocean where no lone human being has ever ventured before. He is being prayed for to every kind of Supreme Being that has a following. If he is lost, it will be the most universally regretted single loss we ever had. But that kid ain't going to fail . . ."[8]

When the *Spirit of St. Louis* touched down at Le Bourget at 10:22 p.m. on May 21, more than 150,000 jubilant Parisians were there to welcome Lindbergh. Undeterred by soldiers and policemen, the crowd swept aside barriers and inundated the field, soon joined by the soldiers and police themselves rushing toward Lindbergh and his plane. At least another million people turned out to cheer him in public events over the next five days. French president Gaston Doumergue awarded him the Légion d'honneur.

Departing Paris in the *Spirit of St. Louis*, Lindbergh twice circled the Eiffel Tower, swooped down low over the Arc de Triomphe, and then followed the Champs Elysees to the Place de la Concorde, where he dropped a French flag from the cockpit. The flag was tied to a sandbag with a handwritten note inside: "Goodbye! Dear Paris. Ten thousand thanks for your kindness to me. Charles A. Lindbergh."[9] After performing a few more spins and rolls, he continued on to Brussels.

Lavish ceremonies and large crowds awaited Lindbergh in Brussels. Albert I, King of the Belgians, pinned the medal of the Chevalier de L'Ordre de Leopold on him at the royal palace. Burgomaster Adolphe Max (a hero of the Belgian resistance in World War I) awarded him the city's gold medal at the guild hall. Auguste Bouillez, the great baritone of the Brussels Opera, sang "The Star-Spangled Banner" as Lindbergh stood at attention. When Bouillez finished, Lindbergh quietly asked him to sing the Belgian national anthem, too. "M. Bouillez obliged, surpassing himself," reported the *New York Times*, "and the heavy oak rafters of the old hall fairly rang with the stirring refrain, '[Le Roi, la Loi, la Liberte]!'"[10]

When Lindbergh departed Brussels for London, he detoured to the town of Waregem, near Ghent, to pay a Memorial Day tribute to the 368 American soldiers buried in the Flanders Field American Cemetery. As he flew over the field, he cut his motor, silently glided down close to the rows of small white crosses, and dropped a bouquet of flowers wrapped in his silk scarf. Then he pulled up, circled the cemetery twice more, and made his way to England.[11]

In London, hundreds of thousands of cheering people turned out to greet him. King George V awarded him the Air Force Cross. During a private visit with the royal family at Buckingham Palace, the king asked, "Now tell me, Captain Lindbergh. There is one thing I long to know. How did you pee?"[12] He also met Queen Mary, their baby granddaughter Princess Elizabeth (the future Queen Elizabeth II), and the Prince of Wales (the future King Edward VIII), as well as Prime Minister Stanley Baldwin and Chancellor of the Exchequer Winston Churchill. "From the little we have seen of him," Churchill reported to Parliament, "we have derived the impression that he represents all that a man should say, all that a man should do, and all that a man should be."[13]

Before he left New York for Paris, Lindbergh hadn't given much thought to how he would get back to the United States, much less to what the next chapter of his life would be. Seeing the reception he received in Europe, he confided to a reporter, "I can't help wondering what will happen to me over there, unless I allow the story to grow a little old before I return."[14]

There was no chance of letting the story grow old, however. President Calvin Coolidge sent a navy cruiser, USS *Memphis*, to Cherbourg, France, to bring Lindbergh and the *Spirit of St. Louis* back to Washington, where more ceremonies and awards awaited him. When the *Memphis* neared Washington on June 11, sixty-five U.S. Army, U.S. Navy, and Air Mail Service airplanes flying in formation and piloted by America's greatest living aviators and World War I pilots, including Lieutenant Jimmy Doolittle and Commander Richard E. Byrd, treated Lindbergh to a spectacular air show. Bombers and pursuit planes roared over the Potomac, then plunged downward in a final salute to Lindbergh before straightening out, zooming by the *Memphis*, rising, and then partially rolling over at the end of the maneuver.

At the Washington Monument, 250,000 people saw President Coolidge award Lindbergh the nation's new Distinguished Flying Cross, as a symbol of the country's appreciation "for what he is and what he has done," and promote him to colonel in the Officers' Reserve Corps. Two days later, more than four million people lined the streets of New York to welcome him home in one of the largest ticker tape parades in history. Later that year Congress passed special legislation to award him the Medal of Honor, even though his heroism had not been displayed in combat, following it up the next year with the Congressional Gold Medal.

The public ardor did not fade. Lindbergh's account of his flight, which he titled *We*, referring to his "spiritual partnership" with the *Spirit of St. Louis*, sold almost 650,000 copies in the first year. Then he embarked on a series of goodwill trips and a three-month tour of the United States to promote aviation, touching down in ninety-two cities in all forty-eight states. In the six months following his return from Paris, thirty million Americans—an astounding 25 percent of the population—had seen Lindbergh in person.[15]

Elinor Smith Sullivan, who became the youngest licensed pilot in the world at the age of sixteen, and who in 1930, at age nineteen, won the Best Woman Aviator of the Year Award, described what Lindbergh and his historic flight meant for aviation:

> [People] seemed to think that we [aviators] were from outer space or something. But after Charles Lindbergh's flight, we could do no wrong. It's hard to describe the impact Lindbergh had on people. Even the first walk on the moon doesn't come close. . . . And it changed aviation forever because all of a sudden the Wall Streeters were banging on doors looking for airplanes to invest in. We'd been standing on our heads trying to get them to notice us but after Lindbergh, suddenly everyone wanted to fly, and there weren't enough planes to carry them.[16]

(The numbers back Smith Sullivan up: in 1926, there were 5,782 U.S. airline passengers; in 1929, there were 173,405.)[17]

Lindbergh was more modest about his contribution to aviation: "I was astonished at the effect my successful landing in France had on the nations of the world. To me, it was like a match lighting a bonfire. I thought thereafter that people confused the light of the bonfire with the flame of the match, and that one individual was credited with doing what, in reality, many groups of individuals had done."[18]

One of the goodwill trips Lindbergh made outside the United States was to Mexico, where he was the guest of the U.S. ambassador, Dwight Morrow. Morrow had been a J. P. Morgan partner when his Amherst College classmate Calvin Coolidge recruited him to try to strengthen relations with America's oil-rich neighbor to the south. It occurred to Morrow that a visit by Lindbergh would be a good way to demonstrate America's friendship with the people of Mexico; he invited Lindbergh to spend Christmas 1927 in Mexico City with his family. There Lindbergh met twenty-one-year-old Anne Morrow, a Smith College senior. She soon became the first—and apparently the only—girl Lindbergh ever took on a date.[19] Anne ignored the advice of a school friend to pass on Lindbergh ("he's just a mechanic"), and the couple married in May 1929.

There were obvious contrasts and some surprising similarities between the two. Where Lindbergh's background was middle-class and small-town Midwestern, Anne had been raised among the ultrarich of the New York suburbs, summering in Maine among the powerful Cabot, Du Pont, and Lamont families. Where Lindbergh's interests were airplanes and inventions, Anne's were books and writing; she would soon launch her literary career by publishing her first poem. At the same time they were both painfully shy, yet both relished adventure, though Anne's willingness to tolerate some danger didn't equal Lindbergh's. Nevertheless she learned to navigate and became a licensed pilot; the couple would fly themselves around the world many times in the coming years, narrowly escaping serious injury on several occasions.

After Anne and Charles married, the awards, ceremonies, and goodwill trips did not cease. They took frequent transcontinental trips to aircraft manufacturers, and Charles often made harrowing test flights. In the early days of aviation, even everyday flights were hardly routine due to weather, poor communications with the ground, and the lack of rudimentary flight maps.

Equally trying for the newlyweds were the unending invitations to spend weekends with Hollywood stars, tycoons, and presidents. By 1930 the word *strain* began to appear in Anne's diary and in letters to her mother and sister. She wrote that people looked upon her and Charles as "monkeys in a cage," admitting to her mother that she had "no patience, no understanding, no sympathy with the people who stare and follow and giggle at us; who ask questions, crowd, want to know about our private life." "It is so wearing," she wrote. "I wonder if it will ever slacken."[20]

The public's fascination with all things Lindbergh was further fueled by the birth of Charles Augustus Lindbergh Jr. ("the Eaglet" to the press) on June 22, 1930. "I am already moved with compassion for the little citizen," wrote columnist Heywood Broun soon after Charlie was born. "He cannot possibly realize yet the price that he must pay for being a front page baby. He will."[21]

Every event in Charlie's young life was news: where he stayed when his parents traveled, how he celebrated his first birthday, the precautions taken to protect him from the polio outbreak in New York. One newspaper reported that Charlie passed much of his time in his playpen on the lawn of the Princeton farmhouse where the Lindberghs lived for a time before completion of the Hopewell house. The farmhouse became such a magnet for the curious, driving by and honking their horns or parking and hoping for a glimpse of the Eaglet and his parents, that the township had to assign a policeman to direct traffic.[22]

Building their own secluded home became the Lindberghs' dream, and searching for the land to build it on became a pleasant diversion. It had to be near enough to Manhattan for Lindbergh to commute by automobile, yet remote and inaccessible enough to discourage curiosity seekers—and there had to be sufficient acreage for a landing strip. Anne and Charles studied maps and flew over possible sites until they found what they were looking for: 425 acres in central New Jersey's Sourland Mountains, made up of thirteen separate small farms, part in Hunterdon County and part in Mercer County. Manhattan was forty-seven miles by automobile, and the nearest town, Hopewell (population not quite fifteen hundred), was three miles away. Distances in the Sourland Mountains often seemed greater than measured, though, because there were few roads; most of them were unpaved, muddy in winter and choked with dust in summer.

Dutch and English pioneers had settled in the area in the late seventeenth and early eighteenth centuries hoping to farm, but the clay soil, rock, and dense woods made farming unrewarding. The terrain was so wild and rugged that the army used it to practice mapping rough topography. Through the years the Sourlands had become known as a haven for people wanting to disappear. During the Revolutionary War, colonial army scouts spied on the British from the higher elevations. Later, slaves escaping to the North via the Underground Railroad hid out in its woods. More recently moonshiners had set up their stills in the woods with little interference from law enforcement. According to locals, though, as soon as the Lindberghs started building their house, Prohibition agents swarmed in and broke up the stills.

By 11:00 p.m. on the night of Charlie's disappearance, a steady stream of police and state troopers headed to Hopewell from Trenton, Lambertville, and other nearby towns. The first reporter arrived fifteen minutes later; by morning, nearly four hundred reporters were wandering around the Lindbergh property and Hopewell. William Randolph Hearst's International News Service hired two ambulances and was having them fitted with portable darkrooms in which to develop photographs as they sped from Hopewell to New York, sirens wailing.[23] State troopers positioned at intervals between the Lindbergh home and the public highway searched all vehicles and their occupants.

The Lindbergh home was not an easy place to get to, especially in the dark, over wet and muddy roads. After turning off the state highway, it was a steep climb up to a clearing at the summit of Sorrel Hill, which at five hundred feet was the highest point around. But the house itself was an easy place to see, "lighted up like a Christmas tree." Without curtains and with the lights on, it was possible to watch almost everything going on inside.

The house was large but not ostentatious: two and a half stories of native fieldstone covered with white stucco in what some described as a mixed French and English Tudor Revival style. There were twenty-three rooms, including the second-floor nursery and four additional bedrooms. From the sky above, it was possible to see that the slates covering the gabled roof were contoured to resemble the dark ripples of the Atlantic Ocean that Lindbergh had seen on his way to Paris. Beyond the clearing surrounding the house, there were dense woods everywhere except where Lindbergh had cleared the ground for his future landing strip.

Darkness blanketed the outside that night until someone thought to illuminate the clearing by lining up police vehicles and turning on their headlamps. Adding to the surreal scene, occasional flare bombs floated down from invisible planes circling overhead, temporarily lighting up small patches of ground.[24] Now and then, a tall, young man in an old cap, worn gray trousers, and a leather flying jacket would come into view, leading small clusters of policemen with a flashlight in one hand and a Springfield rifle in the other.

Lindbergh was no more fond of reporters than Anne, but he already realized the time might come when he would need their help to communicate with the kidnappers or would have to ask them not to publish information that could endanger Charlie's life. He met the first reporters at the front door and invited them in; he thanked them for coming and promised to tell them whatever he could as soon as he could.[25] Anne, Betty Gow, and Elsie Whateley offered them sandwiches and coffee. Before long there was no more room inside the house; later arrivals remained outside. They peered through the windows or walked around the clearing, trying to keep warm in the near-freezing temperature, watching and listening—heedless, apparently, that they could be trampling any forensic evidence the kidnappers might have left behind.

Nevertheless, several clues were discovered during the night. Lindbergh found a handwritten ransom note, demanding $50,000, propped against a window in the nursery, and he and Whateley found a wooden ladder in the woods near the house. Its awkward design and rough craftsmanship suggested it was homemade; the three sections, joined by dowels, allowed the ladder to be extended and collapsed, though not easily. Two of the side rails were split near where one of the dowel pins joined the pieces together.[26] A policeman also found a chisel on the ground nearby. Lindbergh spotted two muddy smudges, possibly footprints, in the nursery and what appeared to be two sets of footprints in the mud beneath the nursery window. Below and to the right of the nursery window, the police discovered two depressions in the mud about the same distance apart as the side rails of the broken ladder. Around midnight the NJSP's fingerprint expert and photographer finally arrived from Morristown to begin processing the crime scene.

At 4:00 a.m. Lindbergh went to see Oscar Bush, an experienced trapper and former sheriff's deputy who lived nearby. He hired Bush and his uncle James Wycoff to look for footprints around the house and track them. They followed the two sets of footprints beneath the nursery window across the clearing and through the woods until they ended two miles away at the unpaved Featherbed Lane. To Bush and Wycoff, it seemed pretty clear that two kidnappers wearing moccasins or padded shoes had taken the child through a wooded area and gotten away by car. They suggested the police make a thorough search of the woods and the many caves near the Lindbergh home.[27]

On Wednesday morning, President Hoover met with Attorney General Mitchell at the White House. The president already knew that the federal government had no authority to prosecute or punish kidnappers because kidnapping was not a federal crime. What he wanted to know was what he *could* do. He was concerned with his legal authority to act, but he also realized the American people would expect the government to do everything possible to find the Lindbergh child. The attorney general's lawyerly answer was not altogether satisfying: barring discovery of evidence that the kidnappers committed other federal crimes in connection with the kidnapping—such as driving a stolen automobile across a state line or using the U.S. Mail unlawfully—the president could only offer the resources of the federal government to the New Jersey authorities to assist them in their investigation. This is what presidents since Theodore Roosevelt had done whenever children were kidnapped and their parents asked for federal assistance. The offer of federal assistance was no small matter. Compared to the law enforcement resources available to individual states, the investigative resources of the federal government were substantial and could be deployed all over the country.

The White House promptly announced that the full resources of the federal government were at the disposal of the NJSP. Immigration officials started searching vehicles going to Mexico and Canada; the Department of Commerce watched train stations and airports; and the Coast Guard patrolled eastern coastlines. The FBI, the Postal Inspection Service, the Secret Service, the Customs and Immigration Service, the Prohibition Enforcement Bureau, the armed services, and the Metropolitan Police Department of the District of Columbia all prepared to help.

Further demonstrating active White House involvement, President Hoover also met that day with Frank J. Loesch, president of the Chicago Crime Commission and one of the country's leading kidnapping experts. Loesch said he believed the kidnappers were professionals, possibly from a Midwest kidnap gang. He struck a pessimistic note when he said America's law enforcement agencies were helpless against professional kidnapping; what was needed was a private vigilante organization operating in secret all over the country. "You have to fight the kidnappers in a different way," he warned.[28]

The attorney general had his own agenda, too. Although he and President Hoover had opposed the recent proposals to make kidnapping a federal crime, it was now clear to him that Congress would pass the legislation overwhelmingly, and he intended for the Department of Justice and the FBI to be in charge of enforcing the law when that happened. That meant grabbing an important role for the FBI in the Lindbergh investigation even if he had to elbow other federal agencies aside to do it. So Mitchell announced that the "whole machinery" of the Justice Department would work in cooperation with the State of New Jersey and that J. Edgar Hoover would be the "backbone" of the federal effort. He specifically mentioned that the FBI's fingerprint identification files and "rogues' gallery" of criminal records would be open to the NJSP. At Mitchell's direction, Hoover wired Colonel Schwarzkopf to offer "100 percent cooperation in any direction the New Jersey authorities considered desirable."

Offers to assist the NJSP also poured in from governors, mayors, and police chiefs throughout the eastern United States. New York City police commissioner Edward P. Mulrooney canceled leaves and ordered all nineteen thousand New York City policemen to search around the clock for the child. He directed every beat patrolman to be on the lookout for newcomers and to stop and question anyone entering a building with a child.[29] New York governor Franklin D. Roosevelt, who would become the Democratic challenger to President Hoover in the 1932 presidential election, offered the services of the New York State Police.

Within twenty-four hours of the kidnapping, an estimated one hundred thousand law enforcement officers and volunteers around the country were looking for little Charlie Lindbergh.[30]

Back at the Hopewell house, officers from the Jersey City, Newark, and Trenton police forces joined the scores of state troopers and members of local police forces that had gathered during the night. There was no chain of command and little coordination; everyone looked to Colonel Lindbergh for direction. Anne found it "impossible to describe the confusion,"[31] but she promised Charles's mother in Detroit that she would write and tell her everything "as I would like it told me and as I *cannot* tell you on the telephone."[32] Her home was "bedlam: hundreds of men stamping in and out, sitting everywhere, on the stairs, on the pantry sink. The telephone goes all day and night. People sleep all over the floors on newspapers and blankets."[33] "At any time I may be routed out of my bed so that a group of detectives may have a conference in the room. It is so terrifically unreal," she would soon write, "that I do not feel anything."[34]

But over the course of that first day, a semblance of organization began to emerge. A security perimeter went up around the house to control access to the property. The state troopers in their horizon-blue tunics and cavalry-yellow-striped riding breeches began guarding the house around the clock. The Lindberghs' three-car garage became a temporary state police headquarters. The automobiles were replaced with army cots, a Teletype machine, a telephone switchboard with seven additional lines, and rows of filing cabinets.

A temporary airstrip was quickly set up in Hopewell, and aviator friends of the Lindberghs, including members of the storied Quiet Birdmen flying fraternity, formed aerial posses to fly policemen and police photographers back and forth across the Sourland Mountains, scouring the wilderness for hiding places and clues. Two airplanes carried photographers with special aerial mapping cameras in hopes the negatives might reveal automobile tracks.[35] They weren't the only traffic in the skies: airliners bound for Washington and New York had begun buzzing overhead, circling the hilltop house and banking steeply so their passengers could have a closer look.[36]

Within hours of the kidnapping, the NJSP had formulated an initial theory of the crime and how it had been committed. A party of "at least two or more persons" had driven a car to the vicinity of the Lindbergh home and parked as close as possible: "Two members of the party had proceeded on foot to the east side of the residence, assembled the three-part ladder, and placed it against the house beside the second-story nursery window. One of the kidnappers then entered the nursery window, abducted the child, and carried him away down the ladder. The two then made their way to the waiting car and away for some place of hiding."[37]

By day's end policemen had searched most of the houses, shacks, and outbuildings within a three-mile radius and were beginning to look for caves and wells. They had begun interviewing neighbors about anything suspicious they might have seen or heard. They had obtained a list of construction workers and suppliers who had made deliveries to the Hopewell house, and they started bringing each one into the garage for questioning. Members of the public had begun offering information, and detectives had begun following leads. The first, frantic efforts to rescue the child were gradually turning into more methodical, investigative work to identify the kidnappers.

Forced to move outside the security perimeter, the reporters had taken over the town of Hopewell. They gathered in bunches around telephones and café tables. They played cards. They waited.

Olly Whateley made regular trips to town for sandwich and coffee supplies. Anne arranged for the staff of twenty-nine at the Morrow home in Englewood to bring extra bedding and three meals a day for forty people.

In Wednesday's fading light, the police on guard duty built bonfires to warm themselves against the cold winds and blowing snow. A few tossed a football around. One of the wire service reporters described the scene as "that of a general staff base in France on the eve of a drive."[38]

News came before nightfall, though not the news the world was waiting to hear. Four hundred miles away, in Niles, Ohio, two men had snatched eleven-year-old James DeJute Jr., son of a wealthy building contractor, as he walked to school that morning. Witnesses said Jimmy fought off the kidnappers once, but they grabbed him a second time and drove away with him. When last seen, he had been wearing his aviator's jacket and a leather "Lindbergh helmet" with goggles.[39]

4

The Colonel's Mission

Hopewell and Trenton, March 1932

From the moment he discovered his son missing, Lindbergh's mission was to bring his son home safely. He didn't panic; he took control. With utmost confidence in his own powers—concentration, ingenuity, and stubbornness—the thirty-year-old Lindbergh believed he would prevail again, no matter the odds. "Single-minded missions were Lindbergh's specialty," wrote his biographer Scott Berg. "From that moment on, he acted as the man in charge of a situation that steadily proved to be beyond his control."[1]

Whatever the mission, Lindbergh surrounded himself with people he trusted to carry out his will. He valued loyalty and competence; he didn't encourage independence or questioning of his judgment. The first person he called after notifying the police of Charlie's disappearance was his lawyer and friend Henry Breckinridge. "Colonel Henry," as he was known at Hopewell, drove from Manhattan that night with his wife, Aida, arriving at 2:30 in the morning.[2]

Breckinridge, a prominent New York lawyer, had represented Lindbergh since shortly after his return from Paris in 1927. Lindbergh got on well with the athletic, slightly graying Breckinridge, sixteen years his senior, and relied on him to review the many business opportunities that came his way. From a distinguished Kentucky family with a long record of military and public service, Breckinridge graduated from Princeton and Harvard Law before beginning law practice in Lexington.

Though his family had been solidly Republican for years, Breckinridge managed Democrat Woodrow Wilson's successful 1912 campaign for president in Kentucky and was rewarded with appointment as assistant secretary of war. At twenty-seven he was the youngest official in the Wilson administration and reportedly "one of the most brilliant of the men holding high office in this administration of young men."[3] During World War I he served with the American Expeditionary Force as a battalion commander and rose to the rank of lieutenant colonel. After the war he was three times a member of the U.S. men's Olympic fencing team.[4] Colonel Henry was the member of Lindbergh's inner circle upon whom Lindbergh most relied.

The concept of an inner circle or executive committee to manage the response to a kidnapping wasn't original with Lindbergh. The families and friends of Dee Kelley and Nell Donnelly utilized them, and Lindbergh had been in the inner circle advising Dwight Morrow when an extortionist threatened to kidnap Anne's fifteen-year-old sister Constance in 1929. He flew Constance and her sisters to safety in Maine.

Another member of Lindbergh's inner circle was Major Thomas Lanphier, a West Point graduate who served in the Army Air Corps in the early days of military aviation during World War I. After the war he commanded the Air Service's oldest airborne combat group, the First Pursuit Squadron, leading it in the air exercises that welcomed Lindbergh to Washington in 1927.[5] The following year, Lanphier and Lindbergh traveled the country together, mapping possible routes for Transcontinental Air Transport, the country's first passenger airline.[6] Lanphier usually worked in the background carrying out Lindbergh and Breckinridge's directions.

Beside Breckinridge and Lanphier, a small handful of others would join—and depart—the inner circle from time to time as Lindbergh saw fit.

When three days passed without the kidnappers making contact to arrange the ransom payment, Lindbergh began to suspect that the heavy police presence around his home would discourage any rational kidnappers from attempting to communicate with him or return Charlie. He decided to reach out directly to the kidnappers by issuing a public statement. "Mrs. Lindbergh and I desire to make a personal contact with the kidnappers of our child," it began. It urged the kidnappers to have their representatives meet whenever and wherever they chose with anyone representing the Lindberghs acceptable to them; he pledged that "we will not try to injure in any way those connected with the return of the child."[7] Such pledges by the families of kidnap victims were fast becoming the new normal. The New Jersey governor, the NJSP, and the prosecutors all announced they wouldn't be bound by the Lindberghs' pledge, which was also standard practice.

Breckinridge followed up the Lindberghs' statement by announcing to reporters that Lindbergh was prepared to meet with the kidnappers "anywhere, under any conditions they may wish to lay down, even to going into the underworld itself, to meet the men who have his baby and arrange for its return."[8] For the many people already concerned that the kidnappers' ultimate target was Lindbergh himself, the prospect of his going to meet with them was horrifying.

Under pressure to show progress or at least activity in the investigation, New Jersey governor Harry Moore tried to buy time by inviting the "best police brains in America" to a conference in Trenton on Saturday morning, March 5.[9]

J. Edgar Hoover hated being on the sidelines of the investigation, yet his several offers of assistance to the NJSP had met with polite expressions of gratitude from Schwarzkopf's subordinates but no requests for help or invitations to participate. Hoover's telephone call to Lindbergh to request the ransom note so a document examiner could analyze it had not been returned.[10] When the attorney general called to suggest that Hoover represent the Justice Department at the governor's conference, Hoover took it as an indication something important was going to happen there. He speculated that Governor Moore might be planning to turn the case over to the FBI.[11] Hoover may not have been the only one who thought he might be in line for a leadership role. In a short piece on the eve of the Trenton meeting, the *New York Times* described Hoover as "one of the world's outstanding authorities on scientific crime detection" and "a firm believer in Sherlockian methods of matching wits with the underworld."[12] It was extravagant praise for the little-known Washington bureaucrat whom some newspapers referred to as "J. Edward Hoover."[13]

Fifty-two representatives from law enforcement organizations of the federal government and every state and major city east of the Mississippi, as well as private detectives from the Pinkertons and Burns agencies, gathered at the New Jersey State House on Saturday morning.[14] Before the conference began, the attendees posed for a group photograph that ran in newspapers across the country the next day.[15]

Hoover's hopes were dashed at the outset when the governor opened the conference by introducing Colonel Schwarzkopf as the man he had chosen to head the investigation.[16] Schwarzkopf briefly summarized the facts and evidence already made public. Then the governor invited those in attendance to share their suggestions and called first on Hoover. Apparently unprepared to take advantage of such an opportunity to describe how the FBI might aid the investigation, Hoover instead lectured the attendees about the need for centralized assignments and recordkeeping and a "rigid policy" against publicity. A state official recommended immediately halting all police searches for Charlie and appointing a committee of lawyers and clergymen to negotiate secretly with the kidnappers; another proposed placing all participating police organizations under a single command, preferably the federal government.[17]

That was it. The conference was over in an hour. Schwarzkopf then invited everyone to board buses for the eighteen-mile trip to the Lindbergh home to view the crime scene and meet Colonel Lindbergh.[18] One of the few who declined that opportunity was the deflated Hoover, who instead instructed Special Agent in Charge Earl Connelley of the New York office to go to Hopewell and offer the FBI's assistance to Lindbergh. Before heading back to Washington, Hoover again offered the FBI's assistance to Schwarzkopf. Schwarzkopf said he didn't need any additional help; indeed he was so inundated with offers from all over the country that he was having a hard time doing anything other than responding to them. In any event, he told Hoover, he fully expected the kidnappers to return the child in the near future.

The *Philadelphia Inquirer* lampooned the governor's do-nothing conference in an imagined interview with "an average American":

Q—Don't you think it might help in avoiding cold trails if police, sleuths, district attorneys, mayors, Governors, etc. agreed to pose for their pictures after the crime had been solved instead of before?

A—I think it would be wonderful, but will America stand for it?

Q—If old-time detectives frequently solved baffling murder mysteries, kidnappings, etc., with nothing but a strand of hair to work on, don't you think it odd that our modern sleuths are so slow doing anything with a clew as big as a stepladder?

A—Not when you stop to consider that when the police arrived there was nobody on the stepladder.[19]

Hoover loved it, scribbling on his copy, "Very good! Absolutely true from what I have seen of it. More energy was expended at Trenton in getting the proper pose for the movies than in solving the crime. I still bear bruises received from the Jersey City mayor's party in the rush for the cameras."[20]

Schwarzkopf and Hoover both sensed a rivalry from the outset, a rivalry neither showed any interest in trying to avert. Schwarzkopf was surely irritated by the buildup Hoover had received from the *New York Times* and no doubt suspected Hoover's supporters of planting it. It is safe to say no one would have thought to compliment Schwarzkopf's crime-solving skills in similar fashion.

The thirty-six-year-old superintendent of the NJSP was an administrator. He had no experience as an investigator or in leading a major criminal investigation successfully, though the NJSP had investigated several less sensational kidnappings, and the FBI had not. Chicken thievery and cattle rustling were the crimes that occupied the biggest chunk of time for the more than two hundred troopers under Schwarzkopf's command responsible for policing seven thousand square miles of rural New Jersey.[21] Knowing Schwarzkopf's limitations and that he, Moore, would be assailed if anything went wrong in the case under Schwarzkopf, the governor arranged for high-ranking detectives of the Jersey City and Newark police departments to assist in the investigation.

A West Point graduate and decorated World War I veteran, Schwarzkopf was the only superintendent the NJSP had ever had. When the State Police were first organized in 1921, he won the appointment because he had military experience and, since he had never voted while in the military, no political ties.[22] As much as possible, he had organized the NJSP along military lines, following military procedures and methods. He designed the troopers' distinctive, military-style uniforms, consisting of brown boots, olive drab riding breeches (soon replaced by canary-striped, cavalry-blue breeches), dark blue fitted shirts, U.S. Cavalry–style campaign hats, and Sam Browne belts. He even chose the rank of colonel for himself because colonels commanded cavalry regiments in the army; he considered the NJSP, with its troops, headquarters, and auxiliary forces, to be like a cavalry regiment.[23] During the first decade of his tenure, he implemented many improvements and advances, including transitioning the NJSP from horses to cars and motorcycles as the principal means of transportation.

Overshadowing Schwarzkopf's achievements, though, were two fiascoes that had made him a target of serious criticism. The first involved the sensational murders of Episcopal rector Edward Wheeler Hall, who was married to a Johnson & Johnson heiress, and his mistress, Eleanor Reinhardt Mills, a member of the church choir, in New Brunswick in 1922. When the sheriffs' departments of two counties made egregious mistakes in handling crime scene evidence and failed to make any arrest in three weeks, the governor ordered Schwarzkopf to go to New Brunswick to find the murderer and not to come back until he did.[24] Schwarzkopf quickly made arrests, including the arrest of the young man who had found the bodies while strolling down a lovers' lane with his girlfriend. Just as quickly, however, the arrests were ridiculed as "an unfortunate mistake" that left New Brunswick "thoroughly skeptical" and "positive" the murders hadn't been solved.[25] The suspects were released; no more arrests were made, in part because the trooper investigating the case for Schwarzkopf admitted accepting a $2,500 bribe to drop the investigation.[26]

The criticisms leveled at Schwarzkopf and the NJSP in the Hall-Mills case were mild compared to the fallout from the tragic confrontation between the NJSP and three poor farmers named Meaney (a sister and two brothers), holed up in their farmhouse near the town of Jutland, in rural Hunterdon County. What began four days before Christmas 1926 as an effort to assist the New Jersey Society for the Prevention of Cruelty to Animals in serving a warrant on the Meaneys to inspect cattle reportedly being starved (a charge found to be meritless) turned into a twelve-hour gun battle between the Meaney brothers and twenty-five state troopers. Though armed with revolvers, rifles, riot guns, and tear gas, the troopers were not in uniform.[27] By the time "the Siege at Jutland" was over, a bullet had shattered James Meaney's knee and fifty-four-year-old Beatrice Meaney lay mortally wounded in the kitchen closet.

Schwarzkopf defended his men and rejected calls for an investigation. "We felt they were harboring criminals there, or that the place was a bootleg distillery or counterfeiting plant because no one would put up that kind of resistance on a cruelty to animals charge," he said.[28] When he finally gave in to demands for an inquiry, he appointed members of his own staff to conduct the investigation.[29] Their conclusions were devastating: the commanding officer's report was full of false statements, and the troopers had manufactured evidence to make it appear that the Meaneys had shot at the troopers from inside the house, including by shooting up a police vehicle and planting spent shotgun shells inside the house.[30]

"If the whole affair had been directed by escaped lunatics it hardly could have been more thoroughly botched," charged the *Atlanta Constitution*.[31] Fourteen troopers were indicted, and two were convicted of manslaughter; the rest were acquitted because they had acted under direct orders from their superiors.

The Hall-Mills case and the Siege at Jutland left Schwarzkopf vulnerable to criticism and unsure of himself in the far bigger and more intensely scrutinized Lindbergh investigation. His admiration for Colonel Lindbergh made him especially deferential; he quickly fell into the habit of looking to Lindbergh to make or approve virtually every significant decision about how the investigation would be conducted. Already Lindbergh had ruled out the use of bloodhounds to search his property and refused to have anyone listen in on his calls or tap his telephone lines. Household staff were not be questioned without his consent and in some cases his presence.

Despite Schwarzkopf's deference to Lindbergh, he was not included in the inner circle. Lindbergh and Breckinridge told him only what they wanted the NJSP to know.

With the FBI having no role in the investigation, Hoover focused his men on lines of inquiry the NJSP was not, insofar as he knew, prioritizing. The FBI, for example, looked into the possibility that the kidnapping was an inside job involving one or more members of the Lindbergh or Morrow household staffs, that it was the work of organized gangs from the Midwest, or possibly some combination of the two. He also assigned a special agent to serve as a contact with the NJSP in Trenton and another with the New York City Police Department (assuming that if the kidnapping was an underworld job, it likely involved New York). Their instructions were to make themselves available for assignments and to report back to Hoover every day.

"We are supposed to be in it and may as well have somebody present even though we are doing nothing on it," he told Special Agent Connelley.[32] Two days later, he sent Connelley himself to Hopewell, "for appearances if nothing else,"[33] so no one could later say that "we merely sent one Agent down there and that is all we did on it."[34]

Unlike Schwarzkopf, the thirty-seven-year-old Hoover had no military experience, which was hardly a minor issue for an able-bodied man of draft age during World War I. What he did have was seven years' experience as director of the FBI and a decent reputation in Washington for cleaning up and beginning to modernize the organization. The Bureau of Investigation he had inherited in 1924 was a small unit of investigators and accountants within the Department of Justice that investigated matters no other federal agency was responsible for, including violations of the antitrust laws and bankruptcy fraud (hence the accountants). Mostly, though, the Bureau investigated alleged violations of the federal laws prohibiting interstate transportation of females for prostitution (the Mann Act) and interstate transportation of stolen motor vehicles (the Dyer Act).

As director, Hoover moved quickly to impose regularity and discipline on the notoriously lax organization and to erase its Harding-era reputation as the "goon squad for the Attorney General."[35] He compiled voluminous manuals of administrative procedures, imposed a strict dress and grooming code, and personally hired all investigators (called "special agents") and most staff. He won the battle to exempt the FBI from civil service regulation and thereby retained complete control over hiring, promotion, and firing, as well as compensation, which enabled the FBI to pay higher salaries than other federal agencies. Even his critics admitted that under Hoover the FBI no longer was a dumping ground for job seekers owed favors by politicians.

Hoover had reason to be proud of what had been accomplished in his first seven years as director, but the greater the strides the FBI made, the larger the chip on his shoulder became. Special agents were investigators but had no authority to make arrests or to carry weapons. The Post Office, Secret Service, and Internal Revenue Bureau all had more investigators than the FBI had.

Hoover knew he could ill afford to remain on the sidelines of the Lindbergh case. The awkward standoff with Schwarzkopf and his failure to establish personal contact with Lindbergh were not a good beginning.

5

....

Lifting the Veil

New York, Hopewell, and Washington, March 1932

After reading about the Lindbergh kidnapping in the morning paper, Manhattan lawyer Robert Thayer went looking for his some-time client Morris "Mickey" Rosner. Rosner was a small-time real estate dealer who moonlighted by peddling information to lawyers about fraudulent financial schemes.[1] More than once he had mentioned to Thayer that he knew people in kidnapping gangs and how to get in touch with them, in case any of his friends got involved in a kidnapping case.[2] Thayer found Rosner that morning at the municipal courthouse on East Thirty-Fifth Street, where he was suing his sister for $500.[3]

Rosner referred to himself as an "underworld emissary."[4] New York City police knew him as a "smart fixer"[5] and a "rather clever individual"[6]—meaning not an ex-con but a man with solid underworld connections. He was currently free on bail facing charges of grand larceny in connection with the sale of stock in a company that promised to insure real estate against declining value. He wore three-piece suits and smart fedoras, and he had friends in high places, including Bob Thayer's mother-in-law, Congresswoman Ruth Pratt, who represented New York's "silk stocking" district, the Seventeenth, in Washington. Oklahoma senator Elmer Thomas, who occasionally used Rosner as an investigator for his Senate committee, said he was "positive that he is extremely trustworthy. In fact, I would trust him with my life."[7]

Rosner promised Thayer he would make a few calls as soon as he could get away from court. That afternoon he reported back to Thayer that the underworld suspected that the veteran kidnapper Abie Wagner had snatched the Lindbergh child. Wagner supposedly had been seen around central New Jersey before the kidnapping but not since.[8] Wagner specialized in kidnapping Broadway racketeers, but he also handled kidnap jobs as the "New York agent" for Detroit's infamous Purple Gang. Rosner offered to send out ten of his own handpicked emissaries to look for Wagner and make contact with kidnap gangs around the country. If Wagner wasn't the Lindbergh kidnapper, his emissaries would find out who was within forty-eight hours.

Thayer discussed Rosner's proposal with the head of his law firm, Colonel William J. "Wild Bill" Donovan, the World War I Congressional Medal of Honor winner. He was representing Lindbergh in a small civil case at the time. Donovan didn't trust Rosner or his underworld connections and wasn't willing to recommend him to Lindbergh, but he agreed Thayer should contact Breckinridge and let him decide.

Breckinridge told Thayer he wanted to meet Rosner and hear what he had to say because he and Lindbergh wanted "all the help possible, from any quarters, because they were absolutely in the dark and would go to any length to get the proper information."[9] That evening, Breckinridge met with Thayer and Rosner in Manhattan. Rosner emphasized that the Lindberghs' only hope of recovering their child was to follow the instructions in the ransom note in every detail and to keep the police out of things, as the kidnappers demanded. It was far more important, he said, "to get their baby back and pay the price, rather than throw the child at the mercy of three police departments, who were fighting for glory."[10]

After hearing Rosner out, Breckinridge was willing to go ahead with his proposal if Lindbergh approved. They all left for Hopewell, arriving at 6:30 the following morning. Lindbergh liked the plan. He added Rosner to the inner circle and gave him his own room in the house with an unmonitored telephone line. Following Lindbergh's lead, Breckinridge and Thayer made no effort to define Rosner's role or supervise his activities. That suited Rosner fine: there was so much chaos in the house and so much "police confusion and blundering" that he preferred to decide for himself how to "tackle this case from the underworld channels."[11]

The first emissary Rosner recruited was Owney "The Killer" Madden, a bootlegger, boxing promoter, and convicted murderer. Madden also owned the celebrated Cotton Club in Harlem, plus interests in over twenty other Manhattan speakeasies and nightclubs. "Sweet, but oh so vicious," was how his girlfriend, entertainer Mae West, described him.[12] Madden was willing to help because he detested kidnappers, having recently had to pay $37,500 to kidnapper Vincent "Mad Dog" Coll for the release of his business partner George "Big Frenchy" DeMange.[13] Madden had conditions, though: "the feds" couldn't be involved, and the Lindberghs had to issue a public statement that they would not assist the prosecution of the kidnappers if Charlie was returned.[14] (This was the statement the Lindberghs issued on March 5.)

Rosner next recruited Salvatore "Salvy" Spitale and his right-hand man, Irving Bitz, to be his emissaries to Italian kidnap gangs. Spitale, a former dance hall bouncer, had profited handsomely in the Brooklyn beer trade during Prohibition as he climbed up the ranks to a status "just below that of the more important racketeers."[15] On the way up, Spitale and Bitz had locked horns with Jack "Legs" Diamond; the police considered them prime suspects in Diamond's unsolved 1931 murder. A "suave and dapper and genial man," Spitale was no longer tied to a particular gang; he was known in the underworld as a man "on the level" who kept his word.[16]

Spitale and Bitz wanted to be more than just Rosner's contacts with Italian gangs; they wanted to be the Lindberghs' designated representatives for all communications with the kidnappers. They convinced Rosner they hated kidnappers and sincerely wanted to help, even offering to pay the ransom themselves. Their motives were admittedly mixed. The search for the Lindbergh child was costing the mobs hundreds of thousands of dollars, Spitale said. "Police are stopping every vehicle on every road in the country and searching them very thoroughly . . . intercepting truckloads of booze. . . . Only last night we lost two truckloads of liquor on the highways which resulted in a net cost to us of $30,000.00, so you can readily see that it would be better for us to pay the ransom and to continue doing our business as in the past."[17] (Bootlegger Abner "Longie" Zwillman, destined to become the "Al Capone of New Jersey," was also frustrated by police searching his liquor trucks for Charlie and offered a $50,000 reward for information leading to the child.) Even more important, Spitale and Bitz faced trial in New York on liquor smuggling charges within a week; they figured the publicity and goodwill associated with being the Lindberghs' representatives couldn't hurt. (They were acquitted on March 12.)

Rosner and Breckinridge accompanied Spitale and Bitz to Hopewell for a final screening by Lindbergh. In the early morning hours of March 6, the Lindberghs issued another brief public statement: "If the kidnappers of our child are unwilling to deal directly, we fully authorize 'Salvy' Spitale and Irving Bitz to act as our go-betweens. We will also follow any other method suggested by the kidnappers that we can be sure will bring the return of our child."[18]

The Lindberghs' announcement that they had reached out to gangsters to represent them in communications with their son's kidnappers produced immediate public reaction. Many people wrote to the president, the attorney general, and the governor of New Jersey expressing concern about the frightful power of the underworld. The publisher of a Long Island newspaper, for example, wrote to President Hoover urging him to impose martial law: "Col. Lindbergh himself is forced to put his faith in the Lords of the Underworld to get his child back because the police of the country are helpless. . . . The true American is patient but once aroused can become the most desperate and believe you me, we shall be compelled to act to protect our homes and families from menaces now shadowing us unless conditions are remedied at once."[19]

Spirits lifted at Hopewell, however. The designation of go-betweens, even gangsters, seemed like tangible progress at last. "I can tell more from [Charles's] actions than from his words," Anne wrote to Lindbergh's mother. "The first two days he looked like a desperate man—I could not speak to him. I was afraid to. But these last two days he is quite himself, only stimulated more than usual."[20]

Of Spitale and Bitz, Anne wrote, "We have come to an understanding with two of the biggest men of the underworld—men who have tremendous power with all gangs. . . . Charles, Col. Henry, and I feel convinced they are sincere and will help us. Isn't it strange, they showed more sincerity in their sympathy than a lot of politicians who've been here."[21]

According to Rosner, his recruits fanned out across the country and reported back to him every day about whom they'd contacted and what they'd learned. Every gang approached for information cooperated, Rosner said. The basic approach was to question mob leaders about any gangsters who were missing from their usual places and then to hunt those gangsters down and question them—more than a hundred in all, he claimed. The gangs themselves spent "thousands" of their own money pursuing their own leads, in one case chartering airplanes in New York and Chicago to send delegations to question members of a Detroit mob.[22] Though Rosner, Madden, Spitale, and Bitz never found Charlie Lindbergh or identified his kidnappers, Rosner maintained their work was valuable nonetheless: "We handled all the chisellers ourselves and cooled them. I guess we busted up a dozen attempts to chisel in and hoist the ransom."[23]

Lindbergh also reached out to New York mobster Frank Costello. Known as the "Prime Minister of the Underworld" for his ties to the Mafia, Tammany Hall, big businessmen, and judges, Costello functioned as a "bridge between the straight world and the mob." He sent his men out and reported back to Breckinridge a few days later that he was satisfied the underworld had not kidnapped the child. He thought Charlie was probably already dead and cautioned Lindbergh not to pay any ransom.[24]

When news of the kidnapping broke, Al Capone was in his cell in Chicago's Cook County Jail, waiting until the final appeal from his income tax conviction was exhausted. He decided to offer a $10,000 reward (over $187,000 in 2020) for information leading to Charlie's return and the capture of his kidnappers. "It's the most outrageous thing I ever heard of," he said. "I know how Mrs. Capone and I would feel if our son was kidnapped." He added, "I have friends all over the country who could aid in running this thing down."[25]

Lindbergh was skeptical, but it was common knowledge that gangsters sometimes intervened to obtain the release of kidnap victims. Aware that Kansas City mob boss Johnny Lazia had sent his men to rescue Nell Donnelly and George Blair from their kidnappers two months before, he called Ogden Mills, secretary of the Treasury, to ask for help from the agents of the Bureau of Internal Revenue who had investigated the case against Capone and might know whether members of his organization could have been involved in the kidnapping.[26] The head of the Bureau of Internal Revenue's Special Intelligence Unit (SIU), Elmer Irey, arrived at Hopewell the following day.

Lindbergh began his meeting with Irey by saying, "Mr. Irey, I wouldn't ask for Capone's release if—even if it would save a life."[27]

"Capone doesn't know who has the child, Colonel Lindbergh," said Irey. "He is simply trying to get out of jail." Irey had already learned from the siu's underworld sources that Capone believed one of his gang, Bob Conroy, was the kidnapper, but the siu knew Conroy was at least two hundred miles away when the kidnapping occurred. His men were looking for Conroy and want to question him, Irey said, but "he didn't do it."[28]

As Irey prepared to leave, Lindbergh said, "I'm at a complete loss, Mr. Irey. I have only policemen to turn to for help. I would like it very much if you folks could stay."[29] Irey told him they would help in any way they could, but the fewer law enforcement personnel around the Lindbergh home while he was trying to communicate with the kidnappers, the better. He promised, though, that he and his men would come back whenever Lindbergh called. In the midst of the chaos and anxiety that day, Irey formed a lasting impression of Lindbergh: "pleasant, stubborn, occasionally gay in an awkward effort to lift the tension, but always in full charge of operations and himself."[30]

When Lindbergh failed to respond to Capone's public overture, Capone began sending a steady stream of intermediaries to privately convey his promise to find Charlie if he was released from jail for forty-eight hours. One of them, Capone's former bodyguard Frank Rio, was recognized at the Lindberghs' front door and turned away.[31] Four men claiming to represent Capone accosted New Jersey governor Harry Moore on the street one night with a proposal for Capone's release, which the governor passed along to Lindbergh.[32] Other intermediaries included prominent lawyers and civic leaders, including Washington lawyer William E. Leahy Jr., Chicago lawyer Edwin H. Cassells, New York lawyer Walter Gordon Merritt, the former president of the U.S. Chamber of Commerce Julius Barnes, and the former president of the Chicago Board of Education H. Wallace Caldwell.[33]

Getting nowhere, Capone went public again on March 10, claiming in an interview with Hearst columnist Arthur Brisbane that he could "reach people in the East who could do more than all the detectives in the country to find the Lindbergh boy." He offered to post a $200,000 bond to guarantee his return to jail.[34]

No one whose opinion mattered was in favor of releasing Capone from jail to rescue Charlie. To the contrary, credible evidence was mounting that he might actually be behind the kidnapping.

Safecracker Morris "Red" Rudensky was in the Atlanta Federal Penitentiary serving twenty-five years for mail robbery when he learned of the kidnapping. He immediately recalled recent conversations he had had with Al's older brother Ralph.

Until two months before, Rudensky had been incarcerated at Leavenworth, where he was known as a "big shot" and was friendly with Ralph Capone, convicted like Al of federal income tax evasion. Before landing in Leavenworth, Rudensky had handled jobs for Capone's Chicago Outfit and had come to know both Capones. When Ralph arrived at Leavenworth, Rudensky took him under his wing and tried to help make it as easy for him there as possible.[35] Then the Bureau of Prisons decided to separate former Capone gang members in the federal prison system by spreading them around in different prisons. Ralph ended up all the way across the country in the federal prison at McNeil Island, Washington.[36]

As soon as he heard about the Lindbergh kidnapping, Rudensky started trying to get word to Special Agent Gus Jones of the FBI's San Antonio office, whom he had met previously, that he had important information for him. After thirteen days and several intermediate stops, the gist of Rudensky's story was set out in a report that landed on Hoover's desk, and Jones was on his way to Atlanta to hear Rudensky tell it in person.

According to Rudensky, he and Ralph often spoke at Leavenworth about Al's prosecution. Ralph had always said that "the

Chief" would never go to prison; if it became clear his conviction would be affirmed on appeal, the mob intended to do something spectacular that would "show up" all the law enforcement agencies in the United States and force them to deal with the Chief. The plan was to kidnap a nationally known figure—possibly one of Attorney General Mitchell's sons—not for money but solely to create a situation where the American people would become incensed that the police couldn't solve the case or rescue the victim.

Capone would then step forward, ostensibly to render a service to the country, and promptly locate the victim and return him to his family. He wouldn't ask for any reward, but he would have performed such a service to the American people that he would transform himself from the world's greatest criminal to a hero, and the people would be so thankful they would demand that the president pardon him for all his crimes.[37] Rudensky warned Jones that law enforcement officials would be "absolutely foolish" to work on any theory other than that the Capone mob was behind the kidnapping.

Jones knew Rudensky was no snitch. He believed him when he said he would never have opened his mouth if Capone's mob had kidnapped an adult, but he wanted to see the Lindbergh baby returned to his parents, and he was willing to help make that happen. Rudensky suggested that the FBI arrange his transfer from Atlanta to a cell near Capone's in the Cook County Jail or to McNeil Island near Ralph; he was confident either one would open up to him and mention the kidnapping if they had had anything to do with it.[38]

Before heading for Washington to brief Hoover, Jones wired him that Rudensky's story was "very convincing."[39]

Two days after Hoover received the initial report of Rudensky's story but before Jones interviewed him, William E. Leahy Jr. asked to meet with Hoover. Leahy was a prominent Washington lawyer, a former federal prosecutor who appeared in many of the major criminal cases in Washington. At the time, he was also dean of the Columbus School of Law in Washington, later part of Catholic University. Hoover sat down with Leahy in his office on Sunday morning, March 13.

Leahy told Hoover that a man closely connected with Al Capone had met with him twice to seek his help in arranging Capone's release from jail to help look for the Lindbergh child. Capone was willing to post a bond to insure his return to jail, drop his appeal, and go back to prison so long as there was an understanding he would be considered for parole after serving one-third of his sentence. Leahy told the man such an agreement would be "unthinkable" for any number of reasons, not least that whenever a sufficiently powerful underworld figure was arrested in the future, his associates could simply kidnap an important target and hold him hostage for the gangster's freedom. Leahy told Hoover he was willing to carry messages back and forth, but he would not represent Capone or accept any fee from him; his only interest was in getting Charlie Lindbergh back safely.[40]

Hoover reported the conversation to Attorney General Mitchell. Mitchell said that while the Justice Department couldn't publicly announce that it refused to even listen to Capone's propositions, releasing Capone from jail was out of the question. He told Hoover to tell Leahy that if Capone had any information, he could give it to the FBI through regular channels.[41]

Two days later, on March 16, Hoover told Special Agent Connelley that Leahy had contacted him again and had reported that "Major Lanphier should be ready with the money at a later date in order to fly by plane to the place where the baby would be designated as being left." As Hoover and Leahy had discussed in their Sunday morning meeting, Leahy had gotten back in touch with the "parties at Chicago" and had listened in on telephone conversations between a Capone lawyer in Washington and a Capone lawyer in Chicago (a "high class member of the Bar") discussing the arrangements for the child's release. Leahy had overheard statements that the child was well and that no harm would come to him because "he was too young to know or see where he is at the present time."

Hoover said he had made clear to Leahy that nothing would be done for Capone to relieve his sentence, but if his people would reveal the child's whereabouts, the FBI would make the arrangements to recover the child and "if they want something in the way of price this can be arranged for when the child is delivered." Leahy told Hoover that "possibly the child would be returned by Tuesday of the present week."[42]

Connelley communicated all of this to Major Lanphier the following day. Lanphier said he could arrange for the money and would fly the plane to get Charlie himself if the arrangements were worked out. Lanphier also told Connelley he would refrain from communicating the details of the plan to the Lindberghs so as not to unduly raise their hopes before knowing whether there really would be a rescue. Nevertheless Lanphier apparently conveyed enough information to Lindbergh that Lindbergh again called Treasury Secretary Mills and asked for Elmer Irey and his men to return to Hopewell to advise him on this further Capone development.[43] Accompanied by SIU investigators A. P. Madden and Frank Wilson, Irey returned to Hopewell on March 18. He again recommended that Lindbergh accept no help from Capone.

The following day, Lanphier told Connelley that Lindbergh and Breckinridge were positive they were now in contact with the real kidnappers and were involved in negotiating arrangements for Charlie's return through an intermediary named Dr. John Condon. Lanphier also reported that Lindbergh and Breckinridge were skeptical about the Capone developments, but glad the FBI was covering those angles.[44]

Despite Lindbergh's assurances to Lanphier that they were in contact with the real kidnappers, a Capone-assisted rescue still remained a possibility. Lanphier accompanied Connelley to Hopewell on March 23 to discuss with Lindbergh, Breckinridge, and Captain Lamb of the NJSP another version of Capone's proposal conveyed by H. Wallace Caldwell, the former president of the Chicago Board of Education.[45] As late as April 26, the *Los Angeles Times* was reporting that Washington officials had ordered that Capone be held incommunicado in his Chicago jail cell while the Lindberghs were considering whether to act on his latest offer. In anticipation of his release, Capone reportedly had already deposited $150,000 in an eastern bank; a dozen of his men were on their way to the East Coast to start their search if his offer was accepted.[46]

Capone's appeals and petitions were finally exhausted when the Supreme Court rejected his last petition on May 2. Arriving at the Atlanta Federal Penitentiary two days later, he was surprised to find that his old friend Red Rudensky was now his cellmate.[47] Capone was never released to look for Charlie; no record has been found that his representatives ever contacted Hoover to say it was time for Major Lanphier to bring the ransom money and pick up Charlie.

From the moment he looked into his son's empty crib, Charles Lindbergh believed, not unreasonably, that gangsters had kidnapped him. No doubt he fervently hoped gangsters were the culprits, for kidnap gangs were in the business of kidnapping for money, and they almost always released their victims unharmed as soon as they collected it. Amateurs were less likely to figure out a workable plan and execute it successfully. The failure of Mickey Rosner, Salvy Spitale, Irving Bitz, and Owney Madden to make contact with the kidnappers was strong evidence the kidnappers weren't gangsters at all. That was sobering.

The Capone episode can be dismissed, in hindsight, as little more than a calculated bet on Capone's part that he could beat law enforcement agencies to the kidnappers even though he didn't know who they were either. Hoover believed there was a good chance he might succeed; he took risks to make it happen, while doing everything he could to conceal his efforts, including within the FBI.

Even without achieving the desired result, the underworld phase of Lindbergh's mission had important consequences. The Lindberghs' announcement that they had chosen gangsters to arrange their son's release lifted a heavy veil of secrecy that finally exposed, as no previous event had, the ugly business of ransom kidnapping in America. By publicly acknowledging the method they had chosen to try to save their son's life, with the counsel of able lawyers, they forced the country to confront the essential nature of the crime that many of America's most prominent families had struggled with for the better part of a decade, often on their own and in secret. And it was Capone's insertion of himself into the unfolding story that caused Lindbergh to request the help of Elmer Irey and his men, which would have profound consequences for the investigation long after the Capone angle had exhausted itself.

6

"Ay, Doctor"

New York and Hopewell, March 1–May 11, 1932

In the first days after the kidnapping, some of the optimists look-ing ahead to Charlie's release began to realize that the extraordi-nary amount of attention focused on the kidnapping would make the task of returning him to his parents even more challenging than usual. Creative suggestions came from unexpected places. The director of the Girl Scouts in Marietta, Ohio, for example, sent a telegram to First Lady Lou Hoover, a former president of the Girl Scouts of the USA. She suggested that President Hoover promise to pardon the kidnappers if they handed Charlie over to any Girl Scout in uniform and that he ask every Girl Scout in America to wear her uniform every day until he was released.[1]

The county prosecutor for Wayne County, Michigan, invited the kidnappers to deliver Charlie to his grandmother Lindbergh's home in the Detroit suburb of Grosse Point. The police cleared traffic from nearby roads, while both police and prosecutor prom-ised to keep their eyes closed. "If I have no official knowledge of the matter, I see no reason for taking any action," announced the prosecutor.[2]

In the Bronx, a retired schoolteacher and principal, Dr. John Condon, came up with another unorthodox idea for getting Charlie back. It would thrust him directly into the epicenter of the unfolding tragedy.

Condon and a handful of his friends were sitting around a table at Bickford's in Fordham Square drinking coffee and discussing world affairs when a newsboy burst inside at midnight hawking papers with the unthinkable headline "LINDBERGH BABY KIDNAPPED."

Colonel Lindbergh was a particular hero to the spry, seventy-two-year-old with the walrus mustache, bushy eyebrows, and sparkling eyes. Condon bought a paper that night and began following every shred of kidnapping news. He fretted about where the country was headed to the point of worrying his family that he had become obsessed. He was stunned when the Lindberghs appointed the gangsters Spitale and Bitz to represent them. When the newspapers said they had done it because they lacked confidence in the police, Condon decided he had to do something himself to bring the Colonel's baby home safely.[3]

That something, he decided, was to write to the editor of his local paper in the Bronx, the *Home News*. In a rambling, emotional letter, he urged the kidnappers to take the Lindbergh baby unharmed to any Catholic priest and confess their crime, for "no Catholic priest in the history of the world has ever betrayed the secrets of the Confessional." He offered to pay them $1,000 of his own money, in addition to the ransom paid by the Lindberghs, and promised "never to utter his or her name to anyone." By the time the *Home News* published the letter on March 8, an editor had rewritten parts of it, turning it into an offer to serve as a go-between for the child's return.[4]

The *Home News* had a circulation at the time of over one hundred thousand, more than dailies in many larger cities, but it was very much a local paper. If Condon's aim was simply to express his thoughts and feelings about the kidnapping, as thousands of others around the world were doing, the *Home News* was a logical place to do it. The publisher was a friend; for years Condon had published opinion letters and even some poetry in the paper. But if his real purpose was to reach the Lindbergh kidnappers to offer his services, what reason did he have to believe they would see his letter in the *Home News*?

In his 1936 book about the kidnapping, *Jafsie Tells All*, Condon offered a convoluted explanation for selecting the *Home News*: a kidnapper eager to escape from Hopewell after the kidnapping probably would have avoided the dense woods of the Sourland Mountains to the north and west and the swampland to the south. By heading northeast instead, he would reach the "populous borough of the Bronx" in under two hours' driving time—"an easy exit and a possible haven."[5] His unconvincing explanation makes the question "Why the *Bronx Home News*?" all the more intriguing. It remains one of the many enduring mysteries surrounding the Lindbergh kidnapping.

When he arrived home on the night of March 9, Condon was astonished to find an envelope addressed to "Mr. Doctor John F. Condon" waiting for him. Inside were two letters, one addressed to him and the other to "Col. Lindbergh, Hopewell." He opened and read the letter addressed to him: "Dear Sir: If you are willing to act as go-between in Lindbergh case please follow strictly instruction. Hand enclosed letter personally to Mr. Lindbergh. It will explain everything. Don't tell anyone about it. As soon as we find out the Press or Police is notified everything are cancel and it will be a further delay."[6] The letter directed Condon to communicate with the kidnappers by placing notices in the classified section of the *New York American*, William Randolph Hearst's morning daily.

Condon didn't know what to make of the letters. Were they really from the kidnappers or was someone playing a cruel joke? After talking it over with friends, he decided to call Colonel Lindbergh. Robert Thayer, the lawyer who had introduced Mickey Rosner to Henry Breckinridge, answered the telephone. After Condon read Thayer the letter addressed to himself, Thayer asked him to read the letter addressed to Lindbergh.[7] He opened it and read aloud: "Dear Sir, Mr. Condon may act as go between. . . . We warn you not to set any trap in any way. If you or someone else will notify the Police there will be a further delay, after we have the money in hand we will tell you where to find your boy. You may have an airplane ready it is about 150 miles away. But before telling you the address a delay of 8 hours will be between."[8]

Condon then mentioned the unusual symbol appearing on the bottom of the letter to Lindbergh. It was composed of two overlapping circles, outlined in blue, with a smaller, solid red circle within the overlapping portion of the larger circles. In addition, there were three holes punched in a straight line across the horizontal diameters of the circles, one hole in the center of the red circle, one to the left of the circles, and one to the right of the circles. "It might have something to do with the Mafia," suggested Condon.[9]

What distinguished Condon's call from the thousands of tips, almost all worthless, telephoned and mailed to the Lindberghs was his mention of the symbol and the holes. Right away, Thayer recognized them as the same symbol and array of holes that appeared on the "Nursery Note," which the kidnappers had left on the windowsill in the nursery. The Nursery Note stated that the symbol and holes would be the kidnappers' authentic "singnature" in all future letters.[10] Thayer asked Condon to bring both letters to Hopewell that night and offered to send a car to the Bronx for him. Condon, who didn't drive, said a friend would drive him.

When Condon arrived at Hopewell, Lindbergh studied the letters carefully and compared them with the Nursery Note. After a few minutes, he pronounced them genuine and accepted Condon's offer to act as go-between. Breckinridge said he would prepare the notices to be placed in the *New York American*; they accepted Condon's suggestion that he submit them using the nom de plume "Jafsie"—a combination of his three initials (J, F, and C) spoken quickly.

No one at Hopewell investigated Condon; no one discussed with Schwarzkopf or any other law enforcement officer his use as a go-between. (They hadn't vetted Mickey Rosner or any gangsters either.) Condon's possession of the letter with the authenticating symbol and holes was all they knew about him and all they felt they needed to know. Had someone looked into his background, though, they would have discovered that Condon had been credited with saving the lives of six people in six different rescues in the past. In one case, that of a boy who fell through the ice of Zeltner's Lake in the Bronx, Congress had awarded him the Gold Lifesaving Medal "in testimony of heroic deeds in saving life from the perils of the sea."[11]

Condon perhaps believed fortune had again called upon him and his remarkable lifesaving powers, but to everyone else the idea that an eccentric, starstruck, old schoolteacher might succeed where law enforcement professionals, private detectives, gangsters, and Wall Street lawyers had so far failed seemed, if not preposterous, at least highly unlikely—unless, of course, Condon was actually working with the kidnappers.

Lindbergh and Breckinridge didn't deny they had their doubts about the strange fellow. If he had been a younger man, Lindbergh later admitted, he would have been immediately suspicious of him. He was enigmatic certainly; also cranky, cantankerous, curmudgeonly, a pest, and a "nut."[12] Yet he was the only person the kidnappers had been willing to deal with. Lindbergh laid his doubts aside, and Breckinridge made as his highest priority keeping a close eye on Condon's every movement. Condon agreed to let Breckinridge move into his home for as long as necessary. Breckinridge would spend almost every night there between March 10 and May 12.[13]

The strange arrival of Condon, the unlikely deus ex machina, convinced the inner circle they were now in contact with the actual kidnappers. Anne took heart. "There *really* is definite prog-ress," she wrote to Lindbergh's mother. "I feel *much* happier today. It does seem to be going ahead. Yesterday things began to move again and it was a great relief to everyone."[14]

The negotiations between Condon and the kidnappers were conducted by means of fourteen notes from the kidnappers and twenty-five "Jafsie" notices (containing nine different messages, some repeated) in the *New York American*.[15]

The kidnappers' March 9 note, the first note sent to Condon with the note to Lindbergh, instructed him to place a notice in the *New York American* reading, "The money is ready" when the ran-som was ready to be paid. On March 11 Jafsie placed this notice in the newspaper. Two notes were delivered to Condon on March 12, providing directions for a meeting that night in Woodlawn Cemetery in the Bronx.

Condon's friend and sometime bodyguard Al Reich, a former sparring partner of Jack Dempsey,[16] drove him to Woodlawn Cem-etery, where Condon met a man who said his name was John. Con-don described him as Scandinavian or German and referred to him as "Cemetery John." The two men sat on a bench and talked for over an hour. Cemetery John told Condon that there were six people involved in the kidnapping.[17] When Cemetery John finally asked, "Did you got it the money?" Condon replied that he couldn't bring the money "until I saw the package."[18] To prove they were the "right parties," Cemetery John offered to send Condon the sleeping suit the child was wearing the night he was taken.[19]

As promised, Condon received a brown paper package on March 16 containing a gray, one-piece Doctor Denton sleeping suit,[20] recently laundered, together with a note saying there would be no more "confidential conferences" in the future ("those arrange-ments too hazardous for us"). The note also rejected a simulta-neous exchange of the money for the child: "circumstances will not allow us to make a transfer like you wish. It is impossible for us." And then, chillingly: "You are willing to pay the 70,000 not 50,000 $ without seeing the baby first or not. Let us know about that in the *New York American*."[21]

Despite the impatient tone of the March 16 note, the kidnappers didn't threaten, and never threatened, to harm Charlie if the money wasn't paid. Most kidnappers used threats to harm their victims as a way of pressuring their families to pay. To a kidnapping expert, the absence of such threats from the kidnappers' notes might have been an indication Charlie was dead, but Lindbergh didn't share the notes with law enforcement officers or other experts.

Lindbergh examined the sleeping suit and said it was like the ones Charlie wore and would have been wearing the night he was kidnapped. The following day, March 17, Jafsie placed a new notice: "I accept. Money is ready. You know they won't let me deliver without getting the package. Let's make it some sort of C.O.D. transaction. Come. You know you can trust Jafsie."[22] The kidnappers responded on March 19 by announcing they wouldn't communicate again until Jafsie placed a notice in the newspaper that their terms were accepted: "We know you have to come to us anyway."[23]

Jafsie placed another notice on March 22, still haggling: "That little package you sent was immediately delivered and accepted as real article. See my position. Over fifty years in business and can I pay without seeing goods? Common sense makes me trust you. Please understand my position."[24]

The kidnappers went silent.

The one consistent piece of advice Lindbergh had received throughout was not to pay the ransom until he had Charlie safely in hand. From the beginning, he had insisted he wouldn't pay until Charlie was returned. At the same time, within the inner circle, he admitted the kidnappers "had him over a barrel"; he hoped, at best, to arrange a simultaneous exchange of the money for the child. Many of the inner circle's thoughts and concerns about the ransom weren't expressed, but as Irey later recalled, Lindbergh "somehow made us realize that he well understood what we all thought but never mentioned."[25]

Receipt of Charlie's sleeping suit was the turning point in the negotiations and in Lindbergh's thinking. It had become clearer as time passed that the underworld emissaries' efforts had failed. Lindbergh's financial advisers at J. P. Morgan were now suggesting that sometimes one must take chances, and this could be one of those times. Condon continued to object to any payment before Charlie's return until Lindbergh explained to him that Mrs. Lindbergh wanted the money to be paid.[26]

Lindbergh finally decided the kidnappers were right: he had no choice. On March 17 he again called Secretary Mills and asked him to send Elmer Irey and his men back to Hopewell again.[27]

The Lindberghs were well off by any measure, but they didn't have $70,000 in cash. Lindbergh directed J. P. Morgan to raise the money by selling shares of stock in his account (acquired at a cost of $350,000)[28] and to prepare the money in the denominations demanded and in strict accordance with the kidnappers' instructions not to mark the bills or take them from a single numerical series.

Irey's investigator Frank Wilson directed the Morgan employees to record the serial numbers of each of the $20, $10, and $5 bills they were assembling because he knew that tracking their expenditures of the ransom money might be the only way to catch the kidnappers. Lindbergh dug in his heels: recording the serial numbers might be viewed as going against his pledge to the kidnappers that he would not try in any way to injure those connected with the child's return.

Irey agreed with Wilson. He raised the issue again with Lindbergh: "Colonel Lindbergh, unless you comply with our suggestion to record the serial numbers, we shall have to withdraw from the case. We cannot compound a felony."[29] (He was alluding to the misdemeanor offense at English common law when a crime victim accepts something of value for agreeing not to prosecute, or for hampering the prosecution of, a felony.) Lindbergh finally relented.

Irey and Wilson also recommended that the ransom money include a large proportion of bills of the gold certificate variety. They explained there was a good chance the president would take the United States off the gold standard and withdraw gold certificates from circulation before long. Gold certificates would then become rare, making their distinctive, gold-colored seals easy to spot. Lindbergh agreed, and the Morgan employees began assembling new packages of ransom money including $35,000 in gold certificates.[30]

Under Wilson's guidance twenty-five Morgan employees manually recorded the serial numbers of the 5,150 ransom bills and wrapped them in packages. When they were finished, they took the packages to the home of Morgan partner Frank Bartow, where the butler locked them in the bedroom closet until they were needed.[31]

On March 28 Jafsie placed a message in the *New York American* indicating that the kidnappers' terms were accepted: "Money is ready. Furnish a simple code for us to use in paper" (to disguise the transaction to prevent the police and others from interfering with the payoff).[32] Breaking the silence they had maintained since March 19, the kidnappers on March 30 wrote that no code was necessary. "If the deal is not closed until the 8th of April we will ask for 30,000 more."[33]

Jafsie responded the next day: "I accept. Money is ready."[34]

The kidnappers' April 1 note instructed Condon to have the money ready, and they would let him know where and how to deliver it the following night, Saturday, April 2.[35] Morgan employees took the money from Bartow's house to Condon's, where $50,000 was

packed in a wooden box. The remaining $20,000 in $50 gold certificates, which didn't fit in the box, was wrapped in a separate
package. That evening, a taxi driver delivered to Condon's home
instructions to go to the Bergen Greenhouse on East Tremont
Avenue in the Bronx, where he would find further instructions
beneath a stone under a table.[36] Strapping on his shoulder holster
and revolver, Lindbergh announced that he would drive Condon
to the rendezvous himself.[37]

At Bergen's, Condon retrieved a note directing him to cross
the street to St. Raymond's Cemetery, alone, and walk along the
edge of the cemetery until Cemetery John met him.[38] While Lindbergh waited in the car with the ransom money, he heard a voice
call out once from the cemetery, "Ay, Doctor." The word "Doctor" was pronounced with a definite accent.[39]

Condon and Cemetery John found each other, but before Condon returned to the car for the money, he had one last item to negotiate. He told Cemetery John that Colonel Lindbergh was not a
rich man; it had been hard enough for him to raise $50,000, but he
couldn't raise the last $20,000. Wouldn't John be decent to him? "If
we can't get $70,000, we'll take $50,000," replied Cemetery John.[40]

Delighted, Condon returned to the car and reported to Lindbergh how he had just saved him $20,000. Then he took the box
containing the $50,000, walked back to the cemetery, and gave
it to Cemetery John. At the same time, John handed Condon a
handwritten note indicating that Charlie was being cared for by
two innocent people on a boat named *Nelly*, anchored between
Horseneck Beach and Gay Head near the Elizabeth Islands off
the coast of Martha's Vineyard. John opened the box and satisfied himself that it was full of money.

"Thank you, Doctor," he said. "Everybody says your work has
been perfect."[41]

They shook hands, and Cemetery John disappeared back into
the pitch-black cemetery.[42]

After the payoff Lindbergh, Breckinridge, and Condon joined Irey, Wilson, and Madden at Mrs. Morrow's Manhattan townhome. Lindbergh finalized arrangements to borrow a Sikorsky amphibious aircraft (a "flying boat"), while Irey contacted the Treasury Department to have the Coast Guard send ships to the Elizabeth Islands.[43]

In the midst of all the excitement, Condon finally got a chance to tell Irey how he had saved the Colonel $20,000. "Look!" he said as he proudly displayed the four hundred $50 gold certificates he hadn't given to Cemetery John. Irey and his men were incredulous. "We could have shot the well-meaning old meddler," he wrote.[44] Those bills were a large portion of the gold certificates they were counting on to be the easiest of the ransom bills to spot when the kidnappers started spending them. Four hundred chances to catch the kidnappers lost.

Lindbergh, Breckinridge, Irey, and Condon prepared to leave for Bridgeport, Connecticut, where they would take off the next morning. Before they left, Lindbergh gathered a few things he thought Charlie might need right away and tied a milk bottle to a bedsheet. It would be just the thing to drop from the plane to signal to the Coast Guard when they spotted the *Nelly*.[45]

At first light, Lindbergh was at the controls of the seaplane heading for Massachusetts. They flew low over the coastline and small harbors searching for the *Nelly*, but there was no *Nelly* anywhere in the vicinity. Lindbergh knew he had been double-crossed, but he kept flying for hours, diving at every boat, and running alongside to check every name.[46]

There was no word from the kidnappers. Four days later, on April 6, Jafsie placed a notice in the *New York American*: "What is wrong? Have you crossed me? Please better directions."[47] He repeated the same notice on April 7 and 8. Cemetery John didn't respond and never again communicated. The odds of ever getting Charlie back alive dropped drastically.

Lindbergh, meanwhile, struggled with the most difficult decision to confront him yet: whether to release the list of ransom money serial numbers to the U.S. Treasury and authorize it to begin immediately searching for ransom money and tracking bills put into circulation. Irey and Wilson urged him not to wait to enlist the facilities of the Treasury and the U.S. banking system. But if Charlie was still alive and the kidnappers learned the money was being tracked, there was a risk they might murder him. He also agonized because he had given his assurances to the kidnappers that he would do nothing to harm them if they returned his son. Of course, they had not met his condition, but keeping his word to those who had taken his son was still important in his thinking.

Lindbergh made up his mind to authorize the SIU and NJSP to begin tracking the ransom money and making every effort to apprehend the kidnappers. On April 4 he wrote a letter to Secretary Mills and gave it to Frank Wilson to deliver: "I have furnished you with a list containing the serial numbers of certain United States currency. . . . I would like very much to determine where that currency now is. . . . If there are any steps that you can properly take in that direction, I shall greatly appreciate your efforts."[48]

The Treasury printed fifty thousand copies of the list of serial numbers and began distributing them to U.S. banks on April 6, with instructions to notify the treasurer of the United States immediately if any bill on the list was discovered.

Anne wasn't ready to give up hope. On April 5 a brush fire swept over two hundred acres of the Lindbergh estate, stopping a few feet from the house. Lindbergh joined the firemen, troopers, and reporters fighting the flames with brooms and shovels for most of the day before the flames were extinguished.[49] The next day she wrote to Lindbergh's mother, referring to the fire: "The exercise was really good for [Charles] and took off the tension. We have had some very disappointing setbacks and think we've got a long wait ahead, but the consensus is that the child is still safe and well."[50]

But when two more days passed without any response from Cemetery John, Anne's confidence seemed to wither: "All the papers here lately say that there is 'an air of great optimism' etc. and predict a speedy return of the child. I don't know where they get that from. We have been rather gloomy lately though the best opinion here is that the child is still safe and all right. We are now living from day to day but realize we must look forward to weeks."[51]

Despite all instructions to the banks to keep the serial numbers and the fact they were watching for ransom money strictly confidential, a bank employee provided a list of serial numbers to a Newark newspaper, which published the list on April 9. Lindbergh insisted on reaching out again to the kidnappers to explain his actions. He worked with Schwarzkopf to write and edit a statement released that night. It disclosed for the first time that the Lindberghs had paid a ransom and that the kidnappers had not released Charlie:

> A ransom of $50,000 was paid to the kidnappers, properly identified as such, upon their agreement to notify [Colonel Lindbergh] as to the exact whereabouts of the baby. The baby was not found at the point designated. Several days were permitted to elapse to give the kidnappers every opportunity to keep their agreement. It was not intended to use the numbers on the specie in which the ransom was paid, but inasmuch as the kidnappers have failed to keep their agreement and have not communicated since the ransom was paid, it is felt that every remaining possible means must be utilized to accomplish the return of the baby and to this end the co-operation of the Federal Government was requested in tracing the bills used.[52]

Paying the ransom and still not getting Charlie back was gut-wrenching, not only for the Lindberghs. Pastors took to their pulpits the day after the shocking revelations to denounce the kidnappers' deception as a second outrage. Unitarian theologian

Reverend Charles Francis Potter told the First Humanist Society of New York, "We might as well face the facts: the Lindbergh case illuminates our whole situation. When the underworld can steal a baby and keep it, take a ransom for it, and still keep it, gangsterdom is thumbing its nose at law and order. The underworld is now the overworld."[53]

April rolled over into May. On May 11 Anne described in her diary the "eternal quality of certain moments in one's life. The baby being lifted out of his crib forever and ever, like Dante's hell. C's set face, carved onto Time for always."[54]

7

....

Competing Investigations

On May 12 William Allen and Orville Wilson were hauling a load of timber on the road from Princeton to Hopewell when Allen pulled the truck off the road near the little village of Mount Rose in farming country. He climbed down and headed for a thicket of maple and locust trees to answer a call of nature. About forty-five feet into the woods, he ducked under a low-hanging tree branch, and when he raised his head he noticed a tiny skull and a little foot sticking up from a shallow trench. Dirt and leaves partially blanketed the trench. He couldn't be sure, but it looked like the badly decomposed body of a baby with blond hair, wearing a little hand-sewn undershirt. The only missing baby Allen had heard about was the Lindbergh baby. He hurried back to the truck, and he and Wilson drove into town to get Deputy Charles Williamson of the Hopewell Police Department and bring him back to their gruesome discovery, less than five miles from the Lindbergh home.[1]

It had been seventy-two days since the kidnapping of Charlie Lindbergh.

Betty Gow identified the undershirt as the one she had made for Charlie to wear under his sleeping suit the night he was taken. Detectives drove her to the morgue in Trenton, where she identified Charlie's remains.[2] As soon as he arrived back at Hopewell from Cape May, New Jersey, where he had been searching offshore for another fictitious boat supposedly holding his son, Lindbergh also identified the remains.

The county coroner and a local undertaker performed an autopsy. They concluded the cause of death was a fractured skull resulting from external violence and that death had probably been instantaneous, approximately two to three months earlier—meaning around the time of the kidnapping or shortly after. The passage of time and state of decomposition made it difficult to be more specific about the nature of the injury or the date of death.

The autopsy findings, together with the splintered ladder found outside the Lindbergh home on the night of the kidnapping, led investigators to theorize that the kidnapper had dropped the child or banged his head with great force as he carried him from the nursery, perhaps when the ladder splintered. Another theory suggested that as the kidnappers were getting away from the home, they looked back and saw police vehicles arriving and realized they would never escape the area with the child. They then clubbed him over the head and hastily buried him in the woods along their escape route.

After Charlie's body was found, the Lindberghs left Hopewell. Lindbergh said they never spent another night in their home.[3] Anne believed there was "no use living in the crime element of this any longer, that is what it is at Hopewell now. Constant reconstruction of the crime. I want to dwell on the boy's happy life, not on the crime that ended it."[4] They both doubted they would ever feel secure there again. Charles told Anne he would "never be able to go away to work—leave me [Anne] and children there without armed protection—and yet we want our children to grow up independent."[5] They moved temporarily back to the Morrow home in Englewood; the following year, they gave the Hopewell house and surrounding land to the State of New Jersey to be used as a home for children.

The discovery of the body removed all remaining restraints on the police in their efforts to find the kidnappers. Likewise, no longer concerned that passing antikidnapping legislation could endanger Charlie's life, Congress passed the bills that had been put on hold at Lindbergh's request after the kidnapping. The on-again, off-again Capone rescue fantasy finally collapsed. The fruitless search Lindbergh was on when he was called back to Hopewell was revealed to be a hoax perpetrated by an amateur extortionist named John Hughes Curtis, who made up the whole story in hopes of selling it to newspapers to raise money to pay off gambling debts.

The morning after Charlie's body was found, President Hoover ordered federal law enforcement and investigative agencies to continue providing assistance to the New Jersey police "in every possible way." In a rare display of emotion, he called in reporters and read to them the words of his order directing federal agencies to make the kidnapping and murder of the Lindbergh baby "a live and never to be forgotten case, never to be relaxed until those criminals are implacably brought to justice."[6] At the president's direction, Attorney General Mitchell announced that J. Edgar Hoover would "coordinate" the services of all the federal agencies.[7]

Schwarzkopf and Irey were incredulous. Irey's SIU was the only federal investigative agency still actively assisting the NJSP at that point. Frank Wilson had been assigned full-time to assist Schwarzkopf and Lindbergh since mid-March; Irey returned to Hopewell whenever he was needed. Hoover and the FBI had never been involved in the investigation in any significant way. That was partly due, at least in the early days, to gangster Owney Madden's advice, which Lindbergh and Breckinridge had taken seriously, to stay away from federal agents so as not to discourage the kidnappers from making contact. But it was also true that, aside from sometimes stationing a token special agent at Hopewell or Trenton to avoid criticism for not showing up at all, Hoover had never tried to integrate the FBI into the NJSP investigation by establishing a continuous presence in New Jersey. He had never reached out directly to Lindbergh or Breckinridge to offer suggestions or resources. Hoover had come to the conclusion that Schwarzkopf never intended to use the FBI as anything other than errand boys to obtain information from immigration and other federal authorities. He didn't want to be anyone's errand boy, especially not Schwarzkopf's. Hoover considered Schwarzkopf a lightweight.

When the ransom was paid and Charlie wasn't returned, Hoover became convinced that a successful outcome was less likely than ever. On April 4, the same day Lindbergh asked the Treasury Department to begin tracking the ransom money and going after the kidnappers, Hoover withdrew the FBI's token agent standing by in Hopewell and Trenton. He ordered his men to "get away" from New Jersey, "leave the case alone," and do no further work unless Lindbergh or Schwarzkopf specifically requested it.[8]

In another indication that Hoover foresaw a bad ending and possible scapegoating, he sent his troubleshooter, Special Agent in Charge J. M. Keith of the Washington office, to New York in April to pull together the facts about the part the FBI had actually played in the NJSP investigation thus far. Keith confirmed what Hoover already knew: Schwarzkopf, Lindbergh, and Breckinridge were tightly controlling everything; they had not shared even basic information with the FBI, like the ransom negotiations, or given the FBI access to any physical evidence, particularly the ransom notes, for scientific analysis. Keith faulted Special Agent Connelley for not pushing more aggressively for access to important information and for accepting what little he was given, usually by Major Lanphier. Keith warned that, as long as the FBI continued handling small projects doled out by Schwarzkopf and Lanphier, the FBI would share blame with the NJSP for a failed investigation. He advised Hoover to get out or get blamed.[9]

On April 11, after the story broke that the ransom had been paid and the child not recovered, Hoover ordered all FBI offices to stop doing any work on the Lindbergh case unless specifically requested by Schwarzkopf and expressly authorized by FBI headquarters in Washington.[10]

Assistant Director Harold "Pop" Nathan, the FBI's second in command, saw to it that the "stop work" order was rigorously enforced. When Lindbergh lawyer Robert Thayer asked for help from the FBI's New York office in understanding certain references in a letter from an informant, Nathan refused the request because Thayer hadn't submitted it to FBI headquarters in Washington.[11] In another, more significant example, St. Louis police chief Joseph Gerk requested that the head of the FBI's St. Louis office obtain authorization from Washington for an agent to accompany St. Louis police officers across the state line into Illinois to interview a woman reported by a reliable police informant to be caring for a kidnapped child that looked like the Lindbergh baby. Nathan turned down that request, too, this time on the ground that the FBI couldn't take any action unless the request came from Schwarzkopf himself. A U.S. postal inspector accompanied the St. Louis police to Illinois instead.[12]

Such was the state of affairs on May 12 when William Allen stumbled across Charlie Lindbergh's body in the woods, and President Hoover selected J. Edgar Hoover to coordinate the activities of all federal agencies assisting the NJSP.

When he learned the president had designated Hoover coordinator of the entire federal effort, Schwarzkopf called Hoover to find out what he had in mind to do. Hoover explained that he expected Schwarzkopf to send all requests for federal assistance to him; he would then issue orders to whichever federal agency he considered best suited to handle each request. Likewise, when a federal agency had information relating to the investigation, he expected the agency to send the information to him, and he would send it to Schwarzkopf. To facilitate the flow of requests and information, he planned to send Special Agent F. X. Fay from New York to Trenton to be the contact man.[13]

The plan seemed overly bureaucratic and unworkable to Schwarzkopf; he feared it would disrupt the good working relationship the NJSP and Lindbergh had developed with Irey and the SIU. In an effort to work out a smoother collaboration, Schwarzkopf invited Hoover to meet with him and his lead investigators in Trenton, along with Irey and his men and anyone else Hoover wanted to bring. They would go over the entire case; Schwarzkopf said he welcomed the benefit of the FBI's experience and advice. Hoover bristled at the mention of another meeting in Trenton and suggested meeting somewhere else instead. When Schwarzkopf said it had to be Trenton, Hoover said he wouldn't attend but would send Harold Nathan in his place.[14] The reason he gave Schwarzkopf for skipping the meeting was that Schwarzkopf and Lindbergh had shown the ransom notes to Irey and Wilson and kept them informed about the ransom negotiations but not shared the same information with the FBI.[15]

The meeting with Schwarzkopf and his lead investigators went forward on May 18, with Nathan representing Hoover and Wilson representing Irey. It got off to a poor start when Nathan began by addressing a list of points presented as facts and suggestions, but that sounded more like demands: the FBI would be the "official and unofficial contact" between all federal agencies and the NJSP; the FBI would "put the case on a scientific basis" and be the "repository of all available information relative to the case"; and the FBI would be the liaison between the NJSP and all other law enforcement agencies throughout the country. Schwarzkopf countered with a proposal for a "board of strategy" composed of representatives of all law enforcement agencies involved in the investigation, including the FBI, that would meet from time to time to share ideas.[16]

The two conceptions of the investigation were polar opposites, but neither man made any effort to win over the other or look for a compromise. On the contrary, the combination of Hoover's snub and Nathan's peremptory approach convinced Schwarzkopf that any attempt to share responsibility with Hoover would only encourage Hoover to take more control, until Schwarzkopf and the NJSP were on the outside looking in. He was already outside Lindbergh's inner circle.

At the end of that same day, his first as Hoover's contact man in Trenton, Special Agent Fay sent a handwritten letter to Hoover on hotel notepaper reporting what he had seen and heard that day. He had seen the SIU's Arthur Madden at Hopewell and believed Frank Wilson was there, too: "I believe both of these babies are still sticking around and 'possibly' 'putting the works in on our outfit.' The sooner they are eliminated from the scene the better and easier I believe it will be for us," he wrote. "The whole thing is quite a mess. . . . It seems a shame that our Bureau should have to waste its time and money on this case." He wasn't keeping a copy of his notes for fear "they may 'frisk' my baggage."[17] It could have been the note of a soldier caught behind enemy lines.

Hoover convened his own meeting of federal agency representatives, including Irey, in his Washington office the next morning. After explaining how he intended to coordinate the federal effort, he directed Irey to withdraw Wilson and Madden from the case "for the time being." Irey said he would comply "for the time being."[18]

Irey and Hoover were bitter enemies in a long-running bureaucratic battle that swept up both their organizations as well. According to Irey's long-time assistant Malachi Harney, "We all had this battle. I always thought Irey was a gentleman and Hoover just simply an alley fighter—a good fighter, let's put it this way. But there was always a contest for this and that or for jurisdiction and so on."[19] It went back at least to 1924, when Irey had lost out to Hoover in the contest to become acting director of the FBI. Though Irey's investigatory credentials as a postal inspector and Treasury agent far outshone Hoover's, Hoover won the job because it was a time to reform the FBI; he was a lawyer, and Irey was not. Since then Irey's success in bringing down Al Capone had brought him renown and mention as a possible replacement for Hoover.

Hoover didn't like Wilson either. Irey had chosen Wilson over all his other accountant investigators to send to Chicago for three years to make the case that Capone had received income he failed to report; Wilson's success in doing that had won him wide respect in law enforcement circles. "Wilson fears nothing that walks," wrote Irey, "he will sit quietly looking at books eighteen hours a day, seven days a week, forever, if he wants to find something in those books."[20] Wilson would investigate his own grandmother if assigned to do it, said a colleague; he sweats ice water, said a suspect he once questioned.[21] For Hoover to despise Wilson, it was enough that Irey and Lindbergh wanted him on their teams.

When Lindbergh learned that Hoover had used his authority as coordinator to fire Wilson and the SIU team from the investigation, he called Treasury Secretary Mills and asked him to reassign Wilson so that he could continue working on the investigation. Mills took the matter up with the president, who agreed to reassign Wilson, but Hoover would remain as the nominal coordinator of the federal effort. Hoover could ask other federal agencies what they were doing in the investigation, but he was to have no authority or control over any federal employees except his own.

Attorney General Mitchell informed Hoover on May 24 of Lindbergh's intervention and the president's decision to reassign Wilson to the investigation. According to Hoover's account, Mitchell also said he, Mitchell, thought it would be "undesirable and unwise" for both Wilson and an FBI contact man to be present at Hopewell and available to assist the NJSP.[22] The following day, Hoover reported to Nathan that the attorney general had authorized him to withdraw Fay from Hopewell as soon as Wilson returned.[23]

Whether it was Hoover's idea or Mitchell's to remove the FBI's contact man from Hopewell may never be known for certain. What is known is that the only thing Mitchell authorized was Fay's withdrawal from Hopewell, not the FBI's withdrawal from the Lindbergh investigation. A few weeks later Schwarzkopf asked Hoover to please send Fay back to Hopewell, where he had been very helpful. Hoover told Schwarzkopf he would like to send Fay back, but he had been withdrawn at Lindbergh's request (not true), and the "next move was up to Colonel Lindbergh."[24]

Even though he had greatly overstepped his coordinator position, Hoover had avoided the humiliation of presidential removal. He had underestimated Lindbergh, though, and it wouldn't be the last time.

The discovery of Charlie's body unleashed a torrent of pent-up criticism against Schwarzkopf and the NJSP. The majority leader of the New Jersey State Senate, Emerson Richards, threatened to open a Senate investigation of the NJSP's mishandling of the case. "The State police is a patrol body to protect rural districts," he said, "and is no more capable of solving crimes of this kind than a traffic policeman down on the corner."[25]

Schwarzkopf's qualifications and experience show that he "lacks anything indicating that he was qualified to adequately handle the greatest criminal investigation of modern history," wrote the *Brooklyn Daily Eagle*.[26] The conclusion is inescapable, wrote the *Daily Eagle*, that the NJSP under Schwarzkopf was "completely blinded to the glare of worldwide attention focused upon them and neglected the obvious and elementary. Even the finding of the body was not the result of police search but the accident of an obscure truckman."[27]

"Boneheaded police from Norman Schwarzkopf down have bungled the Lindbergh case," lamented Congressman Charles Karch of East St. Louis, Illinois, the same congressman who had helped obtain the release of Dr. Dee Kelley and who had offered his services to the Lindbergh team.[28]

President Hoover signed the Federal Kidnapping Act into law on June 22, 1932, the day that would have been Charlie Lindbergh's second birthday. The law, universally known as the "Lindbergh Law," made it a federal crime to transport a ransom kidnap victim across a state line, punishable by imprisonment for a term of years at the judge's discretion. The Extortion Act, signed on July 8, made it a federal crime, punishable by imprisonment for up to twenty years and a $5,000 fine, to send a ransom demand or extortion threat through the mail.

Though Hoover had spent months alternately posting his men to Hopewell and Trenton and pulling them out, shadowing Irey's men, and dodging "menial" assignments offered by Schwarzkopf, he never lost sight of the importance to the FBI's future and to his own career of the Lindbergh case. His early, clumsy efforts to undermine Schwarzkopf, foil Lindbergh, and seize control of the investigation had been counterproductive, but he was a dogged fighter. He quietly set up his own Lindbergh squad in the FBI's New York office and ordered his handpicked special agents to pursue every lead they came upon and to share nothing with the NJSP or the NYPD, who were now actively involved, along with Wilson, in tracking the ransom money as it began turning up.

Few outside the FBI realized it, but Hoover had embarked on a race to beat everyone else to the Lindbergh kidnappers.

Three

To War against Kidnappers

8

....

Call NAtional 8-7117

Cape Cod and Washington, May–July 1933

Bright, bouncy Peggy McMath was ten years old and in the fourth grade at Harwich Centre Grammar School on Cape Cod. She knew she never should have left school with a stranger, but her teacher Miss Flinkman said her father had called the school and asked that she be permitted to leave early with his chauffeur. Peggy also knew, of course, that her family didn't have a chauffeur, but she didn't want to argue with Miss Flinkman. So she picked up her coat and lunch pail and walked out the front door.

Ten-year-old Jack Shaughnessey was playing in the schoolyard. He saw a strange-looking black man grab Peggy, and he heard him tell her to "shut up and get in" his car. Peggy started to cry. The man dragged her into his blue car and made her sit on the seat beside him, and they drove away.[1]

A short while later the man stopped the car at the end of a dirt road near the edge of a cranberry bog.[2] He covered Peggy's head with a black cloth, tied it around her neck with rope, and fastened handcuffs on her wrists. He made her lie down on the back seat and began stuffing dirty clothes into her mouth. Peggy begged him not to gag her and promised she wouldn't scream. He warned that he would chloroform her if she moved or said a word. Then he drove on to an old cranberry shack not far from town, where he left Peggy by herself in the dark, still blindfolded and handcuffed, and hurried back to town to pick up his six-year-old son from school.[3]

The kidnapper returned to the shack at 11:00 that night to get Peggy and move her to a vacant house across the street from his home in Harwich. As he coaxed her into the crawl space under the house, he whispered that he was her friend and that he was hiding her to protect her from kidnappers, but if she moved or said anything he would hurt her parents. When he handed her a ham sandwich, a blanket, and a few burlap bags to sleep on, Peggy noticed his hands were white, not black like his face.[4] Then he left her alone again in the dark. She never let on that she knew the handcuffs were just toys and that she could take them off and put them back on again.[5]

Peggy was born in Detroit and moved to Harwichport in 1931 with her parents, Neil and Margaret McMath, and her brother, Francis, now seven. Both of Peggy's grandfathers were prominent Detroit industrialists and philanthropists who had made sizable fortunes: Francis Charles McMath was a bridge-builder and banker and William R. Kales was the head of a structural steel fabricating company. Her grandmother Alice Gray Kales was the daughter of John S. Gray, one of the founders of the Ford Motor Company. It was to the Kales' sprawling summer home in Harwichport that Peggy's family moved when they left Detroit.

Elite families like the Kales and McMaths were then still reeling from the 1929 kidnapping and murder of David Cass. While the police had broken up several of the Motor City's infamous kidnap gangs since then, Neil McMath could hardly ignore the five letters he reportedly received from extortionists threatening to kidnap Peggy and Francis. He gave up his job as treasurer of

William Kales's company and moved his family to Harwichport, where he became a boatbuilder. It had seemed like a good decision until the afternoon of May 2, 1933, when it got to be 3:30 and Peggy hadn't come home from school on the bus.

Peggy's mother, Margaret, realized right away what had happened. Earlier that afternoon, a caller identifying himself as a telephone lineman had phoned the McMath home and asked her to take the telephone off the hook for ten minutes so he could make some repairs. When she thought back on the call, she remembered she had heard a coin drop during the conversation, indicating that the caller was using a pay phone. Why would a telephone repairman use a pay telephone? Margaret hurried to the school. The principal said the school had permitted Peggy to leave with the McMaths' chauffeur because a man identifying himself as her father had called and authorized it. The school didn't contact the family to confirm, but as Margaret knew, the telephone was off the hook anyway.

Neil decided to handle negotiations with Peggy's kidnappers without involving the police; he didn't want to take the chance they would interfere with paying the ransom and getting Peggy back safely. In a public statement of the sort that had become familiar since the Lindbergh kidnapping, he urged the kidnappers to contact him directly and promised not to aid the police: "I have no desire for revenge or to mete out punishment. If the kidnappers will only get in touch with me I will try to do what they want me to do. They can get in touch with me openly if they want to. I will keep my mouth shut."[6]

Margaret added her own message to the kidnappers: "If it is necessary to take the child in an automobile, it would be wise to have a supply of chewing gum, as she becomes carsick." To Peggy, she said, "Be a good girl and do just what [you are] told to do."[7]

Neil begged the police for a forty-eight-hour moratorium free of police involvement so he could communicate with the kidnappers and clear a path for them to return Peggy. The police would agree only to stay away from the McMath home and not to tap their telephone line during that time.[8] They continued to patrol bridges and highways, while the Coast Guard searched the waters off the New England coast for strange boats that might be hiding a child.[9] Police in Boston, Detroit, New York, and New Jersey also investigated and searched.

The head of the Massachusetts state police, Brigadier General Daniel Needham, announced that solving the McMath case might also lead to a resolution of the Lindbergh case.[10] Though there was no basis for saying that, the tantalizing suggestion drew even more reporters to the little town.

In frustration Neil called the White House and asked whether there was anything President Franklin Roosevelt could do to stop the police and press from interfering and making it difficult for the kidnappers to contact him. White House press secretary Stephen Early contacted Hoover and asked that the FBI do whatever it could to relieve the tension and to tell Peggy's family the FBI was entering the case at the president's request.[11] Special agents in New York and Boston had already contacted the McMaths to offer the FBI's help after reading about the kidnapping in the morning papers, but they had gotten nowhere. Hoover was fuming because his men hadn't gone to Harwichport in person and taken charge.[12] Perhaps the intervention by the White House was the opening the FBI needed.

Hoover sent Assistant Director Harold Nathan to Harwichport and dispatched special agents from New York, Boston, and Charlotte. The McMaths were cordial, but Neil still insisted on handling the situation himself. The agents went to work doing what they could without being too obvious about it: searching headquarters modus operandi files for known African American kidnappers and tracking down Detroit kidnappers and gangsters who were missing from their usual locations, including the fugitive Leonard "Black Leo" Cellura, one of the leaders of the Detroit Mafia, who was dodging a murder warrant.

Meanwhile, with the beginning of the summer season only a few weeks away, Cape Cod residents were horrified by the kidnapping. Boston lawyer Clarence W. Rowley, president of the Law Society of Massachusetts and a summer Cape Cod resident, organized a vigilance committee to look for Peggy's kidnappers. "Gangsters can be tracked down and punished just as were the criminals of pioneer days," he said. "We'll use plenty of rope—not to hang them, but to truss them up and turn them over to the law."[13]

The morning after Peggy's abduction, one of Neil's employees arranged for his friend Cyril Buck to meet with Neil. The forty-one-year-old Buck, owner of a local garage, told Neil that the kidnapper had asked him to serve as go-between and that he was demanding a ransom of $250,000 (over $4.9 million in 2020) in unmarked bills. Neil told Buck that was impossible, and they agreed on $70,000 (over $1.3 million in 2020). Neil also told Buck he wouldn't pay anything unless he received proof that Peggy was alive. He suggested that Buck bring back to him Peggy's answer to the question "What was the name of your dog that died in January?" Buck returned to the McMath home that night with Peggy's lunch pail, a note in her handwriting apologizing to her parents for leaving school without her schoolbooks, and the correct answer to her father's question: Peter the Great.

Neil and Buck finalized the remaining arrangements. Neil's business partner William Lee would fill his boat (the *Bob*) with gas and take it to Wynchmere Harbor in Harwich. Buck would drive Neil, Peggy, the ransom money, and the kidnapper to the *Bob*. There Neil would give the money to the kidnapper. The kidnapper and Buck would then depart. Peggy, Neil, and Lee would remain on the *Bob* at the wharf for another forty-eight hours to give the kidnapper a chance to get away.

Everything went according to plan. Peggy was reunited with Neil, and he handed over the $70,000 to the masked kidnapper on the *Bob*. The kidnapper gave Buck $10,000 of ransom money, but Buck refused to accept it and returned it to Neil "as a gift."

Hours later a Coast Guard boat searching the harbor for strange boats came upon the *Bob*, which appeared unoccupied, and the officers went aboard to take a look. In the cabin below they found Neil, Peggy, and Bill Lee—tired, hungry, and anxious, though relieved to see the Coast Guard and not the kidnapper. The state police took Neil and Lee into custody for questioning, but they refused to allow any FBI agents to attend their questioning or the interviews of any other witnesses. After satisfying themselves that Neil and Lee were not part of a scheme to fake Peggy's kidnapping and extort cash from her grandparents, they released them.

The police also questioned Cyril Buck. He insisted he was not in on the kidnapping and had no prior knowledge of it but had acted solely as a go-between to help return Peggy to her family. During all-night interrogation, he finally admitted the kidnapper was his brother Kenneth, twenty-eight, who had lost his job as a chauffeur the year before and was about to lose his home. Kenneth had tried without success to get a job at Neil's company, which explained why he had blackened his face with burned corks when he snatched Peggy and worn a hood when he met with Neil.[14]

When the police picked up Kenneth at his house, they retrieved $60,000 in $20 and $100 bills with serial numbers matching those on the list prepared by the bank that assembled the ransom money. He confessed to the kidnapping, corroborated Cyril's denial of involvement, and confirmed that he hadn't taken Peggy across a state line. He was convicted of kidnapping and sentenced to not less than twenty-four, nor more than twenty-five, years in state prison. The jury believed Cyril's story that he wasn't part of the kidnapping and had intervened only to return Peggy. He was acquitted of extortion.

Writing afterward to Hoover, Neil praised the FBI's performance: "From the time we first had contact with your men, Mrs.

McMath and I were much easier in our minds and we then felt for the first time some degree of confidence that we would get the little girl back. Their every action and word gave us hope and faith and this hope and faith had a lot to do in making the action which led to the return of Peggy possible." In any future emergency, Neil said, his family would at once get in touch with the FBI, and "we would then feel absolutely certain that everything was being done that human brains and hands could do."[15]

Neil's words confirmed Hoover's belief that the FBI could outperform state and local police in kidnapping cases and that the public would put their trust and confidence in the FBI if only they could see the FBI in action. Establishing a direct, close relationship with every victim's family—actually moving into their home whenever possible—became the FBI's goal in all future cases.

"It is common knowledge, of course, that in the past year there have been perhaps more kidnappings than at any prior time," wrote Hoover in his annual report to the attorney general for 1933.[16] And yet in that first year after passage of the Lindbergh Law, beside the Lindbergh and McMath cases, the FBI had been involved in only two kidnapping and two extortion cases.[17] The new laws didn't seem to be having any significant impact on the total number of kidnappings or on the portion of kidnappings that were federal crimes. If those trends continued, kidnapping might not become the FBI specialty Hoover was looking for.

The main reason the FBI had investigated such a small number of kidnapping cases was that most kidnappings, perhaps 85 percent,[18] were not federal crimes under the Lindbergh Law because the victims were not taken across state lines. Another reason was that the FBI often didn't know that a kidnapping had occurred until after it was over and they read about it in the newspapers. That was because victims' families who reported kidnappings naturally reported them to their local or state police, who usually didn't bother to inform the FBI. Hoover realized he had to figure out a way to get the FBI into many more cases if the FBI was going to become a significant factor in fighting kidnapping.

The Lindbergh Law itself didn't address *when* the interstate transportation requirement had to be met or the consequences, if any, of determining there had been no interstate transportation after the FBI had begun to investigate. One of Hoover's men, V. W. Hughes, consulted Nugent Dodds, the head criminal lawyer in the Justice Department, about when, under the Lindbergh Law, the FBI should enter kidnapping cases.

Dodds chose not to approach the question as one of statutory interpretation. Instead he took a practical view, distinguishing between cases involving adults and cases involving children, though the Lindbergh Law itself made no such distinction. In the case of adult victims, Dodds was of the view that the FBI should wait until there was evidence of interstate transportation before beginning to investigate and "need not be unduly concerned" if it didn't begin investigating until after the kidnapping was concluded, when the FBI could gather the evidence to prove a violation of the law. In the case of children, however, the political realities were different; he believed the FBI could choose to begin investigating at any time after the abduction or could wait until interstate transportation was established. His advice was that "the Bureau should proceed on its own initiative to investigate the cases which it felt should be made the subject of investigation."[19]

Experience in early cases had shown that interstate transportation was hardly ever apparent at the outset, and sometimes wasn't established until the victim was located or the case was solved. Hoover began to question whether it would even matter, for his purposes, if federal jurisdiction was found to be lacking after the FBI had begun to investigate. The Justice Department would have no basis for *prosecuting* such a case as a federal crime, but the FBI's function was to *investigate* cases, not to prosecute them in court, and the best time for the FBI to start investigating was at the beginning. Hoover reasoned that while it might not be apparent at the beginning of a case that it *would* be a federal case, neither was it ordinarily obvious it would *not* be a federal case. That uncertainty, he decided, gave the FBI all the justification it needed to investigate cases that, in Dodds's words, "should be made the subject of investigation."

Hoover had learned a painful lesson from observing Charles Lindbergh's close working relationship with Elmer Irey and Frank Wilson, born of his reliance on their experience and judgment. Harold Nathan's positive experience with Peggy McMath's family enabled him to see that the key to establishing the FBI's leadership in the fight against kidnapping would be persuading the public and state and local police that they *wanted* the FBI's help.

Hoover was not well known outside official Washington. His name was anything but a household word in 1933, but he decided to reach out to the public himself and invite ordinary citizens to call and report *every* kidnapping directly to *him*, in effect bypassing their state and local police. He published the telephone number (NAtional 8-7117, the number of the FBI's Washington DC field office) widely; the line was manned around the clock, seven days a week. More importantly he took every kidnap call personally; late-night calls were referred to his home and returned immediately. It was a bold, brilliant move.

Direct citizen access to Hoover in kidnapping cases did not solve the problem entirely, though. The cases in which victims were never taken across state lines—the 85 percent—were undeniably the sole responsibility of individual states and their state and local law enforcement agencies. Unless families requested FBI involvement, the police had no obligation to work with the FBI, but Hoover wanted the option of participating as a volunteer in those state cases, too, especially the high-profile ones like the Lindbergh and McMath cases.

There was nothing to stop state and local police from accepting or even requesting the FBI's help in kidnapping cases, but they often had little incentive to do that, particularly when monetary rewards were offered for helping catch kidnappers. Hoover didn't allow his men to accept such rewards, but FBI involvement in a case could prevent police from getting the credit that would earn them rewards.

Even when rewards weren't an issue, the FBI and the police often viewed each other as rivals and treated each other with suspicion and hostility. Since FBI agents had no authority to make arrests in any kind of case, they had to suffer the indignity of asking the local police (or United States marshals) to make arrests for them. Friction often resulted. The police resented Hoover's "college kids" who knew little of the ways of criminals, and they loathed the way Hoover claimed credit for every success and only grudgingly shared credit with other law enforcement agencies. Hoover taught his special agents that their training and strict code of conduct set them apart from—and above—ordinary policemen, drumming into them that they were not cops but agents of the United States.[20]

One way to get state and local police to invite the FBI into their cases, despite the bad blood, was to offer them something valuable they could not get elsewhere. That part was easy: the FBI had crime-solving resources that no state or local police department could hope to match. It was the repository of the world's most extensive collection of fingerprints; its new crime laboratory, opened in November 1932, already had more and better scientific and technical resources and capabilities than all but a small handful of state crime laboratories. Even more important, Hoover had at his disposal 353 highly trained special agents stationed all across the country who could be dispatched anywhere in the United States or abroad at a moment's notice to follow a lead, locate a suspect or witness, or track ransom money.[21] The advantages of that capability, when it came to crimes of mobility like kidnapping, were incalculable. So he decided to offer those services free of charge to state and local police seeking the FBI's assistance in kidnapping cases. All they had to do was let the FBI work with them.

"Working with the FBI" had a particular meaning: acquiescing in the FBI's "domination," defined by the FBI's having more agents on the case than state or local officers so that the FBI was in control.[22] As annoying as that surely was, offering FBI technical resources to cooperating state and local agencies was a gift they usually couldn't refuse—and another masterstroke.

With his arrangements in place for resetting the FBI's approach to kidnapping cases, Hoover let the new attorney general, Homer S. Cummings, know that the FBI was no longer waiting for proof of interstate transportation to be established before investigating kidnapping cases. On July 13, in a memorandum updating Cummings on the status of four active kidnapping cases, he noted that interstate transportation was not yet established in any case, but he had decided to enter them all anyway, "as some of these cases may develop into Federal cases and we will then have the advantage of having all information from the beginning." (In only one of the four cases was federal jurisdiction ultimately established.)

One of the cases, he admitted, was definitely not a federal case, but he had decided to investigate it anyway to ensure that the kidnappers were caught. "I do not believe the criminals indulging in kidnapping have as yet begun to draw any line of demarcation between State and Federal violations of law," he explained, "that is to say, a man who will kidnap a person today and not violate the Federal Law may later indulge in another kidnapping which will be a violation of Federal law, and for that reason I believe it desirable to 'smoke out' the nests of individuals who are engaging in this particularly atrocious activity."[23]

Hoover's argument was entirely specious, but who was going to complain that the FBI was trying to catch too many kidnappers?

9

....

Epidemic

Washington, June–August 1933

Inauguration Day, March 4, 1933, was gray, chilly, and somber in the nation's capital. Arthur Krock, dean of the Washington press corps, likened the atmosphere to what might be found in a beleaguered capital in wartime.[1] Flags flew at half-staff in honor of four-term Montana senator Thomas Walsh. Had he not died unexpectedly two days before, Walsh would have been sworn in that day as incoming President Franklin D. Roosevelt's attorney general.

The nation that day faced the greatest challenges to its existence since the Civil War. It was the worst month for joblessness in its history: fifteen and a half million people—30 percent of the workforce—were out of work. Three and a half years after the crash of the U.S. stock market and the beginning of the Great Depression, the Dow Jones Industrial Average was 90 percent below its September 1929 high, and the global economy was mired in depression. Thirty-two states had closed all banks, while another six had closed some of their banks indefinitely. Banks that stayed open severely restricted withdrawals—like in Texas, where the limit was $10 per day. Two banks were robbed every day, on average, somewhere in the country. Adolf Hitler and his Nazi party had come to power in Germany, giving rise, once again, to fears of destabilization in Europe. After a year the Lindbergh case was still unsolved, and kidnappings continued to increase. What little confidence the public had that America would solve its problems and get moving again was constantly undermined by new challenges.

In the cheers of the half-million people lining the route from the White House to the Capitol, Krock detected "a tone of understanding that the motor bore not only two men, not only a Democrat elected to succeed a Republican whom he had defeated, but two antagonistic philosophies of government."[2]

The president's inaugural address was what his fellow citizens, and much of the world, needed to hear. His memorable pronouncement, "the only thing we have to fear is fear itself," set the tone for the short, fifteen-minute address. He promised to rescue the country from its downward economic spiral and vowed that if the powers granted him as president proved insufficient for the task, he would ask Congress for broader executive powers, "as great as the power that would be given to me if we were in fact invaded by a foreign foe."[3]

Within a few days journalist Walter Lippman was praising the new administration's fast start: "It has proceeded rapidly, surely, and boldly, dealing directly with the essentials, accepting responsibility without hesitation."[4] Its greatest achievement so far, he said, was the revival of the public's confidence in themselves and their institutions: "They believe they have a leader whom they can follow. They believe they have a government which can act."[5]

Though hardly of the same magnitude as the other challenges facing the new president, the issue of J. Edgar Hoover also needed addressing. The attorney general–designate, the late Senator Walsh, had already announced plans to reorganize the FBI and clean house from top to bottom; he had told friends he planned to fire Hoover as soon as he took office.[6]

Walsh had distrusted Hoover ever since the infamous Palmer Raids of 1919 and 1920. When anarchists delivered a series of deadly letter and package bombs to the homes of prominent government officials and businessmen in 1919, Attorney General A. Mitchell Palmer, one of the targets, appointed the twenty-four-year-old Hoover to head a new Anti-Radical Division in the Bureau of Investigation. He directed him to find the radicals responsible for the bombs. Under Hoover's direction, simultaneous raids were conducted in thirty-five cities, resulting in almost ten thousand arrests of radicals and immigrants. Two-thirds of those arrests were made without warrants.[7]

The Palmer Raids were widely denounced as overzealous and unconstitutional. Walsh, who caused the Senate Judiciary Committee to hold hearings, called the arrests the "lawless acts of a mob." Federal judge George W. Anderson ruled that the deportation of radicals arrested without warrants was unconstitutional. He condemned the acts of "our supposedly law-enforcing officials." "A mob is a mob," he wrote, "whether made up of government officials acting under instructions from the Department of Justice, or of criminals, loafers, and the vicious classes."[8] Hoover's conduct in the Palmer Raids had left an indelible impression on Walsh, but before he got his chance to dismiss Hoover, the seventy-two-year-old died of a heart attack on the train returning to Washington from his honeymoon.

Don Whitehead, in his authorized history of the FBI, tells the story that the outgoing President Herbert Hoover, aware of the rumors of J. Edgar Hoover's impending replacement, took the opportunity while riding down Pennsylvania Avenue with Roosevelt on Inauguration Day to urge him to stick with "young Hoover."[9] Such solicitude on President Hoover's part that day is questionable, however. Inauguration observers noted instead a taciturn President Hoover enduring "one last torment" riding in the open car beside his successor.[10] Roosevelt, according to one account, filled the frosty void by praising the "lovely steel" at the construction site where the new Department of Commerce building was going up along the route.[11]

In addition to Walsh, several advisers to the president, both inside and outside the administration, wanted Hoover gone. Postmaster General James A. Farley, the president's patronage chief, wanted to replace the nonpartisan Hoover, appointed by Republican president Calvin Coolidge, with a Democrat, while Louis Howe, the president's closest White House adviser, planted the story in a Washington newspaper that the president intended to abolish the FBI.

But Hoover had his supporters, too. Supreme Court Justice Harlan Fiske Stone, who as attorney general had elevated Hoover to acting director in 1924, asked Roosevelt confidant Felix Frankfurter to put in a good word for Hoover. Appointments secretary (today's chief of staff) Edwin "Pa" Watson backed Hoover because he liked having a man at the FBI "who knew which side his bread was buttered on."[12] Roosevelt "Brain Truster" and criminal law expert Raymond Moley supported him because Hoover had done "magnificent work" cleaning up the FBI and introducing modern crime-solving techniques.[13] Press secretary Stephen Early liked the way Hoover had made the White House look good in the Peggy McMath kidnapping and the case of the missing thirteen-year-old Norbun Chandler, whose mother had called the White House for help in April. Norbun turned out to be a runaway rather than a kidnap victim, but the FBI quickly found him and took him home.[14] Hoover's boss, the incoming attorney general Homer Cummings, wasn't ready to take a position on Hoover yet.

While Hoover's fate remained up in the air, early on the morning of June 17, two men with machine guns jumped out of a car parked in front of Kansas City's Union Station. In less than thirty seconds, veteran bank robber Frank "Jelly" Nash lay dead, along with one FBI agent and three police officers escorting Nash back to the federal penitentiary at Leavenworth. The attorney general called the ambush "an outright defiance of a governmental agency which gangdom has long respected."[15]

The question of Hoover's fate went to the back burner.

Peggy McMath's kidnapping in May was soon followed by the headline snatches of twenty-five-year-old Mary McElroy, daughter of Kansas City's city manager; thirty-nine-year-old William A. Hamm, head of the Theodore Hamm Brewing Company in St. Paul; sixty-five-year-old John King Ottley, chairman of the board of the First National Bank of Atlanta; twenty-four-year-old John J. O'Connell, nephew of the Democratic boss of Albany, New York; seventy-eight-year-old August Luer, retired bank president of Alton, Illinois; and fifty-six-year-old Philadelphia real estate broker Frank A. McClatchy, fatally gunned down resisting abduction. Newspapers started calling it a "kidnap epidemic."[16]

The *New York Times* began publishing "Recent Kidnappings in America" as a regular feature, while *Time* magazine reported kidnappings along with notable births, deaths, and other milestones. Lloyd's of London began underwriting kidnap insurance in the United States for persons of "unquestioned reputation" who passed thorough background checks designed to eliminate those considered at risk of faking their own kidnappings. The policies covered ransom payments and injuries to victims during captivity, with maximum limits of $100,000 for adults (over $1.9 million in 2020) and $50,000 for children (over $986,000 in 2020), which was pegged to the amount of the Lindbergh ransom.[17]

Wealthy families and celebrities protected themselves in a variety of ways. Many obtained weapons permits to carry their own guns, while others hired bodyguards and armed chauffeurs. In his history of the J. P. Morgan banking empire, historian Ron Chernow noted that the firm hired "an army of 250 bodyguards" to protect the families of Morgan partners after the Lindbergh kidnapping, and "many of their grandchildren would remember growing up surrounded by opulence and armed guards."[18] Other families— including the Lindberghs, whose second son, Jon, was born in August 1932—got trained guard dogs to watch over their children or installed motion-detecting kidnap alarms in their cribs.[19] Some parents sent their children to Europe for school or summer camp to get them out of harm's way. Thousands of children were fingerprinted and their fingerprints filed with the FBI as a means of identification in case of kidnapping.[20]

Historian John Toland called the Kansas City Massacre the "turning point in the education of the people to the reality of the growing crime wave."[21] The daily reports of gang violence and underworld hits suddenly seemed more threatening when law enforcement officers were the victims and the ambush took place at a busy train station in full daylight. "Crime was suddenly everyone's business," wrote Toland.

Pressure increased on the new administration to add crime to its agenda, specifically kidnapping and other forms of violent crime committed by criminal gangs. Organized crime was spreading beyond New York, Chicago, St. Louis, and Detroit, gaining footholds in other major cities, particularly in the Midwest, where labor racketeering was pervasive and protection rackets often coexisted with the snatch racket. On June 23 Cummings announced that the federal government intended to conduct a "real campaign" against kidnappers and racketeers, without making clear whether he perceived kidnapping and racketeering as different problems or as different examples of the same problem.[22]

Cummings took the first step in that campaign by bringing in Cleveland lawyer Joseph B. Keenan as his assistant, giving him a "roving commission to do anything he can think of that will help."[23] The spunky, square-jawed Keenan had earned a solid reputation battling organized crime in Cleveland as special assistant to the Ohio attorney general. He planned to continue that same fight against racketeers and organized crime on a national scale: "I am going to try to strike at the leadership and at the sources of its huge illicit revenue," he promised. "If you strike at the intelligent gangland leadership and stamp that out, you are on the way, decidedly, to breaking down the whole gang system."[24]

In the midst of the post-McMath "epidemic," the attorney general again addressed the kidnapping problem at his semiweekly press conference on July 13. He urged all Americans to call the FBI immediately if a relative or friend was kidnapped, and he reiterated that the administration was working on a comprehensive legislative package to "exterminate" racketeers and kidnappers, including possibly creating a federal police force.[25] Still short on concrete proposals, he used the language and imagery of war to rally support for federal intervention: "It is almost like a military engagement between the forces of law and order and the underworld army, heavily armed," he said. "It is a campaign to wipe out the public enemy and it will proceed until it succeeds."[26]

Joseph Keenan had been on the job less than a week when he abandoned, at least temporarily, his entire antiracketeering agenda of destroying organized crime gangs from the top down. He pronounced the kidnapping crisis "so acute" that he needed to devote all his time to the war against kidnappers.[27] Echoing the advice of the attorney general, Keenan spoke directly to the public and urged anyone receiving a kidnap threat or whose relative or friend disappeared to place a long-distance call immediately to Hoover. "Don't write," he said, "but telephone or telegraph us. There's no use in giving the kidnappers one or two days' start on us." He said the FBI had "as good detectives as you'll find anywhere" and was "ready to jump into a kidnapping case as soon as it breaks, and that's what we're going to do."[28] Without fanfare Keenan had just announced that the FBI would no longer concern itself with establishing Lindbergh Law jurisdiction by evidence of interstate transportation before entering kidnapping cases—*any* kidnapping cases.

That same day, the Secret Service announced it had placed President Roosevelt's three grandchildren under kidnap guard.[29] The following day, July 14, special agents from the FBI's Chicago office joined Chicago police and Illinois state troopers in guarding the homes of forty wealthy Chicagoans believed to be targets of a notorious Chicago-based kidnapping ring.[30] They were acting on information obtained from recent kidnap victim John (Jake the Barber) Factor, brother of the cosmetics tycoon Max Factor, who reported that the gang that kidnapped him kept a book of kidnap prospects they updated daily.

The Factor kidnapping was later proved to be a hoax and the book of prospects a fiction, but the robust, coordinated law enforcement response to a credible threat of multiple abductions featured a new, proactive attitude on the part of the federal government. Practically overnight, Attorney General Cummings's evolving campaign against racketeers and the structure of organized crime had morphed into a more focused "War against Kidnappers." The FBI, with Cummings's approval, had begun operating under the Hoover-formulated theory that it had all the authority it needed to go after kidnappers anytime, anywhere.[31]

Over the course of the summer of 1933, Cummings and his wife, Mary, grew close to President Roosevelt as they spent many muggy evenings cruising the Potomac on the presidential yacht *Sequoia*. Mary Cummings sometimes served as the president's official hostess when his daughter, Anna Roosevelt Dall, was unavailable. At some point during those days Cummings decided to urge Roosevelt not to fire Hoover—a decision he would later call "one of the biggest mistakes I ever made."[32] The president took his advice. On July 29 Cummings announced that the Justice Department was expanding the FBI (now called the Division of Investigation), not abolishing it: Hoover would continue as director, with increased forces, to crush the bands of kidnappers and racketeers.

The War against Kidnappers was still more a concept than a

plan, but it was now clear that it would be fought on three distinct fronts. The attorney general would focus on drafting new federal criminal laws and seeking new federal powers, if necessary, to defeat kidnapping and other forms of what he began referring to as "predatory" interstate crime. Keenan would lead the Justice Department's prosecution of kidnappers in federal courts across the country. And Hoover and the special agents of the FBI would man the front lines taking the calls of kidnap victims' families, investigating kidnappings, and bringing kidnappers to justice.

On August 1 Cummings spelled out more of his thoughts for the future in a memorandum to Keenan: "In the agenda of things to be considered, when we get around to it, would it not be well to think of having a special prison for racketeers, kidnappers, and others guilty of predatory crimes. . . . It would be in a remote place—on an island, or in Alaska, so that the persons incarcerated would not be in constant communication with friends outside. . . . Please think these things over."[33]

With his job now safe and a war against kidnappers to fight, Hoover reenergized the FBI's Lindbergh investigation. He ordered the Lindbergh squad to pay particular attention to the "most urgent and important" matter of tracking the ransom money as it turned up in circulation. In ordering his men to concentrate on the ransom money, he was well aware that that was already the major task of the NYPD and SIU investigators, working with the NJSP. Only 388 of the original 4,750 ransom bills delivered to Cemetery John had turned up in the year following the kidnapping, but it was only a matter of time until more bills surfaced.[34] As underworld boss and Capone mentor Johnny Torrio put it to the Lindbergh squad: "They have to unload the dough sometime."[35] What the War against Kidnappers needed most now was a signature victory.

10

···

The Road to Paradise

Oklahoma City and Paradise, July–September 1933

Charles and Berenice Urschel were playing bridge with their friends Walter and Clyde Jarrett on Saturday night, July 22. It was typical midsummer Oklahoma City weather, hot and dry, as they sat around the card table on the Urschels' sunporch. Shortly after 11:00 p.m., Berenice's sixteen-year-old daughter, Betty, arrived home, parked in the garage, and stopped to say goodnight before heading upstairs to her room. About fifteen minutes later another car drove into the driveway, and the couples heard two car doors slam. Moments later, the porch door opened, and two "foreign looking" men with "swarthy complexions" walked in.[1]

"Which one is Urschel? We want Urschel," demanded the heavyset man pointing a machine gun at the table. No one said anything.

"Well, then, we'll take you both," he said. Urschel and Jarrett rose without a word and moved toward the door where the other man was standing with a pistol in his hand.

As he backed out from the porch, the man with the machine gun looked back at the wives and said, "Don't move until you hear a car start out in the driveway. If you reach for that telephone before then, I'll blow your brains out."[2]

The gunmen had left the motor running in their car. They ordered Urschel and Jarrett into the back seat, got into the front, and backed out of the driveway. About twelve miles out of town, they stopped the car and took Urschel's and Jarrett's wallets. After checking their identification cards and satisfying themselves that Jarrett wasn't Urschel, they helped themselves to Jarrett's cash and tossed his empty wallet back at him. They told him he could go but warned him to keep his mouth shut.[3] They covered Urschel's eyes with cotton pads, stuffed wads of cotton into his ears, and wound adhesive tape around his head to hold them in place. Then they handcuffed him, forced him down onto the floor, and drove off again.[4]

Berenice and Clyde waited until they heard the kidnappers' car turn into the street before running upstairs to check on Betty and locking themselves in the master bedroom. Berenice called the Oklahoma City police to report the kidnappings and then called J. Edgar Hoover in Washington to report them directly to him.[5] She had read in *Time* magazine about Hoover's new kidnap reporting line and kept the telephone number at her bedside, never imagining she would become the first person to use it to report a kidnapping.[6] Hoover assured her that her husband would be all right. The new "citizen kidnappers" don't usually harm their victims, he said; they collect the ransom and let them go. He promised to send a special agent to her home as soon as he hung up. Within the hour two special agents from the Oklahoma City office were with Berenice in her home.[7]

For the first time in the thirteen months the Lindbergh Law had been in effect, the FBI had the chance to investigate a kidnapping case from the beginning. Hoover personally selected the team to send to Oklahoma City. In addition to Assistant Director Harold Nathan, he assigned the special agents in charge of the Oklahoma City and Dallas offices and supporting agents from twenty offices around the country. To head the team, he picked

Gus T. "Buster" Jones, special agent in charge of the San Antonio office, even though he had to pull him off the Kansas City Massacre investigation to do it. Jones was a no-nonsense former Texas Ranger who wore a tan felt Stetson, marshal-style, and always carried a gun. Hoover constantly nitpicked Jones's paperwork, but he valued his results. Jones was old-school and gritty, and he had a reputation as "the man who brings 'em in alive."[8]

From the moment Berenice Urschel contacted Hoover, the Urschel investigation was an "all hands" operation of highest priority for the FBI. Practically all routine business of the Oklahoma City office came to a halt; "clocks and beds became relics of a bygone age."[9]

Charles and Berenice Urschel were one of the richest couples in Oklahoma. They owned extensive interests in oil fields in Oklahoma, Kansas, Texas, Louisiana, and Mississippi, valued somewhere between $25 and $50 million or more (between $500 million and $1 billion in 2020).[10]

Tall, handsome Charles Urschel, forty-three, had grown up on his family's farm in Ohio. Farming wasn't the life he wanted, though. As soon as he was old enough to go, he left home and put himself through business college. He was working as an accountant when he decided to try the booming oil business, taking a job with a Chicago company that leased land to drill exploratory wells in areas where oil had not yet been discovered (known as "wildcatting"). There he met another ambitious, young "lease man" named Thomas Baker Slick. After years of drilling wells that turned up dry, Slick discovered oil in Oklahoma in 1912 in an area known as the Cushing field. It became the biggest oil field in the country and remained so until 1920, accounting at its peak for 17 percent of U.S. oil production and 3 percent of worldwide production.[11] Known as the "King of the Wildcatters," Slick was the largest independent oil producer in the United States when he died in 1930 at the age of forty-six.[12]

Charles Urschel was Tom Slick's business manager and best friend; together they developed the Cushing field and built their fortunes.[13] He married Tom's sister, Flored. Soon Tom and his wife, Berenice, and Charles and Flored all moved to Oklahoma City to be closer to their oil fields. They bought large, gracious mansions with manicured lawns near each other in prestigious Heritage Hills. Though they lived unpretentiously, their immense wealth was well known. Tom Slick's death and the size of his fortune were national news. Media attention again focused on the Slick and Urschel families and their wealth the following year, when forty-two-year-old Flored Urschel died of a heart attack in her bath. They made headlines again, this time happy ones, in October 1932, when widower Charles Urschel married widow Berenice Slick and moved with his young son into the fourteen-room Slick mansion at 327 Northwest Eighteenth Street.

"Oh, I'm so thankful that it isn't Betty," Berenice told reporters gathered at her home, as news of her husband's kidnapping spread. "I'm not so afraid for Charlie. Charles is a grown man, and he's so resourceful and sensible."[14]

For several years before his death, Tom Slick and their daughter, Betty, had been the target of kidnap threats that the family attributed to crackpots who had seen their pictures in the newspapers. Aside from hiring a night watchman, the Slicks and the Urschels hadn't worried very much about kidnapping. Berenice and Charles had recently fired the night watchman for sleeping on the job and hadn't replaced him.

Hoover's men assured Berenice that her husband's safety was their primary concern. Until he was home, the FBI wouldn't interfere with any of her efforts to obtain his release or do anything else that might jeopardize his life; after he was home, they would shift their focus to catching the kidnappers. According to the report of Ralph Colvin, special agent in charge of the FBI's Oklahoma City office, they asked two things of Berenice. First, the FBI wanted to

be kept informed of every development as it occurred before negotiations with the real kidnappers began, but they didn't want to be
told about actual communications with the kidnappers until after
Urschel was released.[15] Then the FBI expected the family to furnish
to them "every bit of information available." Second, they insisted
that a record be made of the serial numbers of every ransom bill.[16]

I am "in the hands of my government," Berenice replied, and
will do "any and all things the Bureau requests."[17]

Berenice issued a statement drafted by the FBI, inviting the kidnappers to contact her. It was reminiscent of Charles Lindbergh's
statement to Charlie's kidnappers that had raised so many eyebrows
the year before: "I am in no way interested in your capture or prosecution. I care only for the safe return of my husband. To facilitate this I have had police withdrawn from my house, and there is
no one here now except our family. We are sitting beside the telephone waiting for you to call. . . . Arthur Seeligson, my husband's
closest friend, will be in charge. You can trust him. The welfare
of my husband, and his immediate return, is my only concern."[18]

The statement wasn't true, of course. FBI agents remained in
the Urschel home around the clock to intercept communications and listen in on telephone calls. Berenice was soon so inundated with letters, wires, and calls from opportunists and oddballs
that it was "no small task" to "sift the wheat from the chaff."[19] She
refused to dismiss any contact out of hand and met or spoke with
many "desperate characters," including seventeen "convicts or
ex-convicts, escaped, pardoned or paroled."[20] One caller lured
Berenice and Arthur Seeligson to a trap late one night under an
Oklahoma City bridge by promising to bring Urschel's watch as
proof he was the kidnapper. When they arrived he stuck a pistol
in Berenice's face and robbed Seeligson of the $1,000 they had
brought to exchange for the watch.[21]

When five days had passed since the kidnapping and the real
kidnappers had made no contact, Berenice considered enlisting

gangsters or criminal lawyers to help establish communications. Instead she asked reporters to help her get the word out to the kidnappers that they could contact any of the men in the house or, if they preferred, she would deal with them herself. She wanted them to stress that the police were completely out of the way and weren't even secretly watching the house.[22]

Finally, a uniformed Western Union messenger delivered a thick envelope to a friend of Urschel's who lived in Tulsa, oilman John G. Catlett. There was no doubt it was from the real kidnappers: the envelope contained the identification card from Urschel's wallet and letters in his handwriting to Catlett and to Berenice, asking them to arrange the ransom payment.[23] Urschel's letter to Catlett ended with the statement, "This is my final letter to any of my friends or family and if this contact is not successful I fear for my life."[24] His note to Berenice ended with a similarly sobering message: "If the demand is too great, just forget it, it will be O.K. with me."[25]

A third letter in the envelope, typewritten, was from the kidnappers to Urschel's friend and business associate E. E. Kirkpatrick. It demanded $200,000 (over $3.9 million in 2020) in used $20 bills.[26] The amount was greater than any ransom known to have been paid in the United States as of that time. When the money was ready, Kirkpatrick was instructed to place a notice in the *Daily Oklahoman* offering a 160-acre farm "for quick sale" and providing a newspaper box number for replies.

In short order Berenice withdrew the cash from the bank, bank employees recorded the serial numbers, and Kirkpatrick placed the notice in the *Daily Oklahoman*. The next day the kidnappers sent instructions to him to pack the money in a light-colored leather bag, take the 10:00 p.m. "Sooner" train from Oklahoma City to Kansas City on Saturday night, July 29, and look for two fires burning on the right side of the tracks. When the train passed the second fire, he was to throw the bag off the train. If he was unable to execute the plan for any reason, he was to proceed to the Muehlebach Hotel in Kansas City and wait there for a message. If there was any trickery, the kidnappers warned, Urschel would be killed and "some-one very near and dear to the Urschel family is under constant surveillance and will like-wise suffer for your error."[27]

Kirkpatrick and Catlett packed the bag and took the train to Kansas City, but there were no fires alongside the tracks. Disappointed and anxious, they got off at Kansas City and checked into the Muehlebach. The following day a man called the hotel and told Kirkpatrick to take a taxi by himself to the La Salle Hotel, get out, and walk west with the bag in his right hand. Kirkpatrick slipped a .380 Colt automatic into his waistband, grabbed the bag, and hailed a taxi.[28] He got out at the La Salle and walked west with the bag. A burly man with dark skin and hair, in a natty summer suit and a Panama hat with the brim turned down, stepped from a waiting automobile and headed toward him.

"I'll take that grip," said the man, whom Kirkpatrick would later identify as bank robber Machine Gun Kelly.

"How do I know you are the right party?" Kirkpatrick asked.

"Hell, you know damned well I am," Kelly replied. Kirkpatrick handed over the bag stuffed with ten thousand $20 bills.

"Urschel will be home within twelve hours," Kelly said. "Now you turn and walk to the La Salle Hotel and don't look back."[29]

Twelve hours passed but Urschel still wasn't home. The vigil kept by family and friends continued at Northwest Eighteenth Street, though the telephone no longer rang constantly. The quiet was ominous, and the second-guessing began.[30] Was it foolish to believe the kidnappers would keep their promise? Was it a mistake not to let the FBI follow the man who collected the money? Was it a mistake even to call the FBI in the first place?

About 11:30 Monday evening, more than twenty-four hours after the payoff, there was a knock at the back door of the Urschel home. The special agent who answered the door didn't recognize the tall, haggard, somewhat disheveled man standing there, blinking his eyes in the bright light, but Arthur Seeligson's brother Lamar did. He let out a whoop of joy that alerted the whole house.[31]

Charles Urschel was home.

Two days after Urschel was kidnapped, a Fort Worth police detective named Ed Weatherford telephoned the FBI's Dallas office and suggested they take a look at a bank robber named George "Machine Gun" Kelly and his wife, Kathryn, for the Urschel kidnapping: Kelly fit the newspapers' description of the "foreign looking" kidnapper, and snatching someone like Urschel was just the kind of job he would pull.

There was more. The day before, Kathryn had called Weatherford and asked him to come to her Fort Worth home. She mentioned that George would be coming into some money soon, in case Weatherford was running short. While he was there, Weatherford noticed that the wheels of Kathryn's Cadillac were covered in "Oklahoma red dirt dust"; he also saw an Oklahoma newspaper on the front seat, open to a story about the kidnapping. He was convinced Kathryn was trying to find out from him whether Kelly was a suspect in the kidnapping.[32]

For several years Weatherford and his partner J. W. Swinney had heard rumors that George belonged to a gang of bank robbers; they had suspicions about the couple's fancy cars and expensive clothes. Weatherford and Swinney had become drinking buddies with Kathryn and cultivated her as a source of underworld information, some of which they passed along to the FBI in Dallas. It was a two-way street: Kathryn bought them drinks and occasionally gave them cash when they ran short in hopes of finding out what the police knew about George's activities and perhaps getting an early warning if the police were after him. Kathryn's cozy relationship with Weatherford, who bore an amazing resemblance to George, owed much to the fact that she had been on "very intimate terms" with him for over a year by the time Urschel was kidnapped.[33]

Until the Kansas City Massacre in June the FBI hadn't been particularly interested in Kelly and his underworld associates, but that changed with the gunning down of four law enforcement officers. The FBI's Dallas office had asked Weatherford and Swinney to get whatever information they could from Kathryn that might help them identify the Kansas City gunmen.[34]

Based on information about the Kellys provided by Weatherford and Swinney, Special Agent Charles Winstead of the FBI's Dallas office made a reconnaissance trip to a ranch near the town of Paradise in Wise County, Texas, northwest of Fort Worth, on July 13, just nine days before the Urschel kidnapping. He went there to have a quiet look at the ranch, rumored to be a hideout for gangsters. It was owned by R. G. "Boss" Shannon, and his wife, Ora, who was Kathryn Kelly's mother.[35] The Shannons were out of town, though, so Winstead didn't learn very much that day.

Weatherford's tip that the Kellys might be involved in the Urschel kidnapping was sufficiently promising that the FBI's Dallas office set up surveillance of their Fort Worth home, tapping the telephone line and arranging for the telephone operator in Paradise to listen in on conversations to and from the Shannon ranch.[36] They also placed mail covers on the Kellys' and Shannons' mail at both places and had their telegrams intercepted.[37] None of those efforts produced information of value. The Kellys apparently realized their communications could be monitored and were relying primarily on multiple aliases, coded messages, and human messengers.

For the time being at least the FBI seemingly lost interest in information about the Kellys coming from Weatherford and the Dallas office.

Before the Kansas City Massacre and the Urschel kidnapping, George Kelly's criminal activities—primarily bootlegging and bank robbery—had not come within the FBI's purview.[38] Hoover's men knew almost nothing about him, not even what he looked like or the names he went by or who his criminal associates were.

Born George Francis Barnes Jr., Kelly was a big, handsome teddy bear of a man with olive skin, dark hair, and luminous blue eyes. He was intelligent (IQ of 118), affable, and, for most of his thirty-eight years, directionless.[39] Unlike most men who turned to kidnapping during the Great Depression, he had grown up in a comfortable, middle-class home in Memphis, Tennessee, the son of a successful but philandering insurance agent and a devoted mother. His teachers regularly called George out for not "apply-ing himself," but he talked his way into Mississippi A & M College (now Mississippi State University), where he met and married Geneva Ramsey, the daughter of a wealthy construction contrac-tor. College was too much work for George, though. He returned to Memphis to resume his high school business as a "society boot-legger," selling Canadian whiskey to speakeasies and teenagers. About the time Geneva took the couple's two boys and left George, he dropped the surname Barnes and took his mother's maiden name, Kelly, to dodge the police.

Kelly first went to prison in New Mexico for Prohibition viola-tions in 1927. The following year he landed in the federal peniten-tiary at Leavenworth for selling liquor on an Indian reservation.[40] There he ingratiated himself with some of the biggest names in bank robbery—including Frank "Jelly" Nash (killed in the Kansas City Massacre), Francis Keating, Tommy Holden, Wilbur Under-hill, and Verne Miller—by, among other things, helping them escape. They would later help him get his start robbing banks.

After winning early release for good behavior in 1930, Kelly mar-ried Kathryn Thorne and moved into her home in Fort Worth. A bootlegger, convicted shoplifter (of furs), and "woman of easy virtue," Kathryn made her livelihood "in any manner she could other than by physical labor."[41] She was attractive and ambitious; her appetite for jewelry, furs, Chanel gowns, new cars, and Peking-ese puppies was seemingly insatiable. The life of a gangster's moll appealed to her as well; she saw in Kelly, her third husband, the makings of a headline bank robber. She bought him his first machine gun, coached him in shooting walnuts off fence posts, chose his nickname, and handed out spent cartridges at speakeasies to market the "Machine Gun Kelly" brand.[42]

But Kathryn wasn't satisfied for long with a minor bank robber for a husband. Even as she stepped up the pressure on Kelly to make himself a bigger player, they both realized the heyday of the bank robbery business was probably nearing an end. Many banks had failed in the Great Depression, and those that remained open often had less cash than before and usually protected it better with armed guards, silent alarms, and time-locked vaults. By the summer of 1933 Kathryn and George had begun to wonder whether snatching "some rich bastards" and holding them for ransom wouldn't be both easier and more lucrative than robbing banks. Reports that the family of St. Paul brewer William Hamm had paid a $100,000 ransom in June convinced Kathryn they had to try it.

Kelly's two previous forays into kidnapping had been near-disasters, though. According to crime historian Paul Maccabee, he had partnered with a former policeman named Bernard "Big Phil" Phillips in 1930 to kidnap wealthy Chicagoans, but one of them was killed when Phillips's gun accidentally discharged.[43] In 1932 Kelly partnered with bank robber Eddie Doll to kidnap fifty-two-year-old Howard Woolverton, a wealthy South Bend, Indiana, manufacturer and the son of a bank president. They demanded a $50,000 ransom, but Woolverton's father publicly refused to pay any ransom at all and instead offered a $25,000 reward for information leading to the kidnappers' arrest. Young Woolverton convinced Kelly and Doll that he didn't have the money himself but could raise it if they would let him go. They did, and Woolverton never paid a cent.

Despite George's track record, the more he and Kathryn talked about snatching rich men, the more they liked the idea. They envisioned not just one but five kidnappings, at $200,000 each—a fast million dollars and then off to South America.[44] While Kathryn scoured the newspapers to put together a list of possible targets, Kelly talked his buddy Albert Bates—his partner in three bank robberies in 1932—into signing on, despite Bates's misgivings about the dirty business of kidnapping.

The trio set their sights high. First on their list of prospects was Fort Worth oil man Guy Waggoner, one of the heirs to an oil fortune of more than $100 million and to the 520,000-acre Waggoner Ranch, the second largest ranch in the United States.[45] Kathryn even sounded out her detective buddies, Weatherford and Swinney, to see if they might be interested in earning some quick money by helping in case the kidnappers ran into trouble on the Waggoner job, but they begged off (and alerted Waggoner).[46] In July, when Kelly and Bates learned that Waggoner was away from Fort Worth on business, they decided to move on to their second prospect: Charles Urschel.[47]

Now that Urschel was back home safely, the FBI was free to pursue his kidnappers. Ten minutes after Urschel appeared at the back door of his home, Special Agent Gus Jones arrived to begin debriefing him. The nervous, exhausted Urschel wanted to cooperate, but he didn't think he could be much help since he had been blindfolded almost the entire time. From experience, Jones knew that when one of the senses is impaired, the others automatically become more acute. With the right kinds of questions, he told Urschel, he might be able to recall useful information acquired through other senses.[48]

Jones and Urschel proved to be a dream team: a relentless, patient investigator and an intelligent, observant, and courageous witness. The debriefing went on for three days. By the time they were done, Urschel had recalled being driven over both paved and unpaved roads and stopping at three different places before the kidnappers took him to a house somewhere in the country where there was no traffic noise. Then they took him to a fourth location nearby, a small cabin with three rooms, where he was chained to an iron bed. In addition to the kidnappers, two men, one old and one young, took turns guarding him. Over time, the tape covering his eyes loosened, and he could see a wall with a square of wallpaper missing, floorboards running east and west, a baby's high chair, a roof partially caved in, and a cornfield in front of the cabin.[49] He was given plenty of fresh milk to drink and well water that tasted strongly of iron from a rusty metal dipper with the handle broken off. He heard bobwhite and quail, chickens, a bellowing bull, and pigs and hogs that squealed at feeding time.

Jones asked Urschel whether he had heard any other sounds. Just an airplane, Urschel replied. It flew almost directly overhead twice a day, at around 9:45 a.m. and again at 5:45 p.m., except for one day, the day before he was released, when a big thunderstorm blew in with lightning and strong winds. He didn't hear the plane that morning.[50]

Finding the specific locations where the kidnappers had hidden Urschel was a high priority. Even if the kidnappers were no longer there, the locations could be proof that he had been taken across a state line. Like all crime scenes, hideouts usually contained physical evidence, especially fingerprints, that could incriminate the kidnappers.

From stray comments Urschel overheard, the types of roads he traveled, and his estimates of driving times, the FBI deduced that the kidnappers had driven him south from Oklahoma City for a distance of less than six hundred miles. The town of Paradise, Texas, was one of the towns satisfying those criteria. By checking commercial airline schedules, they learned that regularly scheduled flights between Fort Worth and Amarillo passed over Paradise every day around 9:45 a.m. and 5:45 p.m. By checking weather reports and actual flight data, they learned that the flight that usually flew over Paradise at 9:45 had been rerouted and didn't fly over Paradise on the stormy day that Urschel didn't hear the morning plane.

Jones briefed Special Agent Edward Dowd on Urschel's recollections before sending him to Paradise on August 10 to have a look around. Posing as a Fort Worth bank examiner with some paperwork for Boss Shannon to sign, he proceeded to the five-hundred-acre Shannon ranch. He ticked off in his mind as he recognized them many of the features Urschel had described. When he learned that Boss and his wife were out of town, he drove down the road to the small tenant shack where his twenty-year-old son, Armon, lived. He mentioned the paperwork that Shannon needed to sign, and Armon invited him in. From the iron bed to the baby's high chair, the missing wallpaper, the floorboards, and the cornfield, it was precisely as Urschel had described. As he prepared to leave, Dowd asked for a drink of water. Armon drew a fresh bucket from the well and offered him a rusty metal dipper without a handle. Dowd took a long drink, no doubt savoring every drop of the strong iron taste in his mouth.[51]

In the early morning of August 12, just before daybreak, Gus Jones led a raiding party of heavily armed special agents (including sharpshooter Charles Winstead, making a return visit), Dallas and Fort Worth police (including Weatherford and Swinney), and the deputy sheriff of Oklahoma City to the Shannon ranch. Charles Urschel went, too, carrying his own sawed-off shotgun.

Instead of the kidnappers, the raiding party found forty-eight-year-old Harvey Bailey, the most famous bank robber in America and one of a list of suspects in the Kansas City Massacre. He was asleep on a cot under a pecan tree outside Boss Shannon's house, with a loaded .351 Winchester automatic rifle in the bed beside him, a Colt .45 automatic pistol under his pillow, and a Thompson submachine gun and another Colt automatic pistol inside the house. In his pants pocket was $700 of Urschel ransom money.[52] Bailey was cooling off at the ranch for a night or two, still nursing a gunshot wound to his leg sustained when he and ten fellow convicts escaped from the Kansas State Penitentiary in Lansing on May 30.[53] Bailey sometimes laid low at the Shannon ranch, where it was rumored the going rate for gangsters needing refuge was $200 to $300 a night.[54]

Without firing a shot the raiding party also took Boss, Ora, and Armon Shannon into custody. By their voices Urschel identified Boss and Armon as the men who had guarded him. The Shannons identified Kelly and Bates as the kidnappers and admitted to helping guard Urschel. They had no choice, they said. Kelly threatened to kill them if they didn't follow his orders. Charles Urschel's fingerprints were found all over Armon Shannon's shack; he had made a point of planting them on every surface he touched.

Hoover immediately realized what Harvey Bailey's capture could mean for the War against Kidnappers. Aside from his being in the wrong place at the wrong time with a small amount of ransom money from Bates and Kelly to tide him over, there was never any reason to suspect Bailey of participation in the kidnapping. Nevertheless Hoover persuaded federal prosecutors to charge "this super-desperado, kidnapper, jail breaker, machine gun killer and bank robber" as the mastermind of the kidnapping.[55]

For Hoover and Attorney General Cummings, happening upon Bailey in Paradise was manna from heaven. Despite the lack of credible evidence indicating Bailey's involvement in the kidnapping or in the Kansas City Massacre either, they announced that his arrest solved both crimes. The press feasted, too. Such headlines as "Urschel Case Solved with Arrest in Texas of Harvey Bailey, Also Machine Gunner in K.C. Massacre" and "Paradise, Wise County, Hilltop Farmhouse Gives Up Head of K.C. Massacre and Leader of Urschel Kidnap Outrage" brought exactly the kind of publicity they wanted for the War against Kidnappers.[56]

The New York Times hailed the roundup of prisoners as "the first major triumph in the recently undertaken war against kidnapping and racketeering."[57] The *Louisville Courier-Journal*, in a widely reprinted editorial ("A Triumph for Uncle Sam"), focused particularly on Bailey's capture as evidence that the Roosevelt administration had taken definite steps to "strangle" the kidnapping racket and that the public should place its confidence in Hoover and the FBI: "Nothing feasible offers such promise of relief from the national disease as the establishment of confidence among the people in the ability of the United States Government to crush the kidnappers. When such confidence is achieved, the families of kidnap victims may no longer try to hide their dealings from the proper authorities, as they now do most frequently in the hope of negotiating directly with the criminals. The successful handling of the Urschel case should go far to impress the public with Uncle Sam's superior ability to deal with kidnappers."[58]

Hoover and Cummings were quick to claim federal credit for Bailey's capture, though they were less enthusiastic about prosecuting him for kidnapping in federal court. The evidence was lacking, and there was no death penalty under the Lindbergh Law. Instead they tried to persuade Missouri authorities to charge him with murder in the Kansas City Massacre, since murder carried the death penalty in Missouri. But credible evidence of his participation in the Kansas City Massacre was also lacking. The Missouri authorities never charged him.

Before the federals could get him to Oklahoma City for a federal kidnapping trial, the indomitable Bailey escaped from the supposedly escape-proof Dallas County Jail, with help from a deputy sheriff and a jailer. Hoover gave orders to the Dallas office that he wanted Bailey "to be brought in dead and not to take any more chances with him."[59] Despite Hoover's orders, Bailey was recaptured alive the same day by the Ardmore, Oklahoma, police, and was soon on his way to Oklahoma City for trial under heavy guard.

On the same day as the Paradise raid, police picked up a man in a handsome new Buick Victoria coupe that was parked in front of a Denver rooming house. Having received a tip that he was wanted for passing forged American Express checks, they were astonished to learn that the "George Davis" in their custody was actually bank robber Albert Bates ("The Man of Many Names"), suddenly one of the most wanted men in America. Bates was transferred to federal custody and soon was on his way back to Oklahoma City by plane to face kidnapping charges.

Charles and Berenice Urschel, protected by heavily armed federal agents, met the plane in Oklahoma City. "That's him, all right," said Berenice, when the handcuffed Bates appeared. "I'm so glad to see him like that. He didn't have on those gold-rimmed spectacles that night, but he is the one."[60]

Moments later Urschel approached Bates, who was sitting in a police car on the tarmac. "Hello, Albert," he said. "I don't believe I know you," replied Bates. Then, according to a reporter standing nearby, Urschel and Bates both "grinned sheepishly, then laughed. They both seemed embarrassed."[61]

Hoover and the Justice Department considered handing Bates over to Oklahoma authorities so he could be charged with the state crime of highway robbery for emptying the wallets of Jarrett ($60) and Urschel ($50) the night of the kidnapping. The crime carried the death penalty by hanging in Oklahoma, but the prospect of trying and convicting him of kidnapping under the Lindbergh Law won out, even without the death penalty.

After Kelly and Bates released Urschel on the night of July 31, they had gone their separate ways: Bates to Denver, where he was picked up, and Kelly to Minneapolis with Kathryn, to exchange some of their ransom money for clean money. On August 4 Urschel ransom money was used to purchase an $1800 cashier's check in Minneapolis. The FBI had already distributed to banks fifty-page booklets containing the serial numbers of the ten thousand ransom bills. Three "money men" were promptly arrested for aiding and abetting the kidnapping, sending shock waves through the

Twin Cities' underworld and the money conversion facilities on which it depended.[62] The Kellys were already back on the road with the FBI in pursuit.

With the investigation mostly concluded except for catching the Kellys, Hoover sent Jones to Houston to personally handle the attempted kidnapping of twenty-one-year-old Winthrop Rocke-feller, son of John D. Rockefeller Jr., and to Topeka to investigate the plot to kidnap Peggy Anne Landon, sixteen-year-old daughter of Kansas governor Alf Landon (and Republican candidate for president in 1936). Sharpshooter Charles Winstead went back to chasing Clyde Barrow and Bonnie Parker.[63]

In August, in the middle of the FBI's very public chase of the Kellys, the American Bar Association called an extraordinary meeting of its members in Grand Rapids, Michigan, to look for solutions to the "vexing problems" of kidnapping and racketeering.[64] Pat Malloy, the assistant attorney general in charge of the Justice Department's Criminal Division, asked to be put on the agenda to speak.

Malloy, a Tulsa attorney whose early support for Roosevelt in 1932 had earned him his job in the Justice Department, dropped a bombshell at the ABA meeting when he announced that the Justice Department proposed to end the current "reign of terrorism" by placing all law enforcement officers, state militias, and prosecutors in the country under the command of the president and the attorney general to arrest and prosecute kidnappers and racketeers.[65] One after another, horrified lawyers and judges stepped to the podium to denounce the proposal as patently unconstitutional.

Homer Cummings hurried from Washington to quell the uproar in Grand Rapids. Calling the proposal "Malloy's own speech,"[66] he denied there was any plan for Washington to assert command over state and local officials.[67] All the Justice Department had in mind, he said, was better cooperation between the federal government and the states.[68] Just ten days later, however, Cummings himself, in a nationwide radio address, seemed to be advocating the same approach as Malloy: unified law enforcement by local, state, and federal officials operating "when necessary . . . as a unit, and with a maximum degree of efficiency against the common foes of law and order."[69]

Cummings had never had any use for Malloy, whom he considered nothing more than a political appointee parked in the Justice Department. He now saw him as a liability and fired him, though not before Malloy released a letter indicating that Cummings had reviewed and approved his ABA speech in advance.[70]

George and Kathryn Kelly led the FBI on what it later estimated to be a twenty-thousand-mile automobile chase through sixteen states, from Texas to Minnesota and from Oklahoma to Ohio.[71] It finally ended forty-five days later, on September 26, at a little bungalow in Kelly's hometown of Memphis, Tennessee, where the couple surrendered without incident. Pressed to try to explain to Hoover why Kelly was taken alive, a special agent present at the scene reported that they had not seen Kelly "until he was standing with his hands up and therefore did not have an opportunity to shoot him."[72] Machine Gun Kelly never spent another day of his life a free man.

11

....

The Symbol of the Crusade

Oklahoma City, September–October 1933

The first group of defendants to stand trial for the kidnapping of Charles Urschel included kidnapper Albert Bates; Boss and Ora Shannon, owners of the Paradise ranch; Armon Shannon, who helped guard Urschel; Harvey Bailey, who happened to be staying at the Shannon ranch; and seven Minneapolis money dealers who changed some of the hot ransom money into cool spending money. The trial began on September 18 in the new, nine-story Art Deco tower of the federal courthouse in Oklahoma City.[1] Two of the main characters in that drama were missing, however: George and Kathryn Kelly were still at large.

Security was as tight as could be. Marshals and deputies with sawed-off shotguns, machine guns, and rifles took up positions along the streets surrounding the courthouse. Guards patrolled the lobby with machine guns. The elevators to the tower were blocked above the seventh floor so that spectators bound for the courtroom on the ninth floor had to walk up two flights of stairs past more armed guards in the stairwells. Before entering the courtroom, they had to present passes signed by the U.S. marshal and have their bags and purses searched and their clothes patted down.

The Kansas City Massacre and Harvey Bailey's recent escape from the Dallas County Jail had served to warn that the underworld might try to free Bailey and Bates in a bloodbath. The already high threat level escalated when the Kellys sent letters before and during the trial to local newspapers threatening to wipe out the Urschel family, the prosecutors, and the trial judge, Edgar S. Vaught. In a letter to the Justice Department's Joseph Keenan, head of the prosecution team, Kathryn warned that the entire Urschel family and all the prosecution team would be "exterminated" and a "most awful tragedy" and "terrible slaughter" would take place in Oklahoma City "within the next few days" unless Keenan dropped the charges against her mother.[2]

The day before he was to testify, Urschel received a letter from Kelly. Addressed to "Ignorant Charles," Kelly said he was planning to "destroy your so-called mansion, and you and your family immediately after this trial. Are you ignorant enough to think the Government can guard you forever?" "In the event of my arrest," Kelly continued, "I've already formed an outfit to take care of and destroy you and yours the same as if I was there. I am spending *your* money to have you and your family killed—nice—eh?"[3]

None of the threats dissuaded Urschel from testifying. "We still have faith in the ultimate success of the federal government in its struggle with crime," he said in a statement, "and are gambling the safety of every member of our group on that success."[4] An armed deputy sheriff sat beside him throughout the trial, and armed guards escorted Judge Vaught and the government's witnesses to and from court every day. A sharpshooter covered the judge whenever he was on the bench. The family of U.S. attorney Herbert H. Hyde was removed to a safe location in another city after receiving warnings of a gangland plan to kidnap his four-year-old son during the trial.[5]

Neither the threats nor the inconvenience of the security measures discouraged the long lines of people waiting outside the courthouse every morning hoping to get seats or standing room. Most of the spectators were women, many of them from Oklahoma City's upper crust, who came for the day and brought their lunches and thermoses so they wouldn't have to vacate their places at the lunch recess.[6]

The anticipation and the tension were palpable. It was the first time the United States had put kidnappers on trial under the Lindbergh Law. Judge Vaught recognized that history was being made in his courtroom. For that reason he allowed newsreel cameras inside a federal courtroom for the first time. He also realized his rulings would influence the future interpretation of provisions of the Lindbergh Law, which he called "one of the most important laws ever enacted." "There was no reason to pass this law except to stop kidnapping," he said. "I'm going to do all in my power to put teeth into it."[7]

Prosecutor Herbert Hyde called the trial "one of the most important cases ever tried."[8] Joseph Keenan told the jury they had to decide whether "we are to have a government of law and order or abdicate in favor of machine gun gangsters. If the government cannot protect its citizens, then we had better frankly turn it over to the Kellys and the Bateses, the Baileys and the others of the underworld and pay tribute to them through taxes."[9]

The government's evidence against Kelly, Bates, and Boss and Armon Shannon was overwhelming. Bailey and Ora Shannon were swept up into the tidal wave of evidence against the others even though there was no evidence against Bailey other than the relatively small amount of ransom money given him by Kelly and Bates. The evidence against Ora was that she had fried some chickens and baked some biscuits that Charles Urschel remembered as the best meal he had had in Paradise.

The jury took a single ballot and convicted all defendants save five of the accused money dealers for whom the evidence was weak. Bailey, Bates, and Boss and Ora Shannon received sentences of life in prison. Young Armon Shannon got ten years (suspended during good behavior); the two convicted money dealers received five years each.

On September 26, in the middle of the first trial, George and Kathryn Kelly were arrested in Memphis and immediately flown to Oklahoma City under heavy guard. The week after Judge Vaught pronounced sentence on the first group of defendants, he started the Kellys' trial. It was largely a rehash of the earlier trial except that Kathryn took the witness stand to deny that she had advance knowledge of the kidnapping and to blame everything on George, whom she had obeyed, she said, out of fear. The prosecution didn't even bother to cross-examine her, though Judge Vaught in his charge to the jury commented that he would feel "cowardly and derelict in duty" if he failed to point out his conviction that Kathryn's testimony "was not wholly truthful."[10]

The prosecution had mountains of evidence against George, including his own confession and the eyewitness identifications of both Urschels and both Jarretts, but they had little direct evidence to prove Kathryn's knowing participation in the kidnapping. The most incriminating evidence against her was the threatening letters sent before and during the trials. To prove that Kathryn had written two of those letters, the prosecution presented the testimony of D. C. Patterson, an Oklahoma City accountant who claimed to be a handwriting expert. He testified that Kathryn had written the "Ignorant Charles" letter (signed by Kelly) and a second letter sent to the *Daily Oklahoman* threatening the Shannons before they testified.[11] Kathryn's lawyer asked for a recess to give her an opportunity to secure her own handwriting expert to challenge Patterson's conclusions, but Judge Vaught denied the request.[12]

Both Kellys were convicted and sentenced to life in prison—all in just sixteen days after their arrests. An additional nine people were convicted in subsequent trials of various offenses related to the kidnapping, including conspiracy, harboring, and perjury.

The arrest of her mother had shaken Kathryn Kelly, not that she ever seemed to recognize the extreme risk she and Kelly had put her family in when they decided to hide their "rich bastard" at the Shannons' ranch. Nor had she apparently ever considered the possibility that her mother might go to prison for life for preparing Charles Urschel a meal. From the day she was convicted, Kathryn did everything she could to get herself and her mother released from prison, including serving as a confidential informant for the FBI in numerous kidnapping and bank robbery cases. Her applications for parole were always denied, in part due to Urschel's opposition.

In 1958 Kathryn got a new lawyer, who filed a petition in the U.S. District Court in Oklahoma City seeking relief from her conviction on several grounds, including the government's use of false handwriting evidence and Judge Vaught's refusal to allow her time to secure her own handwriting expert. The petition created a dilemma for the FBI. Its own handwriting expert, Charles Appel, had examined the handwriting of those same two letters before the Kellys' trial and concluded that Kathryn could *not* have written either of them: "The handwriting on the letters to the *Oklahomian* [*sic*] and to Urschel is not identical with that of Mrs. Kelly. There are a great many similarities which on casual examination would lead one to think that these handwritings are the same. However, detailed analysis indicates that Mrs. Kelly did not write these letters."[13]

The FBI had kept Appel's potentially exculpatory report under wraps and never disclosed it to the defense, nor, apparently, to the prosecutors. When the court in 1958 ordered the FBI to produce Appel's report, the FBI refused to comply, and Kathryn and Ora were both released from prison.[14] George had died four years earlier in the federal penitentiary at Leavenworth.

It seems obvious the FBI suppressed Appel's handwriting analysis to help ensure Kathryn's conviction. More may have been involved, however. Hoover had a very personal dislike of Kathryn, similar to the intense dislike he would later develop for Ma Barker, that perhaps influenced him to conceal the information. Writing in 1938 he called Kathryn "one of the most coldly deliberate criminals of my experience. Here was a woman who could conceive a kidnapping, and force it through to a conclusion largely through her domination over her husband, who . . . could only bow before her tirades—and do as she bade him. If there ever was a henpecked man, it was George (Machine-gun) Kelly."[15]

The Urschel kidnapping provided the FBI an opportunity to demonstrate that it was a competent and professional law enforcement organization with the resources and the resolve to track kidnappers down all over the country. Hoover was able to showcase many of the powers and resources the FBI could harness to combat kidnapping and, by implication, other crimes: the ability to put special agents on the ground anywhere in the country (and beyond), the capability of tracking ransom money nationwide, and the increasing breadth and depth of experience that came from investigating and analyzing more kidnappings than the police of any individual state were likely to encounter. Simply put, the FBI's nationwide footprint and federal funding gave it a massive comparative advantage over state and local police in mobility, technology, and specialization.

As Hoover boasted at the time, the arrests of Kelly, Bailey, and Bates were the government's "ultimatum to the underworld" that kidnapping was now an extremely unsafe business.[16]

The Urschel kidnapping also provided the near-perfect narrative for the War against Kidnappers: violent, hard-core gangsters with machine guns invading a private home and terrorizing decent citizens. That image forged a powerful link, not previously established, between violent gangs of organized criminals and the kidnapping of law-abiding citizens.

The fact that Kelly and Bates had passed through at least sixteen states in their criminal spree became an important part of the story. Attorney General Cummings frequently used the case to illustrate his dubious claim that crime in America was now "organized on a nationwide basis, and lawbreakers extend their activities over many States."[17] The vast majority of kidnappings did not involve interstate transportation of victims, much less organized gangs of roving criminals. Cummings was laying a foundation for the Roosevelt administration's argument that the federal government needed a whole set of new laws and new powers so it could investigate and prosecute "any number" of "predatory" crimes, like kidnapping, against which "the states cannot adequately protect themselves."[18]

Soon Roosevelt, Cummings, and Hoover were deliberately mixing kidnappers in with armed robbers, roving criminal gangs, and racketeers; they began consciously referring to the War against Kidnappers, the war on crime, and the war on organized crime as interchangeable terms.[19]

New Yorker staff writer Jack Alexander interviewed Hoover for a three-part New Yorker profile in 1937. He wrote that after the Kansas City Massacre, Hoover became convinced it was not enough just to "quiet down" kidnapping and bank robbery. Hoover, according to Alexander, became convinced that "an actual crusade was needed, an enduring campaign that would cover all phases of crime and reduce it ultimately to a minimum." For crime to be conquered, he believed, someone had to become "the symbol of the crusade" and be the individual to put an "abiding fear of sure apprehension . . . in the heart of the felon." Hoover decided he was that someone.[20] His crusade was based on convincing criminals and the public that the FBI was invincible. "Every time we make an arrest or get a conviction in any case it helps put the fear of God and the law into criminals," he once said. "It is this fear and the confidence of the decent people in our work that will do much toward wiping out crime."[21]

One of the tools Hoover found for propagating the invincibility myth was the nickname "G-men." He and the FBI put out the story that Machine Gun Kelly had pleaded, "Don't shoot, G-men! Don't shoot, G-men!" when FBI agents and Memphis police arrived to arrest him. Nothing in the contemporaneous accounts supports that claim; the FBI's website now states that Kelly "allegedly" spoke the famous words.[22] Even if Kelly did use the term "G-men" (short for "Government men"), he was not the first one to do so; nor were FBI agents the only federal agents referred to as G-men.

The point is that Hoover loved the nickname (he named one of his Cairn terriers "G-boy") and embraced it.[23] He correctly guessed the public would associate the term with the superhero-like traits his invincible special agents were supposed to possess. More importantly it helped differentiate Hoover, as leader of the G-men, from the lawyers Cummings and Keenan, also fighting the War against Kidnappers. In Hoover, the public now had a single, recognizable symbol in which to place its trust in the War against Kidnappers and in crime-fighting at the federal level.

Following the headline arrests of Bailey and Bates, Hoover stepped out of the shadows of the Justice Department and started speaking, writing, and giving more interviews. Newspaper stories, magazine articles, books, and movies touting the prowess and integrity of Hoover and his G-men followed. Around the same time he began rewarding journalists and writers like Walter Winchell, Rex Collier, and Don Whitehead, who wrote favorable books and articles about him or the G-men, by offering them access to confidential investigatory files of the FBI. It was a practice he would continue for the rest of his life. Beginning in 1934 he collaborated on a number of ghostwriting and other projects with publicity man and author Courtney Ryley Cooper, Buffalo Bill's former publicist, to create and convey the image of the G-men he wanted to project: professional, fearless, incorruptible.

1. Dr. Isaac Dee Kelley Jr. demonstrates
the taped goggles his kidnappers used to
blindfold him during his captivity. *St. Louis
Post-Dispatch*.

2. Nellie Muench and Dr. Ludwig Muench before Nellie lost her dress shop and suggested that her friends kidnap Dr. Dee Kelley. *St. Louis Post-Dispatch.*

3. (*opposite top*) Peggy McMath in posed photographs appearing as she had when testifying in court the day before against her accused kidnappers. *Boston Globe.*

4. (*opposite bottom*) Harwich Centre Grammar School, from which Peggy McMath was abducted. *Boston Globe.*

5. Home of Armon Shannon near Paradise in Wise County, Texas, where Charles Urschel was held captive. Oklahoma Historical Society, Oklahoma Publishing Company Photography Collection, 2012.201.B1164.0185.

6. Film crews in the courtroom during the first Urschel kidnapping trial. It was the first time newsreel cameras were permitted inside a federal courtroom during trial. Oklahoma Historical Society, Oklahoma Publishing Company Photography Collection, 2012.201.B1164.0509.

7. Berenice and Charles Urschel at the courthouse
during the first Urschel kidnapping trial. Oklahoma
Historical Society, Oklahoma Publishing Company
Photography Collection, 2012.201.B1164.0540.

IF ANYBODY IN YOUR FAMILY EVER IS KIDNAPED—

CALL WASHINGTON!

Upon receipt of threatening letters or the disappearance of a relative or friend ... place a long distance call immediately to Edgar Hoover, director of the federal bureau of investigation (Washington).

Officers will be dispatched to the scene.

—*Assistant Attorney General Keenan.*

Joseph B. Keenan

Joseph B. Keenan, U. S. special assistant attorney general in charge of eliminating kidnapings and rackets, gives suggestions as to what to do if anybody in your family is kidnaped.

8. (*opposite top*) The driveway of the Urschel home in Oklahoma City, leading to the sunporch from which Charles Urschel and Walter Jarrett were abducted. Oklahoma Historical Society, Oklahoma Publishing Company Photography Collection, 2012.201B1164.0481.

9. (*opposite bottom*) An example of the Justice Department's publicity campaign published in many newspapers to encourage the public to report kidnappings directly to J. Edgar Hoover. *Daily Republican*, July 29, 1933.

10. (*above*) Aerial view of Alcatraz Island circa 1928. Federal Bureau of Investigation.

11. William Hamm (*far left*) after release by the Barker-Karpis gang, with go-between W. W. Dunn (*second from left*) and Charles Tierney, Thomas Dahill, and Tom "Big Tom" Brown (*far right*) of the St. Paul Police Department. Minnesota Historical Society.

12. (*opposite top*) Police reenactment of the kidnapping of Edward Bremer after he dropped off his daughter at school in St. Paul, Minnesota. Minnesota Historical Society.

13. (*opposite bottom*) Detectives and reporters examining the three-piece ladder found abandoned at the Lindbergh home on the night of Charlie Lindbergh's abduction. The careless handling of the ladder and other physical evidence would become the subject of much criticism. New Jersey State Police Museum.

14. New Jersey state troopers investigating the kidnappers' possible use of the ladder abandoned near the Lindbergh home as a means of entry into the nursery. New Jersey State Police Museum.

15. Photograph looking toward the entrance to St. Raymond's Cemetery in the Bronx from the greenhouse of the Bergen Nursery on East Tremont Avenue. The photograph is taken from the approximate location where Charles Lindbergh waited in the car while Dr. John Condon paid the ransom to Cemetery John. New Jersey State Police Museum.

Colonel Lindbergh has authorized the statement that a ransom of
$50,000.00 was paid to the kidnapers, properly identified as such,
upon their agreement to notify him as to the exact whereabouts of the
baby within 8 hours after payment. The 8 hours elapsed and the baby
was not found at the point designated. Several days were permitted
to elapse to give the kidnapers every opportunity to keep their
agreement. It was not intended to use the numbers on the specie in
which the ransom was paid but inasmuchas the kidnapers have failed to
keep their agreement, it is felt that every possible means must be
utilized to accomplish the return of the baby and to this end the
co-operation of the Federal Government was requested in tracing it
possible the bills used.

And have not communicated since the ransom was paid

16. Draft of the statement by Charles Lindbergh on April 9, 1932, disclosing that he had paid the ransom and not gotten Charlie back and explaining why the serial numbers of the ransom bills had been provided to banks. Lindbergh's changes are in his handwriting. New Jersey State Police Museum.

FEDERAL RESERVE BANK
OF NEW YORK

CASH DEPARTMENT

DEPOSITED BY

J. J. Faulkner 537 W 149

IN

Federal Reserve Bank of New York

NEW YORK,_____19____

Checks	AMOUNT
	2980
Gold Cert.	
10 x 30	
TOTAL	

WRITE TOTAL AMOUNT OF DEPOSIT HERE

_____DOLLARS

17. (*opposite*) The deposit ticket completed by the individual identifying himself as "J. J. Faulkner" when he exchanged $2,980 in gold certificates at the Federal Reserve Bank of New York on May 1, 1933. New Jersey State Police Museum.

18. (*above*) The Warner-Quinlan gas station in the Bronx where Bruno Richard Hauptmann paid for a tank of gasoline with a $10 ransom gold certificate on September 15, 1934. New Jersey State Police Museum.

19. (*opposite top*) Sketches of Cemetery John
prepared by James T. Berryman in July 1934, based
on information supplied by Dr. John Condon.
New Jersey State Police Museum.

20. (*opposite bottom*) Photograph of Bruno Richard
Hauptmann taken at the New York City Police
Department on September 21, 1934. New Jersey State
Police Museum.

21. (*above*) Charles Lindbergh testifying at the
trial of Bruno Richard Hauptmann. Library of
Congress, LC-USZ62-109416.

22. The rental cottage on Lake Weir in Ocklawaha, Florida, where Ma and Fred Barker died in a gun battle with the FBI on January 16, 1935. Federal Bureau of Investigation.

23. Weapons discovered by the FBI at the Barkers' rental cottage in Ocklawaha the day Ma and Fred Barker died. Federal Bureau of Investigation.

Four

At War

12

The All-American Boy

San Jose, November 1933

The Urschel afterglow was brief.

On November 9, less than a month after the Kellys' convictions, the kidnapping of twenty-two-year-old Brooke Hart stunned San Jose, California. The blond, blue-eyed, all-American boy was the son of the owner of Hart's Department Store, San Jose's largest, where most of the city's families shopped. Brooke had worked there stocking shelves, cashiering, bookkeeping, and selling merchandise on weekends and during vacations since elementary school. Just about everyone in town knew him to speak to. When he graduated from Santa Clara University that September, his father, Alex, promoted him to vice president and held a banquet at the grand Hotel De Anza to announce it to family and employees. The *San Jose Mercury Herald* reported the event along with pictures.[1]

As Brooke drove out of the parking lot after work that Thursday evening in his new Studebaker President roadster—green with yellow wire wheels, a gift from his parents—a stranger named Jack Holmes flagged him down, opened the passenger door, and got in. He pointed a pistol at Brooke and ordered him to keep driving. They headed north toward Milpitas, a small farming community just beyond the city, where another stranger named Harold Thurmond met them. Holmes and Thurmond placed a pillowcase over Brooke's head and pushed him into the back of Thurmond's Chevrolet. Then they drove away, abandoning the roadster on the side of the road. Brooke thought it was all some kind of joke and played along. He'd never been held up before, he said, and he was getting a thrill out of his first experience being kidnapped.[2]

Alex Hart knew something was wrong when Brooke failed to pick him up after work and drive him to a meeting as they had planned. He went straight to the San Jose Police Department to report Brooke's disappearance. Chief John Black, who knew the family, sensed right away that Brooke had been kidnapped and wasted no time getting the telephone company to trace all calls to the Hart home. Then he called Reed Vetterli, special agent in charge of the FBI's San Francisco office, for help.[3] Vetterli sent Special Agent William Ramsey to the Hart home with instructions to move in, take charge of the family, and monitor every communication into and out of the home. Within the hour Ramsey was settling into the sprawling white mansion on The Alameda, the tree-lined boulevard where many of the city's wealthiest and most prominent citizens lived. Built to look like the Petit Trianon palace at Versailles, it was a San Jose landmark.

The telephone rang at the Hart home about 9:30, before Alex got there, and Brooke's sister Aleese answered. Kidnapper Harold Thurmond told her that her brother had been kidnapped, and the family would hear from him again. Then he hung up. An hour later he called back and told Brooke's sister Miriam that her brother was safe, but it would cost $40,000 (about $790,000 in 2020) to get him back. He warned her against contacting the police and said the family would receive additional instructions. The telephone company traced the first call to a speakeasy on

Market Street in San Francisco and the second to a pay phone in a nearby Market Street hotel.[4]

Already there were strong indications Brooke's kidnappers were amateurs. Experienced kidnappers would have needed more time before contacting the family to transport the victim to a hideout far enough away to reduce the risk that the victim would recognize the location, and they wouldn't have risked contacting the family twice before providing the all-important instructions for delivering the ransom. Lack of experience usually meant poor planning, poor execution, and often a poor outcome.

Just after midnight a Milpitas resident driving home from work came upon a Studebaker roadster parked at an odd angle on the side of the road with its lights on. He saw that it was empty and called the Santa Clara County sheriff's office, which discovered the license plate was registered to Brooke Hart.

On Monday, November 13, an envelope addressed to Alex, postmarked Sacramento, arrived with the department store's morning mail. Inside was a handwritten postcard instructing Alex to put the ransom money—five hundred $20 bills, two thousand $10s, and two thousand $5s—in a black satchel and prepare to take a weeklong trip in Brooke's car.[5] There was no proof he was dealing with the real kidnappers, but Alex got the money anyway.[6] The FBI prepared a statement for him to hand out to reporters in which he promised to pay the ransom as soon as the kidnappers provided evidence they were holding his son.[7]

Another letter and additional telephone calls told Alex to drive to Los Angeles and watch for a man wearing a white mask who would approach him and take the money. They told him to place a small sign containing the numeral "1" in the store's Market Street window when the money was ready.[8] Since Alex didn't know how to drive, as experienced kidnappers would have discovered in planning the snatch, he put a sign in the store window with the words "I CANNOT DRIVE" in large black letters. Thurmond called back with new instructions: Alex was to take the 9:30 train to Los Angeles that night. Alex said he had to have proof Thurmond actually had Brooke. Thurmond hung up.[9]

Holmes and Thurmond were running out of options. On Wednesday, November 15, they decided to risk another telephone call to try to persuade Alex to take the train to Los Angeles that night. About 8:00, they drove to the Plaza Garage in downtown San Jose. Thurmond went inside to use the pay telephone. He gave the operator the number of the Hart home. Alex answered. After listening patiently to Thurmond's new plan, he took his time explaining in detail that the money was ready and he would pay as soon as he had proof he was dealing with the real kidnappers. Alex managed to keep Thurmond on the line long enough for the telephone company to contact the police with the address of the pay phone where the call was coming from and for the police and FBI to get to the garage and arrest Thurmond. Holmes was still waiting in his car outside the garage. He finally realized something was wrong and quietly slipped away.[10]

Jittery, wild-eyed Harold Thurmond, twenty-seven, came across as slow and somewhat simpleminded. His family said he had never been right since suffering a childhood head injury. He had dropped out of high school in San Jose and drifted from job to job during the Depression, working in a lumberyard, a paint store, and a gas station while his keener siblings held down jobs as a pastor, schoolteacher, organist, accountant, and stenographer.[11] The only girlfriend he'd ever had turned down his marriage proposal because she didn't think he would be able to make a living. Thurmond didn't have a criminal record, but he and his new friend Jack Holmes had recently robbed two messengers for a total of over $1,400.[12] The police had never questioned them about either robbery, so they were feeling pretty good about their little crime spree when they began planning the kidnapping of Brooke Hart.

Within hours of his arrest Thurmond made a stunning confession. After abandoning Brooke's car in Milpitas and switching to the Chevrolet, he and Holmes drove Brooke north to the San Mateo Bridge, which crossed over San Francisco Bay near Hayward in the East Bay, about twenty-five miles from San Jose. Holmes stopped the car on the bridge and ordered Brooke to get out. At some point they took Brooke's wallet and cash. As Holmes pulled out his pistol and grabbed a bundle of clothesline wire from the car, Brooke began yelling for help. Holmes beat him over the head with the butt of his gun, knocking him to the pavement, and held him down while Thurmond wrapped wire around his arms and feet. With the remaining wire, he attached two cement blocks, twenty-two pounds each, to his chest and back. Together they lifted Brooke up and pushed him over the railing, cement blocks and all, into San Francisco Bay. Hearing several feeble cries for help after Brooke hit the water, they both fired bullets at the spot where he went under.[13]

Holmes and Thurmond then drove back to San Jose. They arrived in time for Holmes to accompany his wife and another couple to see Walt Disney's new movie *The Three Little Pigs*. Thurmond changed clothes and drove up to San Francisco, where he placed two telephone calls to Brooke's family before heading up to Sacramento to mail the first ransom note to Alex Hart.

At some point one of the kidnappers took Brooke's wallet and identification cards to Pier 32 on the San Francisco waterfront and tossed them into the water, apparently unaware that he was throwing away valuable proof they were the real kidnappers.[14] Another mistake of inexperience.

After signing his confession in the early morning hours of November 16, Thurmond led police and FBI agents to the California Hotel, behind the Plaza Garage, where Jack Holmes had been staying in an SRO room for several days. Holmes at first denied involvement in Brooke's kidnapping and murder, but soon broke down under questioning and confessed everything, telling much the same story as Thurmond. They disagreed principally on who the mastermind was and how many shots each had fired at Brooke as he struggled to keep himself afloat in the water. When the detectives asked Holmes what they were thinking about when they demanded a ransom after murdering Brooke, Holmes was nonchalant. "It made no difference to us that Hart was dead. We still thought we could collect the $40,000," he said.[15]

Handsome, fiery Jack Holmes, twenty-nine, was from a good, middle-class San Jose family. Jack's mother, Hulda, belonged to the venerable San Jose Woman's Club; his father, Maurice, a tailor, was on familiar terms with most of San Jose society. Maurice and Jack were both Masons and members of the same lodge as Santa Clara County sheriff William Emig, who had custody of Holmes and Thurmond.[16] Like Thurmond, Holmes had dropped out of high school. He had worked as a salesman for several oil companies until recently losing his job. Married and the father of two young children, he had left home and checked into the California Hotel the day after the kidnapping, ostensibly because his wife could no longer tolerate his infatuation with a former girlfriend. He, too, had no criminal record, but he was an avid reader of crime magazines. He had been obsessed for several years with planning the perfect crime.

The arrests brought a new wave of shock and anger as the realization set in that Brooke Hart was never coming home. The disclosures that the kidnappers had planned all along to murder Brooke and might plead not guilty by reason of insanity enraged the public even more. They called to mind the infamous case of Chicago teenagers Nathan Leopold and Richard Loeb, who murdered young Bobby Franks in 1924 and then demanded a $10,000 ransom from his father.[17]

As soon as word of the arrests got out, people began milling around the sixty-two-year-old Santa Clara County Jail. Sheriff Emig didn't like the mood of the bystanders and wasn't confident his men would be able to defend the jail and protect the prisoners if violence erupted. He decided to find a safer place to hold Holmes and Thurmond. On the morning of November 16, they were driven to the San Francisco City Prison, located in the Hall of Justice.[18] When crowds gathered there, FBI agents took the prisoners to the FBI's San Francisco office for further questioning.[19] A crowd gathered there, too. When Thurmond was led away from the building to return to the City Prison, the crowd shouted, "Lynch him! Lynch him!"[20] Hoover read about it the next morning in the *New York Times* and scribbled an order to an assistant to call Vetterli "at once & tell him to stop taking these two criminals out of jail. If they should be lynched while in our custody it would be terrible."[21]

The pressing question now was what charges to bring against Holmes and Thurmond. The only available federal charge was using the mail to make a kidnap threat, which was not a capital crime. California, however, could charge the state crimes of kidnapping, which carried the death penalty when bodily harm occurred, and murder, which also carried the death penalty. State and federal authorities agreed that the state charges should be tried first and the federal charges held in abeyance, but there was still the question whether to charge murder or kidnapping or both.

The legal principle of corpus delicti ("body of the crime") ordinarily requires the existence of a corpse in a murder case to prove that the alleged victim actually died and hadn't just disappeared, but despite intensive searching by divers, Coast Guard boats, airplanes, and a navy blimp, Brooke's body had not yet been found.[22] Under more normal circumstances the county prosecutor might have waited a bit longer for the body to turn up, but he yielded to public pressure for swift action and decided to proceed with the state kidnapping charge alone.

Late on the night of Wednesday, November 22, Sheriff Emig sent four cars of deputies armed with machine guns and tear gas to the City Prison to bring Holmes and Thurmond back to the Santa Clara County Jail to await trial.

The San Jose City Council passed a resolution expressing hope that "justice will be sure and swift and that the subterfuges and technicalities of law that frequently thwart or delay justice"—including sanity determinations, legal motions, and appeals—"will not be taken in this instance."[23] The *San Francisco Chronicle* urged that Holmes and Thurmond be executed "at the earliest legal date without the law's endless delays."[24]

Ambiguous references to "swift justice" began to sound like calls for vigilante action. On November 16, the *San Jose Evening Times* published an incendiary editorial titled "Human Devils": "If mob violence could ever be justified it would be in a case like this"; the confessions of Holmes and Thurmond make one "feel like he wanted to go out and be a part of that mob." The piece also contained a clear warning: "Unless these two prisoners are kept safely away from San Jose there is likely to be a hanging without waiting for the courts of justice."[25]

On Saturday, November 25, Royce Brier of the *San Francisco Chronicle*, who would win a Pulitzer Prize for his reporting on the case, wrote that talk of a "necktie party" is "coming more and more into the open on San Jose streets," and that a vigilante committee was being organized to "see justice done." More than sixty people had already signed secret pledges to "take adequate action" against Holmes and Thurmond as soon as Brooke Hart's body was found, he reported.[26]

Fearing the worst, Sheriff Emig stocked up on extra canisters of tear gas, rifles, shotguns, handguns, and ammunition. He called California governor James Rolph to find out whether he could count on Rolph to send the National Guard to help protect the prisoners if necessary. Rolph's answer was "no," which was the same answer he gave the lawyer Maurice Holmes hired to represent his son. "If they lynch those fellows, I'll pardon the lynchers," Rolph vowed.[27]

Jim Rolph was known as "Sunny" for his optimistic, positive disposition; he had never been considered an extremist or a grandstander. A successful businessman and bank president, he first came to public attention for organizing massive relief efforts to feed and clothe victims of the earthquake and fire that destroyed much of San Francisco in 1906. His efforts thereafter to rebuild the city's infrastructure won him five consecutive terms as mayor (1912–30), making him the longest-serving mayor in San Francisco history. Elected governor of California in 1930, Rolph was serving as chairman of the National Governors Association when he refused to call out the National Guard to protect Brooke Hart's murderers.

On Sunday morning, the 26th, the fog was thick over San Francisco Bay as two duck hunters out in a skiff spotted a body floating in shallow water, a half mile south of the San Mateo Bridge. They covered it with a tarpaulin and towed it to shore.

After seventeen days in the water, there wasn't much left of the body. Sharks and crabs had eaten away the hands and feet. There was nothing but a skeleton from the waist up, but three Hart's Department Store employees and a friend of Brooke's were able to identify his remains from items of clothing from the store and the pocketknife in his pocket.[28] The autopsy found head wounds but no skull fracture or bullet holes, indicating that Brooke had been beaten over the head before dying an agonizing death by drowning.[29]

By noon word was out that Brooke's body had been found, and large crowds began to gather near the jail.[30] Radio stations reported rumors that a lynching would take place that night at St. James Park across the street from the jail.[31] Sheriff Emig called in fifty extra deputies and distributed tear gas bombs and rifles. Governor Rolph canceled plans to attend a western governors' conference in Boise, Idaho, because he "didn't dare leave the state because [the lieutenant governor] might have called out the troops."[32]

By 9:30 the crowd had grown to several thousand, mostly men and boys, but women and children, too, chanting "Brookie *Hart!*

Brookie *Hart*!" Too late, the sheriff called the San Francisco and Oakland police for additional officers. About 11:00 p.m., eighteen-year-old Anthony Cataldi decided to take the lead. Climbing onto the roof of a nearby shed, he shouted, "Come on, fellows. Let's go get 'em."[33]

Dozens of men in business suits, ties, and felt hats grabbed a large steel pipe from a nearby construction site and hauled it over to the jail, where they used it as a battering ram to break down the doors. Others picked up bricks, stones, and pieces of construction debris and hurled them at the jail windows. Officers inside the jail tossed tear gas bombs out the windows into the mob until they ran out. When he realized the jail doors couldn't hold much longer, Sheriff Emig ordered his men not to shoot—an order some would later say averted a bloodbath. The doors finally gave way, and the mob poured in. They knocked the sheriff down, took his keys, and roamed the hallways searching for Holmes and Thurmond.

They found them in their cells. Thurmond was standing on the toilet trying to climb out through the roof. The mob beat and kicked them in the head, tore their clothes, and dragged them across the street to the park. It was now filled with an angry, noisy crowd estimated at between three thousand and fifteen thousand. John Young, an off-duty reporter for the *San Jose Mercury Herald*, described a "frightful number of presumably decent citizens turned into a pack of hyenas. There were all kinds—well-dressed businessmen and housewives, students, bums from the slums, professional people, people of all races and nationalities, a cross-section of the city to its everlasting shame."[34] The famous child actor Jackie Coogan, a friend of Brooke's from Santa Clara University, was spotted holding a coiled rope.

Thurmond was unconscious and possibly already dead from a fractured skull when the mob strung him up over the branch of an elm tree. Holmes was naked when he was hanged from a nearby tree. A man in the crowd ignited his cigarette lighter and tried to set fire to their dangling feet as mothers lifted up little children for a better view.[35] A San Francisco radio station broadcast everything live.

Though Alex Hart had warned he would fire any Hart's Department Store employee who took part in any violence, many store employees were present in the park that night.[36] "I was perfectly satisfied that the law should take its course against the two men who killed my son," Alex said afterward, "but it brings me comfort to feel that my fellow citizens took violent action because they loved Brookie."[37]

Governor Rolph praised the mob and called the lynchings the "best lesson California has ever given the country."[38] He defended his refusal to call out the National Guard by arguing that there would be swifter justice and fewer kidnappings if citizens were confident that troops wouldn't be called out to "mow them down" when they acted to protect themselves against kidnappers. He again vowed to pardon anyone charged with lynching and added that he would like to release all kidnappers then in California prisons to the custody of "those fine, patriotic San Jose citizens who knew how to handle such a situation."[39] Several suspects would later be arrested, but no one was ever tried for the murders of Holmes and Thurmond.

From across the country came expressions of sympathy and support for the lynch mob and for Governor Rolph's stand. Will Rogers wrote, "All the Californians I have met are going around proud today."[40] The Reverend Dr. Henry Darlington, rector of the Protestant Episcopal Church of the Heavenly Rest in New York, telegraphed the governor: "Congratulations on the stand you have taken."[41] (He later expressed regret for the telegram.)[42] The *Harvard Crimson*, the university newspaper, called Rolph a "keen observer of popular trends" in praising the mob's "spectacular demonstration of rising public intolerance with an emasculated system of criminal law."[43] Hollywood actress Jean Harlow, herself a target of kidnap threats, said Hollywood stars now would rest easier because the "San Jose affair" would make those planning kidnappings think twice.[44]

There were twenty-eight lynchings in the United States in 1933. Only four of the victims were white,[45] but the San Jose lynchings and Governor Rolph's conduct injected new energy into the national conversation about lynching. The board of the American Civil Liberties Union expressed "the indignation of thousands who deplore and condemn kidnapping, but who abhor lynching and mob violence more."[46] Denouncing Rolph's "astounding attitude," Mrs. Jessie Daniel Ames, executive director of the Association of Southern Women for the Prevention of Lynching, said, "We are grateful no Southern Governor of today has made himself a public defender and protector of lynchers."[47]

President Roosevelt, who had thus far resisted speaking out against lynching, came under renewed pressure from civil rights groups and First Lady Eleanor Roosevelt to say something. In a nationally broadcast speech to the Federal Council of the Churches of Christ in America, he called lynching a "vile form of collective murder" and without singling out Rolph said, "We do not excuse those in high places or in low who condone lynch law."[48] It wasn't much, but it was perhaps a start.

Brooke Hart's kidnapping was another headline kidnapping of another elite citizen, another murdered victim. This time, though, it was harder to fault the law enforcement effort, federal or state, in apprehending the kidnappers. Yet the lynchings were a powerful display of public intolerance toward kidnappers and impatience toward the legal system and the constitutional protections it affords to all accused, even kidnappers.

13

···

Framing God's Bagman

St. Paul, September–November 1933

Two days after the San Jose lynchings, a St. Paul, Minnesota, jury acquitted four Chicago gangsters of the kidnapping of St. Paul brewer William A. Hamm Jr. It was the first time the United States government had lost a case brought under the Lindbergh Law.

Alvin Karpis already knew he wanted to be a criminal when he stole his first gun at the age of ten.[1] By the time he was eighteen, he had escaped from a Kansas reformatory where he was serving time for burglary. The theft of a car landed him back at the reformatory and earned him a transfer to the big leagues of the Kansas State Penitentiary at Lansing. There he met a twenty-four-year-old bank robber named Fred Barker. He was the youngest of the four sons of Arizona "Ma" Barker of Tulsa, all convicted felons.[2]

A few days after Karpis arrived at Lansing, Fred approached him in the dinner line and invited him to eat with him. Soon Fred was supplying Karpis with marijuana from the prison farm and arranging to have Karpis transferred to his cell. More than forty years later, Karpis still remembered how impressed he'd been with Fred's cell, with his writing table and bookshelf stocked with supplies of canned sardines, jams, and crackers. "Freddie liked his luxuries, and he was a generous host," he recalled. "Freddie used to set up lunches in the yard—I don't know how—that featured treats like canned chicken, fresh bread, and pies and pastries."[3] There was another, vicious side to Fred, too, as Karpis would learn: he was a "natural killer" who never seemed to mind "gunning down anybody who stood in his way, whether it was a cop or a hood or an ordinary guy on the street."[4]

If the Barkers had a special talent, it was for getting out of jails and prisons. Fred was released from Lansing in 1930 after serving only three years of a five-to-ten-year sentence.[5] When Karpis finished serving his sentence in May 1931, they got together again and started burglarizing stores around Tulsa. After Fred was caught breaking into a jewelry store, he escaped from jail, and they relocated to Thayer, Missouri, in the Ozarks, where Ma was renting a farm. From there they continued burglarizing jewelry and clothing stores in Missouri and Kansas.[6]

In October they broke into the Peoples Bank of Mountain View, Missouri, at 3:00 one morning and waited for the employees to arrive at 9:00. After forcing them to empty the safe of nearly $7,000, Fred and Karpis locked the employees in the vault and ran out the back. As they sped away they sprinkled roofing tacks on the road behind them.[7] The *Mountain View Standard* called it the "most sensational, daring and well planned bank robbery ever staged in this part of the Ozarks."[8]

Two months later they broke into C. C. McCallon's clothing store in West Plains, Missouri, and loaded $2,000 worth of clothing into Karpis's blue DeSoto. The next morning they returned to West Plains to case the bank and get their tires patched. One of the garage mechanics spotted Sheriff Roy Kelly across the street and slipped away to let him know there were two strangers in the garage who were wearing some of McCallon's merchandise.[9] The sheriff went to take a look. When he approached the DeSoto, Fred stepped out. Without a word he jabbed his pistol into Kelly's chest and shot him in the heart; Kelly dropped dead as Karpis and Fred got away.[10] Within days Fred and Karpis were identified as suspects in the sheriff's murder, and a $1,200 reward was offered. Their pictures were sent to police and newspapers all over the country.[11] Fred and Karpis were "hot" now. The place to go was St. Paul.

America had a number of "good towns" in the early 1930s where criminals who played by the local rules were welcomed with open arms—places like Atlantic City, Reno, Kansas City, Toledo, Hot Springs, Joplin, and Cicero, Illinois. The most notorious of all was St. Paul, Minnesota. Hands down.

Since Police Chief John J. O'Connor first opened St. Paul to criminals in 1900, the city had operated under the unwritten "O'Connor System" (sometimes referred to as the "O'Connor Layover Agreement"). The rules were simple: fugitives could stay in St. Paul without being arrested or extradited as long as they checked in with the police or their representatives when they arrived, paid the stipulated bribes, and didn't commit any violent crimes within the city limits. O'Connor ran St. Paul "as a sort of prisoner's base," observed columnist Westbrook Pegler, "which is a way of saying that as long as a lawless character, in from elsewhere, led a blameless life in St. Paul he was free to stay there and spend his money, and was more or less immune to extradition." Indeed, if another state tried to extradite a visiting criminal who was behaving himself, "O'Connor would hide him and supply hair dye and false whiskers."[12]

St. Paul's elaborate underworld infrastructure made it easy for criminals to go about their business. Mail drops, message centers, guns, and women were provided. Referrals were made to doctors, lawyers, apartments, and golf clubs that welcomed them. Visitors with criminal skills were matched up with jobs that could use them. Money men changed their "hot" money and "hot" bonds into "cool" money, and personal "bankers" held their cash in safes that were safer than banks. As historian Paul Maccabee said, St. Paul was "like a Walmart for criminals."[13]

"The fix was in from top to bottom," recalled Karpis. "You could relax in its joints and speakeasies without any fear of arrest, and when you were planning a score, you could have your pick of all the top men at all the top crimes." It was a real "crook's haven."[14] Surprisingly, perhaps, the law-abiding citizens of St. Paul liked it, too. Freedom from violent crime was good for business and for family life.

Two of the fixers who handled bribes and served as bridges between the criminals and the city were Jack Peifer and Harry Sawyer, both bootleggers who rode the coattails of Prohibition to power.[15] It took a great deal of money to fund all the payoffs necessary to make the O'Connor System work: for police to tip off the criminals, for prosecutors and judges to be bought, for juries to be fixed, and for paroles and pardons to be rigged. The money came from the bribes paid by visiting criminals and by the enormous revenues generated by Prohibition and the other rackets controlled by the underworld. By 1933, however, the future of the O'Connor System was in doubt. Congress had passed legislation in February to begin the process of ending Prohibition; on December 5 the last state ratified the Twenty-First Amendment to the Constitution, which repealed the Eighteenth. Prohibition was over.

One afternoon in April 1933, fixer Jack Peifer invited Karpis and Fred to stop by his Hollyhocks Club on a bluff overlooking the Mississippi River. There the well-heeled from all over the Midwest came to enjoy thick, juicy steaks and decent wines before heading upstairs for craps, blackjack, and roulette. The Hollyhocks's real draw, though, was the opportunity for the law-abiding and famous criminals to hobnob with each other in what passed for a glamor spot.[16] For 20 percent of the club's net profits delivered in a bag each week, Peifer and his guests had no worries about the St. Paul police and politicians.[17]

As Karpis later told the story, Peifer laid out a proposition for them that afternoon: kidnap William Hamm Jr. and collect $100,000—$10,000 for Peifer and the other $90,000 for their kidnap team. Hamm, thirty-nine, was president of the Theodore Hamm Brewing Company and the scion of one of St. Paul's most prominent families. He was called at the time "the most eligible bachelor in the Midwest."[18]

Peifer promised the snatch would be safe: his police contacts would let him know what was happening in the investigation, and he would pass the information along to them.[19] Karpis and Barker didn't need much convincing: a safe $90,000 job was easily worth several bank robberies. The odd thing was that it was Peifer, who was supposed to be *enforcing* the O'Connor System, who was offering them a job to be pulled in St. Paul.

Peifer had already lined up freelance bank robber and kidnapper Fred Goetz (also known as "Shotgun George Ziegler") and his sidekick, Byron "Monty" Bolton. Ziegler had studied engineering and played football at the University of Illinois before being charged with the attempted rape of a seven-year-old girl while working as a lifeguard in Chicago. He absconded, joined up with the Capone Outfit, and settled into a life of crime. Both Ziegler and Bolton were suspects in the infamous but unsolved St. Valentine's Day Massacre of 1929, in which seven members of Bugs Moran's Chicago gang were gunned down.

In addition to Ziegler and Bolton, Fred and Karpis recruited veteran bank robber Charles Fitzgerald and Fred's mean, trigger-happy brother Doc Barker, recently released from the Oklahoma State Penitentiary, where he had been serving a life sentence for murder. He had received a "banishment pardon," bought from Oklahoma governor William "Alfalfa Bill" Murray, on the condition that he leave the state immediately and never return.[20]

Though it is customary now to refer to the "Barker-Karpis gang" as if it were an organization with identifiable members, that wasn't quite the case. The "gang" was two men: Alvin Karpis, the more cerebral one, and Fred Barker, the one with the more established criminal reputation, at least initially. Other individuals worked with them from time to time, job by job. Ma Barker, who was always closer to Fred (and to Karpis) than to her other sons, often traveled with them, renting the apartments and houses where they stayed.

The Hamm kidnap team, plus Ma and a Japanese cook, spent May and early June in a vacation cottage at Bald Eagle Lake outside St. Paul, arranged by Peifer, where they meticulously planned the kidnapping. They traveled back and forth to St. Paul to observe Hamm's home and the brewery, charted their escape route, and rehearsed the duties of each team member. "We got to know so much about [Hamm] that I was sick of him long before the kidnapping," wrote Karpis.[21]

On June 15 Hamm left his office at 12:45 p.m., as usual, to walk to his mother's home for lunch. As he made his way up the hill toward the redbrick mansion, a black Hudson with four men inside pulled over to the sidewalk. Fitzgerald, a kindly looking gentleman in his sixties with gray hair and a boardroom face, crossed the street and approached Hamm. He stuck out his hand and said, "Mr. Hamm, I wonder if I might speak to you on a rather important business matter." With a grip on Hamm's arm, he guided him toward the Hudson parked nearby.

Hamm kept shaking hands and nodding around without seeming to understand what was happening until he was inside the car and on the floor, sandwiched between Fitzgerald and Bolton. Karpis, in a chauffeur's cap, was at the wheel with Doc beside him. They drove Hamm to the home of Edward Bartholmey and his family in Bensenville, Illinois, a Chicago suburb, where they had arranged to hide out until the ransom was paid. Bartholmey was a member of the Bensenville school board and was soon to become postmaster of Bensenville.

Two days later Hamm's family paid the kidnappers $100,000 (over $1.9 million in 2020). Two days after that Karpis, Doc, and

Bolton drove Hamm to Wyoming, Minnesota, forty-five miles north of St. Paul, and released him. By dropping him off in Minnesota, they hoped to trick the FBI into believing Hamm had never left the state.[22] It was a smooth, professional, by-the-book snatch, well planned and executed.

Before releasing Hamm, Karpis secretly removed four $20 bills from Hamm's wallet and substituted four $20 bills of ransom money. The plan was for the kidnappers to refrain temporarily from spending any of the ransom money so that Hamm would be the first person to pass a ransom bill. If the serial numbers of the ransom bills had been recorded and provided to banks, the banks receiving ransom bills passed by Hamm would notify the FBI, and the newspapers would likely report that ransom money had turned up. The kidnappers would then know the serial numbers had been recorded and that they had to be careful how they spent the money.[23]

After waiting a few days and not reading about any Hamm money turning up, the gang was itching to start spending, even though they still weren't sure it was safe. They decided to handle it like any other hot money: sell it to money dealers, hopefully for no more than the usual 5 percent fee. Karpis flew to Reno and sold it to dealers he knew there, cautiously confident that "Reno money was safer money, even if it was $5,000 less than Hamm money."[24]

After his release, Hamm professed willingness to cooperate with the police, but he claimed he had been blindfolded most of the time and didn't get a good look at any of his kidnappers. He showed little interest in pursuing his kidnappers. For years there had been rumors that the St. Paul police and the Ramsey County district attorney's office had close ties with the underworld. It was also more or less common knowledge that the city's breweries had underworld connections, particularly breweries like Hamm's that were managing to survive during Prohibition. Two months passed without a break in the case.

Then, in August, Dan "Tubbo" Gilbert, head investigator in the Cook County state's attorney's office, gave Melvin Purvis, special agent in charge of the FBI's Chicago office, a tip: Roger Touhy's Chicago gang of bootleggers had kidnapped both Hamm and John (Jake the Barber) Factor, brother of cosmetics mogul Max Factor.[25]

Touhy was known as "God's Bagman" for his financial support of his favorite parish priest.[26] Since Capone had gone to prison, Touhy and his gang had been locked in a fierce struggle with the Capone Outfit for organized crime supremacy in Chicago. Gilbert, who had ties to the Outfit, saw a golden opportunity to use the sometimes gullible Purvis and the FBI to frame Touhy and his gang for the Hamm and Factor kidnappings.

Though Hamm couldn't identify any of the four accused gang members and two of them had solid alibis, Purvis convinced Hoover to go for indictments on the basis of a shaky eyewitness identification and the presence of loaded revolvers, a rifle, and "bandages for kidnapping purposes" found in the gang's car when they were arrested. When the U.S. attorney in St. Paul charged Touhy's gang in August, the Barker-Karpis gang relaxed; they could hardly believe their good luck.

As the trial date approached the U.S. attorney and Justice Department lawyers grew increasingly reluctant to go to trial without stronger evidence. Hoover convened a summit meeting in Washington with the special agents who had put the case together. After the meeting, he urged the trial lawyers to proceed with the trial.

Just as the lawyers had warned, the evidence at trial was weak and unconvincing: no ransom money had been found; there were no fingerprints or other forensic evidence linking Hamm to any of the defendants, their automobiles or a hideout; and Hamm still couldn't identify any of the gangsters on trial. On November 28, two days after the San Jose lynchings, the jury acquitted all four members of the Touhy gang.

The foreman of the jury, sixty-nine-year-old T. O. Sundry, was a farmer and a veteran of twenty trials. "Knowing them to be gangsters, we would have preferred to find them guilty," he said after the trial, but Hamm testified that the kidnapper who accosted him was taller and had finer features than the defendants. "If that doesn't constitute reasonable doubt," said Sundry, "then I and the other jurors don't know what does."[27]

Joseph Keenan, one of the government lawyers who had been reluctant to go to trial in the first place, insisted after the verdict that the Justice Department was "entirely convinced" the defendants were guilty.[28] "If a jury of citizens decides to turn these men loose upon this community there is nothing we can do about it," he said.[29] St. Paul police chief Thomas Dahill said, "If that's the attitude of American jurors toward kidnapping, I applaud the action of San Jose, California citizens in taking justice into their own hands."[30]

The *Minneapolis Star* in a scathing editorial called the acquittal of the Touhy gang a good example of why the San Jose mob had lynched Holmes and Thurmond and Governor Rolph had sympathized with them: "These gentry have roamed the country with their private arsenals, their aliases, their big rolls of money and without visible source of honest income, yet they don't even condescend to take the witness stand in their own defense and the federal government's only charges against them are pronounced false by a jury."[31]

It was a setback for the War against Kidnappers and the credibility of the FBI, but an entirely avoidable one. In September the FBI crime laboratory had lifted three latent fingerprints from the Hamm ransom notes using the new (to the FBI) silver nitrate technique. They were not the fingerprints of any Touhy gang members, though. They were the fingerprints of Karpis, Doc Barker, and Charles Fitzgerald. The already weak case against the Touhy gang members was now untenable, but the FBI kept quiet and didn't provide the fingerprint evidence to the defense or, apparently, to the prosecution. To this day the FBI describes its identification of the Barker-Karpis gang's fingerprints on the Hamm ransom notes as a noteworthy accomplishment. The FBI website calls the latent fingerprints "hard evidence that the Karpis gang was behind the kidnapping," but fails to mention that the government still went forward and tried the members of the Touhy gang for Hamm's kidnapping two months later.[32]

Hoover was now in a bind. He knew that the Barker-Karpis gang was implicated in the Hamm kidnapping, but admitting the FBI had made a mistake in trying to pin it on the Touhy gang would undermine the G-men's nascent reputation for invincibility. So the FBI continued to maintain that it had solved the Hamm case and that God's Bagman and his men were guilty. They left the Barker-Karpis gang alone.

14

....

"Like a Damned Albatross around My Neck"

St. Paul and Chicago, January–May 1934

The Hamm kidnapping was the fifth in St. Paul in less than two years, more than enough to put wealthy families unaccustomed to violent crime on edge.[1] To calm nerves the St. Paul police formed a special kidnap squad under former police chief Thomas "Big Tom" Brown, recently demoted to chief of detectives. Brown met personally with prominent families to explain what to do in a kidnapping and to review their daily activities and suggest protective measures. What the families didn't realize, however, was that he was also identifying possible kidnap targets and passing their information along to finger men like Jack Peifer and Harry Sawyer, in return for a sizable cut of each ransom. One of the prominent St. Paulites Brown met with was Edward Bremer, the thirty-seven-year-old president of the Commercial State Bank.

Whenever Alvin Karpis and Fred Barker were in St. Paul, they spent a lot of time at the Green Lantern speakeasy operated by fixer Harry Sawyer. The entrance to the Green Lantern was through a cigar store on Wabasha Street leading to a back room lined with dark wooden booths. There customers relaxed, did business, and guzzled real beer brewed by the Schmidt Brewing Company. It was also where visiting criminals checked in to let the police know they were in town and to pay their bribes. Karpis liked to refer to it as his "personal headquarters in St. Paul."[2]

One day in the fall of 1933 Sawyer told Karpis he wanted Edward Bremer grabbed. All the kidnappers would have to do was hold Bremer for a couple of days and collect $200,000 (over $3.7 million in 2020). Sawyer promised it would be safe and easy: his police contacts would let him know what the police knew and what to watch out for. Except for doubling the amount of the ransom, Sawyer's spiel was pretty much the same one Peifer had given them before the Hamm snatch.

"Forget the cops," Karpis told Sawyer. "This will be strictly a government thing. We'll have the G to deal with."[3] Karpis understood immediately that snatching Bremer would be an entirely different matter than Hamm. A second kidnapping in the same city within six months would be tempting fate, but especially so given the Bremer family's powerful connections. Edward's father, Adolph, was president of the Schmidt Brewing Company. He also controlled the Commercial State Bank run by Edward. So many racketeers were rumored to have accounts there under assumed names that it was called the "Racketeer Bank of St. Paul."[4] Adolph's brother, Otto Bremer, was chairman of the American National Bank of St. Paul and one of the Midwest's most prominent bankers.[5] Both Adolph and Otto were leaders of St. Paul's Democratic Party; Adolph, a personal friend of President Roosevelt,[6] had reportedly contributed $350,000 (over $6.5 million in 2020) to his 1932 presidential campaign.[7] As far as the G-men went, Karpis knew they couldn't expect them to be as distracted and gullible as they had been during the Hamm investigation.

After weighing the pros and cons, Karpis and Fred decided "what the hell" and started planning the kidnapping of Bremer.[8] In addition to themselves and Hamm veterans Doc, Ziegler, and

Bolton, the team included bank robbers William "Lapland Willie" Weaver, Harry Campbell, and Volney "Curley" Davis, who had been serving a life sentence for the same murder that landed Doc in the Oklahoma State Penitentiary. He was the beneficiary of one of Governor "Alfalfa Bill" Murray's two-year "leave of absence" paroles, and hadn't returned to prison when his time was up.[9]

When Edward Bremer met with Big Tom Brown to discuss how to protect his family from kidnappers, he described the route he took each weekday morning to drive his nine-year-old daughter, Betty, to school and then continue to the bank. Brown recommended a bodyguard, but Edward thought that might frighten Betty. He finally accepted Brown's suggestion that a bodyguard meet him at his downtown parking garage and accompany him from there to his office and for the rest of his day. Not long after he hired the bodyguard, there were rumors that kidnappers would be coming for Edward next. Brown recommended that the St. Paul police take over his protection, and Edward let the bodyguard go.[10]

On the morning of January 17, 1934, Edward dropped Betty off at the Summit School on Goodrich Avenue and continued in his black Lincoln to the intersection of Goodrich and Lexington Parkway. When he stopped at the stop sign, a car with Fred and Harry Campbell rolled forward and blocked his path from the front, while a second car with Doc, Davis, and Karpis closed in from the back. Doc and Davis opened the front doors of the Lincoln and tried to force Edward into the back, but Edward resisted. Doc clubbed him over the head with the butt end of his automatic pistol multiple times before finally subduing him. The three cars then headed out of town to rendezvous with Ziegler.[11]

Ziegler's role, as the college-educated "brain," was to handle communications with Bremer's family. He had already prepared three typewritten ransom notes, which he put before Edward and forced him to sign by the side of the road. The kidnappers then blindfolded Edward and shoved him down onto the floor of their car. Ziegler returned to St. Paul with Fred to deliver the first ransom note and prepare for negotiations with Adolph. The rest of the gang set out with Edward for Bensenville, where they planned to hide out while awaiting delivery of the ransom. They abandoned the Lincoln with Edward's bloodstains on the upholstery by the side of the road.

Two hours after the kidnapping Ziegler telephoned the home of St. Paul building contractor Walter Magee. He told him that Edward had been kidnapped and that a note from the kidnappers was waiting for him at his office. Magee retrieved the note, one of those signed by Edward, and took it to Adolph. It demanded $200,000 in $5 and $10 bills (over $3.8 million in 2020)—"no new money—no consecutive numbers—large variety of issues"—and instructed Magee to place the message "We are ready Alice" in the *Minneapolis Tribune* when the money was ready.[12]

Magee was a natural choice for a go-between. A long-time friend of Adolph Bremer, he was described in an FBI memorandum as "a rather shady character" and "a species of panderer."[13] Before going into the contracting business, he had operated a saloon and hotel (a "joint") and worked as a chauffeur for Adolph.

Adolph contacted St. Paul police chief Thomas Dahill but didn't see any reason to involve the FBI. Dahill himself called the FBI into the investigation that morning. After receiving assurances that Edward's safety would be the FBI's priority until he was returned, Adolph reluctantly agreed to permit the FBI to station agents in his and Edward's homes around the clock to cover the telephones.[14]

Adolph also agreed to turn the ransom note over to the FBI for forensic examination. Two days later the FBI's document examination specialist, Charles Appel, reported that the writing style and format of the Bremer note were substantially similar to the three Hamm ransom notes previously examined by the FBI and that all the Hamm and Bremer notes had been typed on a Corona typewriter with pica type.[15] Further examination led Appel to conclude on January 23 that the same individual was the author of all four notes, and the same typewriter probably typed them all.[16]

The FBI laboratory was unable to lift any fingerprints from the Bremer note, but it had previously lifted the fingerprints of Karpis, Doc, and Fitzgerald from the Hamm notes. Putting it all together, the FBI now had strong evidence that the Barker-Karpis gang was responsible for both the Hamm and the Bremer kidnappings. It did not share that information with the St. Paul police.

The kidnapping of Edward Bremer outside the posh Summit School at drop-off time in the morning rocked the "decent citizens" of St. Paul. As the *New York Times* put it, "The thunderbolts of crime have hit their friends, their neighbors, and maybe them."[17]

It baffled Adolph. He couldn't understand why the kidnappers were demanding a ransom double that paid for Hamm and equal to the Urschel ransom, the highest on record. Nor could he understand why his ties to the St. Paul police and to the underworld had not protected his family. Adolph claimed credit for using his influence to place both Chief Dahill and Big Tom Brown in their positions. And while most St. Paul brewers had underworld connections, his were tighter and deeper than most. His brewery, Schmidt's, supplied *real* beer, not near-beer or the home-brewed stuff, to Harry Sawyer's Green Lantern during Prohibition. It was rumored that Schmidt's may even have owned the Green Lantern.[18] According to St. Paul historian Tim Mahoney, "The beer was secretly piped underground to a home near the brewery, barreled, and driven at night to the Green Lantern. Harry's deal with the Bremer family gave him distribution rights to other speakeasies."[19]

Whether Adolph knew it was Sawyer who had plotted Edward's kidnapping or that Big Tom Brown had supplied information and talked Edward into giving up his bodyguard is unclear, but the Bremer family's extensive police and underworld connections suggest that the reasons behind Edward's kidnapping were complicated. Karpis later claimed he never knew "what Sawyer's beef was, but he sure didn't like Bremer."[20]

Adolph tried to negotiate a reduced ransom. Edward even tried to gain his own release by offering to finger other potential targets—like the St. Paul man he knew who had put $250,000 in a safe deposit box for his wife to use if he was kidnapped.[21] Neither succeeded. When Ziegler threatened to raise the demand to $500,000 if the ransom wasn't paid immediately, Adolph finally gave up and borrowed the money. Otto followed the FBI's advice and arranged to have the serial numbers of the ransom bills recorded.

Walter Magee drove the money to the designated drop site near Zumbrota, Minnesota, sixty miles from St. Paul. He followed the kidnappers' instructions and left it in two packages by the side of the road. Adolph included a personal note in one of the packages: "I've done my part and kept my word 100 percent just as I said I would. This money is not marked and is the full amount asked for. And now boys, I am counting on your honor. Be sports and do the square thing by turning Edward loose at once."[22]

The "sports" drove Edward to Rochester, Minnesota, and released him on February 7. From there, he caught a train and a bus back to St. Paul.

Once Edward was back home, Harold Nathan informed Chief Dahill that the FBI was taking full charge of the case.[23] The location of the hideout was still unknown, and there was no other evidence yet that Edward had crossed a state line. Nothing required the St. Paul police to step aside, but Dahill, described in an FBI memorandum as "honest, dumb, and afraid of his own soul," was relieved to hand off the hot potato.[24] He had his own suspicions that Big Tom Brown was involved in both the Hamm and Bremer kidnappings.[25]

Hoover sent Inspector William Rorer, the G-man who had nabbed Machine Gun Kelly, to St. Paul to debrief Edward. Rorer found him to be nervous, tearful, and hostile, visibly traumatized by the kidnappers' threats to return for him or Betty if he talked to the G-men.[26] Rorer insisted that it was still his duty to answer questions, to which Edward responded, "To hell with duty."[27] Only after Rorer showed Edward the statement the FBI intended to give the press about his lack of cooperation did he begin to answer a few questions.

As Rorer took him through the FBI catalog of questions for kidnap victims, Edward gradually divulged small facts, details he considered unimportant, like the pattern of the wallpaper in the room where he was held. He mentioned in passing that about halfway back on the long drive from the hideout (he had no idea where it was located) to Rochester, where he was released, the kidnappers had stopped alongside a country road to refuel their cars from gasoline cans stashed there in advance; he assumed they left the empties there when they finished. (The gang had learned from robbing banks that the police liked to shoot holes in their gas tanks, so they made a habit of carrying corks to plug the leaks and stashing full gas cans along their escape routes.)[28] Before the FBI could begin looking for the discarded cans, two farmers reported finding four five-gallon cans and a funnel on the side of the road near Portage, Wisconsin. An alert sheriff notified the FBI, and the G-men rushed the cans and funnel to Washington. Fingerprint identification specialists lifted a latent fingerprint and identified it as the right index finger of Doc Barker.[29]

The FBI, meanwhile, had located three abandoned flashlights with red lenses near Zumbrota, fitting the description of the red signal lights used to guide Walter Magee to the drop spot. Soon thereafter, a salesclerk at the F&W Grand Silver Store in St. Paul identified a photograph of Karpis as the man who purchased the flashlights three days before the ransom was delivered.[30]

Hoover was now ready to go after the members of the Barker-Karpis gang. On February 21 the FBI issued orders to agents in the field to apprehend Karpis and Doc, who had been positively identified, and Fred, Volney Davis, and Harry Campbell on the mistaken assumption that "all five have always worked together."[31] He also authorized the use of "strong-arm methods" in dealing with reluctant witnesses, "in the event it appeared to be desirable."[32]

Two days after Edward's release, the FBI began distributing lists of the serial numbers of the Bremer ransom bills to all banks in the United States and selected foreign countries, along with the request that they notify the nearest FBI office immediately if they received any of the ransom bills.[33] Prompt distribution of the lists was a great improvement over prior efforts. The listing of serial numbers in numerical order was an even greater improvement, since bank employees, understandably, were far more likely to take time to check the bills if the serial numbers—all 28,400 of them in this case—were listed in numerical order. With the use of four borrowed keypunch machines, twelve keypunchers, each punching about two thousand serial numbers per shift, completed the job in just two and a half days.[34]

The FBI was now ready and eager for the Barker-Karpis gang to start spending the Bremer ransom money.

Even though Adolph's note to the kidnappers said the ransom money wasn't marked, the gang couldn't assume the serial numbers hadn't been recorded. Doc took the money to Reno to sell it to the same money dealers who had bought the Hamm money, but they wouldn't touch it—nor would anyone else. It was "too damned hot."[35] Karpis wasn't yet ready to panic. He assumed they would be able to spend the money sometime, though he worried that the FBI, so soon after the government lost the Hamm trial, would be determined to pin the Bremer case on somebody. As long as he had Bremer money in his possession. Karpis knew he could easily be that somebody.

"It was like a damned albatross around my neck," he realized.[36]

Karpis believed his and Fred's mugshots and fingerprints were on display in every police station and FBI office in the country, or soon would be. As the two of them lay low in Chicago, fuming about the stacks of ransom money they didn't dare spend, they considered having their appearances and fingerprints altered. Plastic surgery had become popular since World War I, and both the underworld and law enforcement were abuzz with reports that Theodore "Handsome Jack" Klutas, head of Chicago's "College Kidnappers" gang, had successfully obliterated his fingerprints by slashing the skin of the balls of his fingers.[37] Karpis asked around and learned that Dr. Joseph P. Moran was the man to see in Chicago.

A Tufts medical school graduate and World War I pilot, Moran had lost his medical license and ended up in prison for performing abortions. There he befriended inmates who would later help him get a new start in Chicago as a labor union doctor. In his off-hours, he patched up gangsters and dabbled in plastic surgery and fingerprint obliteration. In early March Karpis and Fred paid Moran $1,250 to give them new faces and remove their fingerprints. Despite heavy doses of morphine, the surgeries were excruciating; worse still, they were mostly ineffective.

On March 20 Shotgun George Ziegler was executed in a drive-by shooting outside a Cicero, Illinois, restaurant. Ziegler had a reputation for talking too much; some suspected the Barker-Karpis gang had murdered him to keep him from implicating them in the Hamm and Bremer kidnappings, but the police never solved the case. Whether or not the gang was responsible for the hit, Chicago was a dangerous place for them to be, with the G-men hunting them. In hopes of making it harder for the FBI to pick up their trail, they decided the remaining members of the kidnap team should split up and the ransom money should not be divided until it had been exchanged for clean money. Karpis and the Barkers took the money and headed for Toledo.

Desperate to exchange at least some of the ransom money, Karpis and Fred sent Doc back to Chicago to see Dr. Moran in April. Moran said he could unload $10,000 through some of his patients, and arranged for John J. "Boss" McLaughlin, an old-time Democratic ward heeler, to take it. McLaughlin passed most of it along to a bookie named William Vidler and a bartender named Philip Delaney with instructions to exchange it in small quantities at various Chicago banks; he gave about $85 of the ransom money to his seventeen-year-old son, Jack, to spend.

Eight days later the Uptown State Bank in Chicago contacted the FBI to report that a man had come to the bank that day and exchanged $900 in $5 bills and $100 in $10 and $20 bills for ten $100 bills. The cashier's suspicion was aroused because the same individual had made a similar exchange the week before. He checked the serial numbers of some of the smaller bills and found them on the Bremer list. He also took a good look at the man and later was able to give a detailed description to the FBI: "weight 190 pounds, 40 years of age, 5'10" in height, very fair complexion, wears dark tortoise shell glasses, medium shade brown felt hat with rim turned down all around, light tan camel's hair coat, neat appearing, apparently an American, stocky build."[38]

Three days later the City National Bank and Trust Company in Chicago reported to the FBI that a man subsequently identified as William Vidler had exchanged ten $10 bills of Bremer money for a $100 bill. The man had also mentioned that he was a bookie.[39] The G-men drove around from bookmaking establishment to bookmaking establishment until they found Vidler, who had $2,265 of Bremer ransom money in his possession at the time. He admitted knowingly exchanging Bremer money at several banks, identifying Boss McLaughlin as the source of the money and Philip Delaney as the man who drove him around to the banks.[40]

On May 4 a federal grand jury in St. Paul indicted fugitives Alvin Karpis and Doc Barker for the kidnapping of Edward Bremer. It also indicted the two McLaughlins, Vidler, and Delaney for conspiracy to violate the Lindbergh Law by exchanging ransom money for clean money.

There was no evidence the accused money exchangers knew about the kidnapping in advance or participated in any way in the alleged conspiracy until after Bremer was released. Their indictments, therefore, depended on the government's legal position that a criminal conspiracy continues until the attainment of its objectives. In the case of a kidnapping for ransom, the government contended that the conspiracy to kidnap would continue until the last ransom bill had been converted into spending money. What that meant in practical terms was that money exchangers could be convicted of conspiracy to kidnap under the Lindbergh Law even though they had no knowledge of the kidnapping before it occurred and didn't become involved in exchange activity until long after the kidnap victim had been released, as in the Bremer case.

If the government's position held up in court, it could be the end of the efficient conversion of hot ransom money into cool spending money.

15

Fifty-Three Crates of Furniture

Manitowish Waters, Chicago, and Alcatraz Island, March–August 1934

Crime sells newspapers and always has. No crime story ever sold better than the Lindbergh kidnapping, but as the search for the kidnappers dragged on, the news buzz began to wear off. Reporters hunted for fresh, new stories with bold enough crimes or glamorous enough criminals to pull readers in. Most of the criminals who became celebrities in the early 1930s were bank robbers, who became popular in large measure because the banks themselves were so unpopular.

Three years into the Great Depression, mortgage defaults and foreclosures were at all-time highs. One-third of American farmers lost their farms through foreclosure between 1929 and 1933; over 40 percent of home mortgages in urban areas were in default by the beginning of 1934.[1] Many Americans had come to view banks as instruments by which the rich robbed the poor. Alvin Karpis observed it firsthand when he and the Barkers robbed the bank in Wahpeton, North Dakota, in October 1932. To prevent their getaway, the police shot up their back tires. The gang took two young women from the bank as shields and drove the car on its

rims for a mile until they spotted an old Essex parked in a farm-
yard. The wary farmer, Ed Lindberg, came out of his house. Karpis told him they had robbed the bank in town and needed his
Essex to make their getaway.

"You robbed the bank, did you?" said Lindberg. "Well, I don't
care. All the banks ever do is foreclose on us farmers."[2]

Some bank robbers ingratiated themselves with the public by
making a point of destroying mortgage records or handing out dol-
lar bills to customers during robberies. Pseudo–Robin Hoods like
Pretty Boy Floyd ("Robin Hood of the Cooksons")[3] and handsome,
courteous John Dillinger were favorites of reporters who chron-
icled their crime sprees like multipart adventure series. Youthful
Clyde Champion Barrow and Bonnie Parker turned themselves
into fan favorites by projecting the image of romantic, carefree
thrill-seekers, with their stylish clothes, fast cars, and fancy guns.

Most of all, bank robbers provided entertainment, which was a
much-valued commodity in the drab, fun-less years of the Great
Depression. Moviegoers cheered when newsreels featured Dillinger's exploits, infuriating President Roosevelt and Attorney
General Cummings.

In January 1934 Cummings kept the promise he had made at the
start of the War against Kidnappers to propose an entire package
of new federal laws to strengthen the government's hand against
kidnappers, racketeers, and other predatory criminals. To toughen
the Lindbergh Law, he proposed the death penalty for kidnappers who didn't return their victims unharmed. He also proposed
expanding the crime of sending a ransom demand by mail to
include delivery by any means. He asked Congress to amend the
law to create a presumption that victims had been transported
across state lines if they weren't returned within seven days. The
creation of that presumption effectively eliminated the interstate
transportation requirement for establishing federal jurisdiction.
None of those proposals were controversial.

The attorney general's other anticrime proposals were a different story. Some—robbing a federal bank, escaping from a federal prison, and assaulting a federal officer—made federal crimes of three more forms of crime against federal interests that were of current concern. Other proposals followed the Lindbergh Law's example by taking an existing state crime and turning it into a federal crime by adding the requirement of interstate transportation: for example, crossing a state line to avoid arrest and transporting stolen property worth more than $5,000 across a state line. Federalizing those garden-variety state crimes was consistent with the attorney general's frequent, though questionable, assertion that such crimes were now being "organized on a nationwide basis."[4]

There was widespread recognition in Congress, as in the country, that violent crime was a problem, but there was little consensus that the attorney general's proposals were the right solution. The principal objection was that most violent crimes are local, not interstate or national, in character. State and local law enforcement agencies, with their greater knowledge of local people and conditions, are better able to investigate and punish such crimes, went the argument. State and local law enforcement agencies should be improved, not supplanted by a giant federal bureaucracy. On this argument, states' rights advocates, who nearly always objected to taking powers away from the states and handing them over to the federal government, found common ground with other opponents. When the attorney general's proposals reached the House Judiciary Committee, its chairman, Texas congressman Hatton Sumners, a staunch defender of states' rights, did nothing to move them forward.[5]

John Dillinger (his family pronounced it with a hard *g*) served more than nine years in the Indiana prison system for robbing a grocery store owner of $50. His close friends behind bars were mostly bank robbers. They taught him what they knew and made plans to rob banks with him when they got out.

Dillinger was paroled on May 10, 1933, at the age of twenty-nine. Five weeks later, he robbed his first bank, the New Carlisle National Bank of New Carlisle, Ohio. He and his two partners entered the bank through a window the night before and waited inside until the employees arrived the next morning. Wearing handkerchiefs over their faces and flashing handguns, they ordered the employees to open the vault and empty out all the bills—over $10,000. Then they tied the employees up, forced them down onto the floor, and scooted out the back to their car. As they got away, they scattered roofing nails along the road, blowing out the tires of several excited motorists following the action.[6]

In the next twelve months Dillinger and members of the eleven-man group that came to be known as the "Dillinger gang" robbed at least thirteen banks;[7] other gang members probably robbed at least another eleven banks that year. They also broke into two Indiana police stations and stole machine guns, rifles, handguns, ammunition, and bulletproof vests. Police and sheriff's departments all over the Midwest were after them, but until Dillinger escaped from the jail in Crown Point, Indiana (using a fake wooden gun and stolen machine guns), and drove a stolen car (the sheriff's) across the state line into Illinois on March 3, 1934, he wasn't wanted for any federal crime, and the FBI wasn't looking for him. The cocky bandit's escapes and taunts had embarrassed so many police chiefs and sheriffs that Hoover was content to watch from the sidelines and pass along occasional bits of Dillinger information to friendly police departments. After Crown Point, armed with a warrant for Dillinger's arrest for violation of the Dyer Act, the FBI officially joined the hunt.

Among the many reports of possible Dillinger sightings was an ambiguous tip from Daisy Coffey, the owner of the Lincoln Court Apartments in St. Paul. She told the St. Paul police that the couple in Apartment 303 (the "Hellmans") was behaving strangely: they rarely left their apartment, and when they did, they always used the building's back entrance; they kept their window shades lowered; and they wouldn't let the handyman in to make repairs.[8] When FBI agents and a St. Paul detective went to investigate on March 31, they found Dillinger and his girlfriend Evelyn Frechette in the apartment, where Dillinger was recuperating from a bullet wound to the shoulder sustained during the recent robbery of the First National Bank of Mason City, Iowa. Both sides began shooting in the hallway. A bullet caught Dillinger in the leg, possibly his own shot ricocheting off a wall. Dillinger, Frechette, and gang member Homer Van Meter still managed to reach their car, which was parked in the garage in the alley behind the apartment, and get away. The FBI and police had neglected to watch the alley and the rear entrance to the apartment house, the one Daisy Coffey said the Hellmans always used.

Cornering Dillinger and then letting him slip away during a shootout was exactly the sort of humiliation Hoover had tried to avoid in keeping the FBI out of the Dillinger hunt until then. Now that it happened, he considered it so damaging to the G-men's reputation that he declared Dillinger the FBI's highest priority and appointed a special Dillinger squad to hunt him down under Special Agent in Charge Melvin Purvis of the Chicago office.

Hoover sent a handwritten note to Purvis: "Get Dillinger for me, and the world is yours."[9]

After the shootout at the Lincoln Court Apartments, Dillinger and Frechette headed for his father's farm in Mooresville, Indiana, six hundred miles away, to recuperate. The FBI and police had had the farm under surveillance off and on, but apparently not while Dillinger and Frechette were visiting. And not when family members gathered for a Sunday afternoon reunion with their adored Johnnie.[10] "I made him coconut cream pie, fried chicken, everything that goes with it," recalled his sister, Audrey Hancock, who had been Dillinger's primary caregiver after his mother died when he was three. "All our family was there. There must have been a dozen of us."[11]

Two weeks later the G-men caught up with Dillinger again, this time at the Little Bohemia Lodge on Little Star Lake near Manitowish Waters, Wisconsin. Gang members were spending the weekend there with their girlfriends, trying to regroup and figure out how they were going to stay ahead of the growing number of law enforcement agencies after them.

A friend of the Little Bohemia's owner tipped off the FBI that Dillinger and his men were there. The FBI chartered three planes to fly seventeen special agents from Chicago and St. Paul to the nearest airfield in Rhinelander, Wisconsin, fifty miles from Manitowish Waters. Once on the ground they learned that Dillinger and his gang were planning to have an early dinner and then leave. After commandeering five private automobiles to transport them, the agents piled into the cars and set out for the lodge over roads covered with melting snow, ice, mud, and potholes. Two of the cars broke down, and eight G-men had to ride on the running boards of the three functional cars, hanging on to the car with one hand and their weapons with the other.[12]

It was already dark when they arrived at the Little Bohemia. They hid in the woods around the lodge waiting for the gangsters to come out. Before long three men walked out the front, got into an automobile, and started driving away with their radio blaring. The agents ordered them to halt, but they apparently didn't hear the order. Mistaking the young men out for a beer for Dillinger gang members, the G-men opened fire, killing one and wounding another. Meanwhile the gangsters, alerted by barking dogs and gunfire, jumped out of the second-story windows and escaped into the woods through the unguarded rear of the lodge.

Later that night Special Agents Carter Baum and Jay Newman and local constable Carl Christensen set out from the lodge to let the sheriff know that the Dillinger gang was in the area. They came upon Baby Face Nelson making his getaway. Nelson opened fire, killing Baum and wounding Newman and Christensen. When the sun came up the next morning Purvis entered the lodge and confirmed that Dillinger and all the members of his gang had escaped without injury, leaving behind three women.

Little Bohemia was the most mortifying episode in the FBI's pursuit of Dillinger—some said in the history of the FBI to date. Local citizens circulated a petition calling for Purvis's suspension pending a full investigation of the "irresponsible conduct" of the FBI in raiding the Little Bohemia "in such a stupid manner as to bring about the deaths of two men and injury to four others, none of whom were gangsters."[13] Will Rogers ridiculed the G-men: "They had Dillinger surrounded and was all ready to shoot him when he come out, but another bunch of folks came out ahead, so they just shot them instead."[14]

The day after the debacle President Roosevelt sat down at the White House with Congressman Sumners and made his case that the country urgently needed Congress to pass his anticrime proposals to deal with Dillinger and his ilk. Sumners called his committee into session the next morning, and they reported out the first six bills favorably.[15]

Congress ultimately passed seventeen anticrime bills, which the president signed into law in May and June. In addition to the Lindbergh Law amendments and the bills creating new federal crimes for bank robbery, transportation of stolen property, prison escape, flight to avoid prosecution, and assault on federal officers, the attorney general was authorized to offer rewards of up to $25,000 for the capture of dangerous criminals, and FBI agents were authorized for the first time to make arrests and carry weapons. No longer would the G-men have to swallow their pride and ask the local police or federal marshals to step in and make arrests for them or comply with varying state and local weapons laws concerning permits, concealed carry, and the like.[16]

At the signing of the first six bills the president issued a statement calling on the American people to cooperate in cracking down on the underworld. Without referring to any of the celebrity criminals by name, it was clear he had them and their cheering fans in mind when he said that law enforcement would never be effective as long as a substantial part of the public "looks with tolerance upon known criminals . . . or applauds efforts to romanticize crime."[17]

Hoover had permitted special agents to carry weapons for "defensive use" since at least 1929. Following the Kansas City Massacre, he had issued .38 Special Police Positive Revolvers and holsters to all special agents.[18] The shootout had made it impossible to ignore any longer the substantial disparity between the weapons available to criminals and those available to FBI agents. The special agent in charge of the Kansas City office, Ralph Colvin, discreetly but forcefully complained to Hoover that the "small light pistols" the FBI had previously furnished were "entirely inadequate." He pressed specifically for a Thompson submachine gun, a couple of high-powered rifles and sawed-off shotguns, four .45 caliber Colt automatic pistols, and adequate ammunition. "I hate to send agents out after these outlaws unless we can meet them on equal footing," he told Hoover. "As we are now situated, we have to scramble round and borrow guns if called for a tough job."[19]

With passage of the new legislation, the FBI procured and distributed to its field offices submachine guns and Colt Monitor automatic rifles designed to penetrate armored vehicles. Congress also funded the purchase of two hundred fast cars and 110 two-way automobile radios.[20] The transformation of the FBI from an investigatory agency to a law enforcement agency, which had begun with passage of the Lindbergh Law, was now essentially complete. A new, militant phase in the war on crime commenced.

On the eve of the president's signing of the first of the new laws, Joseph Keenan promised that the federal government now would "go after every man and woman in this country guilty of crime of violence—highway robbery, bank robbery, kidnapping and homicide." The only effective instrument for capturing criminals "as they race from State to State, escaping detection by local authorities, would be a mobile detective force which would establish the identity of the criminal and follow him night and day. That is the work we are undertaking tomorrow," he said.[21]

On June 23 Attorney General Cummings offered a $10,000 reward for the capture of Dillinger and $5,000 for the capture of Nelson (born Lester Gillis).[22] He reportedly commented to FBI agents at the time that the government's policy was "shoot to kill—then count to ten."[23] It wasn't the first time a Justice Department official had implied they didn't intend for the FBI to take Dillinger alive. Three months before, Keenan had said of Dillinger, "I don't know where or when we will get him, but we will get him. I hope we get him under such circumstances that the government won't have to stand the expense of a trial."[24]

On the night of July 22 Melvin Purvis led a team of twenty special agents and five East Chicago, Indiana, policemen to the Biograph Theater near Chicago's Lincoln Park.[25] Brothel madam Ana Sage, a friend of Dillinger's girlfriend Polly Hamilton, had offered to tell Purvis and an East Chicago detective she knew where Dillinger would be that night in return for the attorney general's reward money and relief from the outstanding order for her deportation to Romania. Upon Purvis's assurance that she would be taken care of if her information was good, Sage disclosed that she and Hamilton would accompany Dillinger that evening to the Biograph Theater for the 9:00 showing of MGM's hit movie *Manhattan Melodrama*.

The movie was over a little before 11:00. Dillinger, wearing a straw hat and glasses, walked out with the two women past Purvis, who was standing in front of the theater. When he spotted Dillinger, Purvis struck a match and lit his cigar to give the prearranged signal to his men. Three special agents then closed in on Dillinger. Hamilton sensed danger and grabbed his shirt. He reached into his pocket for his Colt automatic pistol but never got off a shot. Special Agent Charles Winstead, the former Texas Ranger considered the FBI's finest shooter, immediately fired, followed quickly by five more shots from him and the other two agents, also sharpshooters.

A total of five bullets hit Dillinger. The fifth, fired by Winstead, entered through the back of his neck and traveled through one vertebra, his spinal cord, and his brain before exiting below his right eye.[26] He was dead before hitting the ground.[27] Two female bystanders received non-life-threatening bullet wounds.[28] Eyewitnesses reported thinking Dillinger was the victim of a sidewalk holdup and that the agents made no attempt to take him alive.

Hoover was satisfied that the FBI had redeemed itself: "He was just a yellow rat that the country may consider itself fortunate to be rid of," he said. "There are other rats still to be gotten, however, and we are not taking any time off to celebrate about Dillinger."[29]

Early on the morning of August 19, five prison guards roused Al Capone from his bed at the Atlanta Federal Penitentiary. "Let's go, Al. Leave all your personal things in there," said one. "You're going to the Rock, Al, a nice long ride to Alcatraz," said another. Just like that, Capone learned he was headed for the government's new supermax prison on Alcatraz Island in San Francisco Bay.

"You dirty S.O.B.! You'll never take me out of here!" snarled Capone as they dragged him away. "Where in hell are those $200-an-hour lawyers, and the big politicians, and lobbyists with all the pull?"[30]

In leg irons and handcuffs, Capone joined fifty-two other prisoners in shackles loaded into two specially constructed coaches on a special train switched into the prison yard to load its passengers. The "Forty Thieves Special," as one paper referred to it,[31] was bound for New Orleans and on to Houston, El Paso, Yuma, Los Angeles, and, finally—after three and a half miserable, stifling days—Tiburon, California. Despite extraordinary security measures and an embargo on information about the train's passengers and destination, word got out. Excited spectators lined station platforms along the way, eager to catch a glimpse of Scarface Al, though the train's windows were barred and it didn't stop at passenger stations.[32]

At Tiburon the locomotive was detached and the coaches were loaded onto a barge and towed across San Francisco Bay to Alcatraz Island.[33] Guards removed the prisoners' leg irons and handcuffed them in pairs to trudge up the steep path from the dock to the cell house, the equivalent of a twelve-story climb.[34] Later that afternoon when the prisoners were all accounted for, bathed, dressed, and locked in their individual cells, Warden James Johnston wired the director of the Bureau of Prisons: "Fifty three crates furniture from Atlanta received in good condition, installed—no breakage."[35]

The Roosevelt administration viewed the establishment of the government's first supermax prison vital to the War against Kidnappers and its drive to defeat organized crime. They had two specific goals in mind. First, Cummings and Hoover wanted to make sure that the kidnappers and gangsters the federal government was putting behind bars would not escape from federal custody. Second, they knew that a disproportionate number of violent crimes generally were committed by convicted felons who had escaped from prison or been released early on parole or pardon by corrupt officials, and they wanted a place of confinement for the "worst of the worst" federal prisoners that was as near to escape-proof as possible.

Machine Gun Kelly and other celebrity criminals had boasted that no prison could hold them. When Harvey Bailey and Albert Bates became the first big-name criminals convicted under the Lindbergh Law, Cummings had been so concerned they would escape that he wrote to the warden at Leavenworth, where they were confined before Alcatraz opened, to say he was holding him personally responsible for seeing that they didn't escape: "It would be a shock to the country should either of these men escape. I shall expect, therefore, that you give personal attention to these men. I am informed that you have ample means to keep them in confinement. I shall hold you personally responsible for their safe-keeping."[36]

Though he also considered a remote site in Alaska for the prison, Cummings ultimately chose to take over an existing facility the army was abandoning on Alcatraz Island. The rocky, twelve-acre island had been used for a fort since 1858 and as a military prison since the Civil War. With a surprisingly modest amount of retrofitting—toughening of doors and windows, construction of new towers and galleries for armed guards, new locks, and barbed wire fences around the shoreline—the massive concrete cell house, built in 1912 to accommodate over six hundred military prisoners, was converted into a prison of 270 individual cells.

There were no bridges between the island and the mainland, and no airstrip; the only way to get there or get away was by boat or to swim the 1.25 miles in frigid waters with strong currents that swarmed around the island in five different directions. The swim was daunting but not impossible, as two teenage girls protesting the prison's proximity to San Francisco demonstrated when they swam from the shore to the island in under an hour; a third swam to the island, around it, and back again in just two hours.[37] Cummings was unfazed. "The fact that some young lady out there swam clear around the island and back again is, of course, a matter of no consequence one way or the other," he said.[38]

Nor was the prison facility itself impossible to get out of. A number of inmates would succeed in future years in getting out of the cell house before they were caught, killed or drowned. Officially it is the Bureau of Prisons' position that "no one ever succeeded in escaping from Alcatraz, although to this day there are five prisoners listed as 'missing, presumed drowned.'"[39]

Cummings and Hoover also believed that making Alcatraz as undesirable as possible for the inmates would have deterrent effect.

Its West Coast location was undesirable for most inmates because it made family visits very difficult, but the harsh, dehumanizing rules and policies were even more objectionable. According to the Bureau of Prisons, an Alcatraz inmate had four rights: "food, clothing, shelter, and medical care. Everything else was a privilege that had to be earned."[40] Even when small privileges could be earned, like writing to family or access to the prison library, the overall prison environment and system of control were designed to destroy the "big shot" image of kidnappers and gangsters, to eliminate the special privileges that powerful inmates enjoyed at other prisons, and to cut off all contact between inmates and their former criminal associates.[41] To these ends prison officials called Alcatraz inmates by their prison numbers, not their names. There were no newspapers, radios, or movies; no canteen for purchases of cigarettes, toiletries, or food. Inmates were forbidden to speak with each other except at mealtime, during supervised recreation time once a week, and when necessary for performing their prison jobs. No one could visit unless approved in advance by the warden and then only once a month for an hour.

The first prisoners transferred to Alcatraz included the "worst of the worst" in federal custody at the time: convicted kidnappers Machine Gun Kelly, Harvey Bailey, Albert Bates, and Gordon Alcorn, as well as members of seven criminal gangs, eleven escape artists, eight "writ writers" who drafted legal papers for other inmates, and other "troublemakers." More than a third of the original inmates fit none of the categories of prisoners too dangerous for the other federal prisons; they were sent there because they were needed to staff the prison laundry and kitchen and to cook and clean for the warden.[42] Still, there were only 210 prisoners in 1934, far fewer than the 270 available cells.[43]

Penologists and prison reformers criticized Alcatraz's focus on punitive isolation and deprivation from the very beginning. To them it was an anachronism before it opened, a throwback that disregarded current thinking about the proper role of rehabilitation in incarceration. Sanford Bates, the first director of the U.S. Bureau of Prisons, tried to dissuade Cummings from rejecting rehabilitation as an aim of Alcatraz before it opened, not only because of the effect it would have on Alcatraz inmates, but also on the entire federal prison system. As he pointed out in a letter to Cummings, the federal prison system was "built upon the hope that every man has the germ of reform somewhere in him." He had misgivings, he said, about establishing a prison like Alcatraz, "which is becoming notorious," to handle the very few prisoners of the "Machine Gun Kelly type" when the vast majority of federal prisoners were "more of the reformable type." "I cannot help recording my belief," he wrote, "that this small number of men [like Kelly] should not be brought into such prominence in the public imagination that the fear of them should blind people to the importance of the Federal prison work as an opportunity for rehabilitation."[44]

The criticisms of Alcatraz didn't bother Cummings or Hoover in the least. They saw no point in trying to rehabilitate the "worst of the worst." Many inmates (although by no means all) were not expected to be released for years, if ever. Moreover Alcatraz was never intended to be a model for humane or progressive penal institutions. It was, as Cummings often said, a symbol of the government's determination to reestablish law and order in American society.

Alcatraz soon earned its intended reputation as the least desirable place to serve time in the federal prison system. Cummings had been right about the deterrent effect of its dreadful conditions.[45] The knowledge that a Lindbergh Law conviction now meant either execution or a one-way ticket to the nation's most miserable federal prison would prove a powerful disincentive to professional criminals.

Five

Turning the Tide

16

....

"Johnny, We've Got to Solve That Lindbergh Case"

Washington and New York, October 1932–August 1934

Every ransom bill that passes through the hands of a kidnapper has the potential to reveal information that can help identify
him: fingerprints, other residues on the surface, the kidnapper's
spending patterns or habits, eyewitnesses to the passage—the
possibilities are limitless. With a total of 4,750 Lindbergh ransom bills—$50,000 worth—investigators were looking at 4,750
potential sources of useful information.

The first Lindbergh ransom bill turned up two days after Dr.
Condon delivered it to Cemetery John at St. Raymond's Cemetery in the Bronx. It was a $20 bill discovered at the East River
Savings Bank on New York's Upper West Side. Ten days later a $5
ransom bill was found at the Bank of Manhattan on Wall Street
in the consolidated deposit of five Schrafft's restaurants. On May
19 a $5 ransom bill was discovered at a Chase National Bank in
Midtown in a deposit made by Bickford's all-night cafeteria on
West 42nd Street. The night cashier at Bickford's remembered
receiving it from a customer who purchased a food item for fifteen cents between 3:00 a.m. and 6:00 a.m. Another $5 ransom

bill found the same day at the Central Hanover Bank & Trust Co. at Madison Avenue and 42nd Street was traced to a Sinclair Oil station in Brooklyn.[1]

By October 1932 a total of thirteen ransom bills had turned up in New York banks, usually days or sometimes weeks after they had been passed at cafeterias, a gas station, a candy store, and the Consolidated Gas Company office near Grand Central. Acting Lieutenant James J. Finn, a detective with the NYPD, personally investigated each one.

Fifty-year-old Jimmy Finn was short, slight, and wiry, every inch the scrappy Irish Catholic cop from Queens with sandy hair, icy blue eyes, and a taste for three-piece suits and high-domed bowler hats. Most of his NYPD colleagues found the intense but friendly Finn easy to work with, but his assignment to the Lindbergh investigation put him in almost daily contact with NJSP detectives who didn't care for him at all. To them, he was more a competitor than a colleague.

Finn had been one of the NYPD officers chosen to guard Charles Lindbergh when he visited New York after returning from Paris in 1927. They remained in touch after that, and Finn contacted Lindbergh after the kidnapping to offer his help. Lindbergh asked him to come to Hopewell and accepted him right away into the inner circle, to Schwarzkopf's displeasure. At Lindbergh's request, Police Commissioner Edward Mulrooney assigned Finn to the investigation full-time. When the ransom money was delivered in the Bronx, the NYPD opened its own criminal investigation, with Finn in day-to-day charge.

It is unlikely Jimmy Finn—or anyone else in the NYPD, NJSP, or FBI—had any actual experience tracking ransom money; it was something that law enforcement agencies hadn't done in any systematic way before the Lindbergh kidnapping. Banks and private detectives occasionally recorded the serial numbers of ransom bills or marked ransom money as a way to identify it when found in the possession of a suspect, but recording serial numbers for the purpose of tracing ransom bills back to an unknown kidnapper was a new and innovative method of investigating kidnappings.

Jimmy Finn and Frank Wilson of the Internal Revenue Bureau's Special Intelligence Unit (SIU) developed a simple, logical procedure for tracking the Lindbergh ransom money that turned up. A record was kept of the denomination and type (federal note or gold certificate) of each ransom bill and the location where it first appeared. Detectives tried to identify and find every person or establishment that touched that bill; Finn interviewed each one himself. Occasionally, a witness recalled something about the person who passed the bill: a facial characteristic, an item of clothing, a mannerism, an unusual odor. Several people, for instance, recalled that the man passing a Lindbergh ransom bill had purchased something costing only a few cents, like a head of cabbage, and then left with the rest in change. Some remembered that the bills had been folded neatly into eight sections.

During his interviews of bank employees Finn also learned that the lists of Lindbergh serial numbers distributed to banks by the Treasury Department were printed on large sheets of paper and folded several times, but only one list had been provided to each bank. Tellers often couldn't, or didn't, take the time to scan the list while the customer waited; by the time they got around to checking the list and realized they had received a ransom bill, the customer was long gone, and the teller had little, if any, recollection of which customer it was, what he or she looked like, or how they behaved.[2]

Finn covered the walls in his office with large maps of New York City's five boroughs. Each time a ransom bill was discovered, he stuck a straight pin with a colored head into the map to mark the location where it had been passed—green for $20 bills, red for $10 bills, and black for $5 bills—like using colored pins to mark troop locations during wartime. It was a tedious process, but gradually pins with colored heads began to cluster around particular neighborhoods.

According to journalist Sidney Whipple, who covered the Lindbergh case from beginning to end, Jimmy Finn had one obsession throughout the investigation: he believed the kidnapper would be caught by passing ransom money, specifically by using it to buy gasoline. He asked the owners of gas stations in all forty-eight states to do the impossible and record the serial numbers of every $5, $10, and $20 bill they received and the license number of every car into which the gasoline purchased by those bills was pumped. "The early results were slow and disappointing," noted Whipple.[3]

On October 4, 1932, David Bari deposited $5 in cash into his thrift account with Perrin Durbrow Life Associates in New York. Two days later Perrin Durbrow made a deposit containing Bari's $5 bill into its account at the Chase National Bank on Maiden Lane near the New York Stock Exchange.[4] Bank employees examining the deposit money spotted the serial number of the $5 bill on the Lindbergh ransom list and contacted the FBI's New York office. It was the first time the discovery of a Lindbergh bill was reported directly to the FBI. Although it had withdrawn from the NJSP investigation the previous June, the FBI was still pursuing its own leads and following up information the public provided. The Lindbergh squad decided to investigate Bari without informing Finn or the NJSP that the ransom bill had turned up.

There were several things about twenty-eight-year-old David Bari that interested the FBI. He lived in the Bronx, where the ransom was paid. He was a carpenter, and the investigators believed the kidnappers' handmade ladder had been built by a carpenter. He was from Austria, and handwriting experts believed the writer of the ransom notes had been educated in Germany or a country adjacent to Germany, such as Austria.

On the morning of October 11 FBI agents searched Bari's home and took him to the FBI's office on Lexington Avenue for questioning. He explained that he had received the $5 bill as part of his wages from his employer, Joseph Koretsky, which proved to be true. Koretsky said he had obtained it as part of a $45 withdrawal from the Public National Bank & Trust Company, which was also true. The FBI obtained writing samples from Bari by dictating language from some of the ransom notes to him. They submitted those samples to handwriting experts Albert S. Osborn and his son Albert D. Osborn. The Osborns said Bari's handwriting was the closest to the handwriting of the Lindbergh ransom notes of all the samples they had compared, but they needed more samples from Bari to give a definite opinion.

The FBI didn't want to release Bari before receiving the Osborns' final opinion; neither did they want to take the chance that NYPD or NJSP detectives might see Bari in the FBI's office and learn why he was being questioned. So while the Osborns examined the additional writing samples, the Lindbergh squad took Bari out to dinner and stayed overnight with him in a hotel.[5] Hoover gave orders that the NJSP and NYPD were not to be told about Bari and that he was to be informed immediately if the Osborns said Bari had written the ransom notes so he could get to New York to make the public announcement.[6]

Meanwhile Jimmy Finn appeared at the FBI's office late in the afternoon of October 11 as the agents were questioning Bari. He went there because Bari's family had gone to the NYPD to find out what had happened to him after he was taken from their home that morning for questioning about the Lindbergh ransom money. Finn was surprised that the FBI, which wasn't supposed to be investigating the case anymore, was questioning a possible suspect about ransom money without his knowledge, but he chose to treat the situation as a teachable moment. He explained to Special Agent T. D. Quinn that he and Wilson were tracking every ransom bill that turned up—twenty-six so far—and that the person passing them appeared to be doing so on a regular basis around the second and sixteenth of each month. Any publicity now about the lookout for ransom bills or about the questioning of Bari could discourage the kidnappers from passing more bills in the near future. Quinn understood Finn's point; he promised there would be no publicity about Bari from the FBI.

Finn also mentioned that he was surprised Chase had contacted the FBI because he had asked all New York banks to report ransom bills to the NYPD. He didn't dwell on the point, other than to remark, "This case is big enough for all of us." He asked Quinn to provide him the serial numbers of all ransom bills passed by Bari, as well as any others called to the FBI's attention, so his tracking data would be complete. He promised in turn to provide all his data to the FBI.[7]

The following day the Osborns reported that there were enough dissimilarities between Bari's handwriting and the handwriting of the ransom notes that they couldn't say Bari had written the notes. The FBI released Bari. Jimmy Finn and his work tracking the ransom money had made quite an impression on the Lindbergh squad, however.[8]

On May 2, 1933, the Money Department of the New York City branch of the Federal Reserve Bank discovered 296 $10 gold certificates and one $20 gold certificate in the previous day's deposits—all Lindbergh ransom money. They had been received at the bank in a single exchange transaction of $2,980. The deposit ticket for that transaction contained the customer's name (J. J. Faulkner) and address (537 West 149th Street, New York) in the customer's handwriting. When questioned, the teller who handled the transaction, James Estey, said he remembered receiving the "goldies," strapping them, and forwarding them to the Money Department, but he couldn't recall anything else about the exchange, not even the gender of the customer.

NYPD and NJSP detectives, along with Frank Wilson, immediately began trying to find "J. J. Faulkner." No one named Faulkner resided at 537 West 149th Street, which was the address of the

Plymouth Apartment House in the Hamilton Heights neighbor-hood of Harlem. They tried to identify and locate every tenant and employee of the Plymouth Apartments since it opened in 1910, and they investigated every person named Faulkner in the New York area. They obtained dozens of handwriting samples from people with any connection, however slight, to the name or to the address, which they submitted to handwriting experts for comparison with the ransom notes. Despite several tantalizing coincidences, they never found "J. J. Faulkner" or any evidence sufficient to warrant criminal charges against any individual.

A bulk exchange of ransom gold certificates on or shortly before May 1, 1933, such as the Faulkner transaction, was not unexpected. May 1 was the deadline President Roosevelt had set for turning in all gold bullion, gold coins, and gold certificates to Federal Reserve Banks in exchange for other currency in accordance with his executive order forbidding the private hoarding of gold and gold certificates.[9] Wilson and Finn had foreseen that the kidnap-pers might attempt a last-minute exchange of a large amount of ransom money and planned to have NYPD detectives stationed at the Federal Reserve Bank of New York that day. For reasons never made clear, the NYPD failed to appear.

After discovery of the J. J. Faulkner transaction, investigation revealed that it wasn't the only bulk exchange of Lindbergh ransom bills on the eve of the May 1 deadline. Twenty-four $10 gold cer-tificates bearing Lindbergh serial numbers had been surrendered at the Chemical National Bank at Cortland Street and Broadway on or about April 27, 1933, and another twenty-six $10 gold cer-tificates at the same bank between April 27 and 29. Fifty $10 gold certificates were surrendered at the Manufacturers Trust Co. on Broadway between April 27 and 29.[10] Efforts to obtain informa-tion about the customers in each case and to match deposit slips with these exchanges were expedited, but failed to produce use-ful information.

The surrender of 297 ransom bills at one time suggested two possibilities: either "J. J. Faulkner" was one of the kidnappers (or a surrogate) or the kidnappers had transferred a sizable portion of the ransom money to others. In either event it was the best clue yet in the Lindbergh investigation. In all probability, one of the kidnappers or a coconspirator had made the J. J. Faulkner exchange. With any luck, that person could have been apprehended at the Federal Reserve Bank on May 1. The blunder was devastating.

Hoover decided to take full advantage. The FBI sent a circular to New York banks asking them to notify the FBI's New York office if they received any Lindbergh ransom bills.[11] Their mistake also made the NYPD and NJSP realize they needed to trace each ransom money transaction to the individual passing the bill much more quickly, even if it meant they had to get additional manpower from the FBI to do it. In July the three agencies began conducting immediate investigations of every ransom bill discovery, working in three-man teams of one NYPD detective, one NJSP detective, and one FBI agent.

Hoover was now more convinced than ever that the ransom money would lead to the kidnappers and that it was the "most urgent and important" part of the investigation.[12] Though he agreed to the FBI's participation in the three-way investigations, he was afraid the NYPD would do what the FBI had done when it investigated David Bari: keep "hot" leads to itself. He ordered the Lindbergh squad to stay in "intimate contact" with Jimmy Finn and his men to learn what they were working on each and every day.[13]

President Roosevelt called Hoover to the White House on the afternoon of September 13. He said he had been discussing kidnapping with Attorney General Cummings, and he wanted to find out from Hoover about the Lindbergh case. Specifically, he wanted to know why the FBI had withdrawn from the investigation after the Lindbergh child's body was found and why the

Special Intelligence Unit of the Internal Revenue Bureau was the only federal agency involved in the case.[14]

According to Hoover's report of the meeting to Cummings, he told the president that President Hoover had designated the FBI as the clearing house for all federal work in support of the NJSP and directed other federal agencies providing services to the NJSP to clear all information they received through the FBI. After those arrangements were put into effect, however, Colonel Lindbergh asked for the SIU to be reassigned to the case, and President Hoover had approved it. The previous attorney general then decided that there might be "crossing of wires" if two federal agencies were working on the same case, so he directed the FBI to withdraw and "stand by merely to render such aid as was requested of us by the New Jersey State authorities, and not actively lead in the investigation."

If Hoover's report accurately summarizes the conversation, he omitted crucial parts of the story: it was Hoover's order to Elmer Irey to remove Wilson and the SIU from the investigation that caused Lindbergh to request Wilson's reassignment, and Attorney General Mitchell had never authorized Hoover to do anything other than withdraw his contact man, Special Agent Fay, from Hopewell. Mitchell had never authorized the FBI's withdrawal from assisting the NJSP. Hoover also failed to tell the president that when he had stopped the FBI from assisting the NJSP's investigation, he set up his own Lindbergh squad and began investigating the kidnapping independently.

The president also asked Hoover whether anyone had investigated the J. J. Faulkner surrender of gold certificates. Hoover pleaded ignorance of anything about it other than hearing indirectly that three or four thousand dollars of ransom money had been turned in. The president asked whether the Treasury Department had investigated it; Hoover said he didn't know, but he assumed that "some investigative steps must necessarily have been initiated." Again, according to his own report of the meeting, Hoover didn't mention the extensive investigations the NJSP, NYPD, and Wilson had undertaken or the investigation his own Lindbergh squad had conducted at his direction. Nor did he say that, as a result of the Faulkner episode, three-way ransom money tracking investigations had been underway since July.

To the extent Roosevelt needed convincing that the NJSP were not on a path to solving the Lindbergh case, Hoover apparently convinced him that day. According to the version of the story Hoover later told Assistant Director Hugh Clegg, the president was resting in bed during their meeting. "He always called Mr. Hoover Johnny," Clegg recalled. "He said, 'Johnny, we've got to solve that Lindbergh case. Get in it. Do whatever needs to be done to solve the case.'"[15]

After the meeting the president directed Cummings to have the FBI replace the SIU, and he ordered that all future work by federal investigators be done exclusively by the FBI. Six months into his presidency Roosevelt was on a mission to restore public confidence in government; once again he demonstrated that he wouldn't shy away from intervening when states didn't seem capable of handling their problems.

Cummings announced the president's decision on October 19. It had been apparent for some time, he said, that the search for the guilty parties in the Lindbergh case was "lagging," but with Hoover in charge it would be "pressed intensively" in the future. The change was "no reflection" on the investigators of the Internal Revenue Bureau, he added.[16]

The wording of the announcement was confusing to anyone not fully conversant with the fact that no agency of the federal government had any jurisdiction over the Lindbergh case and that the only official investigations were those conducted by the NJSP and the NYPD. Headlines like "Department of Justice Takes over Full Probe of Lindbergh Kidnapping: Action Sanctioned by Roosevelt—Lone Income Tax Division Investigator Is Withdrawn—J. Edgar Hoover to Assume Charge of U.S. Search for

Kidnappers" confused matters still further.[17] Most of the public naturally assumed that the president had put Hoover in charge of the entire, and the only, Lindbergh investigation.

Schwarzkopf was humiliated and angry, not only because he believed the announcement made him appear incompetent and ineffective, but also because he considered the removal of Wilson, upon whom he and Lindbergh depended heavily, an affront to both. The Lindberghs were on a five-month, thirty-thousand-mile trip by air to Europe, Asia, and South America, and didn't learn in real time that Irey and his men had been sacked. When word caught up with Lindbergh, he contacted the new secretary of the Treasury, William Woodin. The secretary, a close friend of Roosevelt, was perhaps unlikely to challenge the president on a personal matter such as this even if he had not been gravely ill at the time, as he was. The removal would stand.

The FBI now had Jimmy Finn's complete record of every ransom bill that had surfaced, when and where it had turned up, as well as the additional pieces of information he had collected that were beginning to fill in the ransom money puzzle. Wilson and Irey were once again out of Hoover's way, and he had the full backing of the president. Only Schwarzkopf remained to be dealt with.

Hoover dispatched Harold Nathan to Trenton on November 1 to respond to complaints Schwarzkopf had been alluding to recently but not articulating. Nathan asked what his "squawks" were. Schwarzkopf said the FBI had been "favoring" the NYPD in the three-way tracking investigations ("absurd," said Nathan) and "holding out" on the NJSP and keeping information from them (again, "absurd"). Schwarzkopf then spoke "quite feelingly," Nathan reported to Hoover, about the publicity coming from Washington about the FBI's taking over the investigation.

That was the cue for Nathan to unleash the message Hoover had sent him to deliver: the FBI was not taking over the NJSP's nineteen-month-old investigation, implying that it was a hopeless mess ("we had many other cases in hand that would bring us all the glory we needed"); the FBI was going to do its own, independent investigation and would no longer be relegated to "office boy status." He spoke in generalities, but his meaning was clear to Schwarzkopf: Hoover was now in open competition with him— let the chips fall where they may.

"We always have trouble in cases of this kind where we have to work with other agencies," Nathan told Schwarzkopf. "The average police officer is extremely jealous and is concerned with publicity only, and many police organizations would rather have a case unsolved than have it solved by an organization other than their own. . . . We are accustomed to being unpopular, in fact are rather proud of it."[18]

The rancor of the meeting stemmed from two unmentioned, but nonetheless overarching, realities: the heart of the Lindbergh investigation had shifted from New Jersey to New York, where almost every new lead of any consequence was coming from tracking the ransom money, and budget constraints had long since forced Schwarzkopf to cut back to a total of ten detectives assigned to the entire case. Without the help of Wilson and the SIU going forward, the NJSP would have even less to contribute to the ransom money investigation than before.

Schwarzkopf could complain about favoritism and mistreatment as much as he liked, but unless he could come to an understanding with the FBI and the NYPD that would enable them to work together as a team, the NJSP was likely to miss out altogether on catching the kidnappers. So he did what he had to do: he agreed to share information with the FBI and the NYPD. In return the NYPD agreed to continue allowing the NJSP to come into New York to investigate, and the three-way ransom money investigations would resume.

As far as Hoover and Nathan were concerned, the J. J. Faulkner exchange was the "principal problem" to be solved in the case and the FBI's highest priority.[19] Despite the NJSP's objection to the FBI's revisiting the Faulkner investigation in December, Hoover ordered the Lindbergh squad to plow ahead and assigned additional special agents to the task.[20]

The FBI also intensified its efforts to remind New York banks to be on the lookout for Lindbergh ransom money and to contact the FBI's New York office if they received any ransom bills. (The NYPD and NJSP were also asking banks to contact them.) In November the FBI distributed revised lists of serial numbers in conveniently sized booklets in sufficient numbers to supply one to every employee handling money in every bank in Greater New York and Westchester County.[21]

In January an opportunity arose for a possible "redo" of the Faulkner episode, but with better results. The secretary of the Treasury had in December instructed banks to continue accepting gold certificates for exchange until midnight on January 17.[22] Extension of the deadline raised the possibility that "J. J. Faulkner" might surrender more of his "goldies" on or before that date. The FBI advised banks in Greater New York to maintain an "extremely close lookout" on January 17; FBI agents were stationed that day in the Federal Reserve Bank and a number of other banks in the Bronx, where they believed a bulk exchange would be most likely to occur. But "J. J. Faulkner" didn't appear, nor did any ransom bills.[23]

As of the end of January 1934, Jimmy Finn's borough maps displayed 449 colored pins.[24] The FBI began to worry that the kidnappers might decide they had passed too many ransom bills in the New York area and begin passing them outside the area or in other types of places than previously. On February 26 the FBI instructed the special agents in charge of all field offices to personally contact Federal Reserve Banks in their areas, provide copies of the serial number booklets for every employee handling currency, and remind them of the importance of carefully scrutinizing the bills they received.[25]

Two days later the FBI distributed more than four thousand booklets of serial numbers in Greater New York to Western Union offices, post offices, railroad stations, bus stations, cigar stores, chain groceries, movie theaters, subway offices, insurance companies, public utility companies, chain restaurants, department stores, airline ticket offices, and Northern New Jersey banks.[26] In May the Federal Reserve Bank of New York withdrew from circulation one million $5 bills of the same series as the Lindbergh ransom money in hopes the reduction in the quantity of $5 bills in circulation might make the search for ransom bills easier.[27]

During lulls in the ransom money investigation the FBI began interviewing the thousands of employees and former employees of cemeteries in the Bronx, where the two meetings between Dr. Condon and Cemetery John had taken place. NJSP detectives objected, and it was reported to Hoover. "I do not care about the sensibilities of the N.J. police," he wrote on his copy of the report. "Tell [Special Agent] Sisk to pay no attention to them (police)."[28] He also followed up with a letter to Sisk, who was now supervising the Lindbergh squad: "The responsibility of the solution of this case rests upon the [FBI] and I want you to go forward with this investigation, independent of any other law enforcement agency and regardless of their sensibilities in the matter."[29]

With the ransom money tracking process proceeding mostly smoothly with Finn and the FBI in control, Hoover decided it was time to pressure Schwarzkopf into ceding other areas of the investigation to the FBI as well. He had specifically set his sights on getting a crack at the physical evidence in the case, over which Schwarzkopf had maintained tight control from the beginning, particularly the original ransom notes and any latent fingerprints. With its new, state-of-the-art crime laboratory, the FBI had a clear advantage over the NJSP in the scientific analysis of evidence. Hoover decided it was high time to put it to use.

On March 6 Hoover wrote to Schwarzkopf requesting a list of all the physical evidence in the case and photographic copies of the evidence, as well as any latent prints lifted from the ransom notes or other evidence for comparison with fingerprints on file at FBI headquarters.[30] Schwarzkopf replied that it was the policy of the NJSP not to release physical evidence from its custody, but he offered to have the NJSP perform any comparisons Hoover requested. He added that no latent prints had been developed from any of the ransom notes, and all other fingerprints had already been sent to Washington for comparison.[31]

Hoover wrote back to say, disingenuously, that the FBI needed the descriptions of the physical evidence because it maintained a collection of the descriptions of physical evidence in all kidnapping cases and wanted to include a description of the physical evidence in the Lindbergh case as well.[32] Schwarzkopf held firm: "When the Lindbergh case is finished, I will be very glad to give you everything you wish, and will do my utmost to help you complete your files."[33]

They had dueled to a draw. Hoover moved on, filing the episode away for future use against Schwarzkopf.

On May 15 the NJSP suddenly announced they would no longer participate alongside the FBI in the three-way ransom money tracking investigations and would no longer permit FBI agents to ride in New Jersey state vehicles during any joint activities. The New Jersey detectives had just discovered that the FBI had obtained the actual J. J. Faulkner ransom bills from the Federal Reserve Bank of New York and sent them to Washington for forensic examination without informing the NJSP.[34] The ransom money investigations continued, but as two separate teams (NJSP and NYPD, NYPD and FBI).

A few weeks later the FBI learned that the original J. J. Faulkner deposit ticket was also still on file at the Federal Reserve Bank. Once again, without informing the NJSP, they obtained the deposit ticket and sent it to Washington for forensic analysis even though, just two days before, Lindbergh had telephoned Hoover to express concern that poor relations between the NJSP and the FBI were impeding the search for the kidnappers. In response Hoover complained that Schwarzkopf had refused to share information with the FBI or permit the FBI to examine evidence. Not satisfied with Hoover's response, Lindbergh said he wanted a representative of the NJSP to be present in the future whenever the FBI conferred with him.[35]

On June 14 Schwarzkopf finally took his complaints about Hoover's sharp elbows to Attorney General Cummings, accompanied by New Jersey senator William Barbour and Congressman Lane Powers of Trenton. Citing as an example the FBI's removal of the Faulkner ransom money from the Federal Reserve Bank for examination, he said he couldn't understand the FBI's conduct because he had always tried to cooperate with the FBI to the fullest. Then Hoover listed some of his own complaints about Schwarzkopf's refusal to make evidence available to the FBI for scientific testing.

Cummings had heard enough and cut it short by saying that he had read the correspondence between the two, and it was clear to him that Schwarzkopf had refused to provide the FBI the information it had requested. He said he expected the fullest cooperation between the two organizations, not bickering, but Schwarzkopf must understand that cooperation was not one-sided. Then he sent them both to another room to try to figure out a way to work together.[36]

The meeting did nothing to reduce the deep distrust Schwarzkopf and Hoover harbored for each other or prevent it from permeating both of their organizations. Even though some of their complaints had merit, they were standing in the way of progress. It remained to be seen whether they were willing or able to move beyond those complaints in the interest of the investigation. Three-way ransom money investigations resumed. On July

24 the NJSP for the first time invited Special Agent Tom Sisk to the Hopewell house for a tour of the crime scene.

None of the forensic tests the FBI performed on the much-handled Faulkner ransom money and deposit ticket yielded fingerprints, chemical residues, or other useful evidence. The FBI compared handwriting samples of hundreds of known criminals with the ransom notes, without a match. Comparisons of John Condon's handwriting with the ransom notes produced conflicting opinions, with at least one expert believing he might have written the notes and at least one other inclined to think not—neither was certain. The handwriting of every prisoner sent to Sing Sing and certain other state and federal prisons after the FBI took over the federal investigation—more than five thousand prisoners—was reportedly compared with facsimiles of the ransom notes without a match.[37]

Extensive background investigations of Condon and his family and friends were unproductive, as was the FBI's investigations into Lindbergh's boyhood in Little Falls, Minnesota, and the extortionist who sent a kidnap threat to Anne Lindbergh's sister Constance Morrow in 1929. Exhaustive but futile efforts were made all over the East Coast to find boats named *Nelly* and boat owners named Faulkner.[38]

Dr. Condon reviewed mugshots on many occasions without spotting any that looked much like Cemetery John, but he could recall many of Cemetery John's facial features. It was more than twenty-five years before the Identikit technique would be widely used to produce likenesses from the recollections of eyewitnesses, but artists were sometimes enlisted to prepare sketches for this purpose. The FBI had no sketch artist, but a special agent in Washington knew a young sports cartoonist for the *Washington Evening Star* named James T. Berryman, who would later win the Pulitzer Prize for one of his editorial cartoons.

Berryman reviewed summaries of Condon's previous descriptions of Cemetery John, and he went to New York and sat down for hours with Condon going over all the details he could remember. Based on this information Berryman produced two sketches, one a front view and the other a side view, which Condon pronounced the "nearest likeness to him I've seen yet."[39] Assistant Director Edward Tamm assured Hoover that the NJSP "will not be advised that the [FBI] is in possession of these sketches."[40]

The investigation was mostly quiet in August: fewer interagency squabbles, but no breaks.

17

....

Dragnet

New York, August 20–September 27, 1934

So few Lindbergh ransom bills were showing up in July and August
that the FBI assigned its point man for tracking the ransom money,
Special Agent W. F. Seery, to another matter, and Jimmy Finn took
a five-week vacation.[1] Everything changed on August 20, when
the Federal Reserve Bank of New York discovered a $10 gold cer-
tificate with a Lindbergh serial number in a deposit by the Bank
of Sicily Trust Company in the East Village. It was the first $10
ransom gold certificate discovered in more than six months. Two
more turned up in bank deposits the following week.

In checking the serial numbers of all the $10 gold certificates
found so far against J. P. Morgan's original listing of the serial
numbers of the Lindbergh ransom bills, the FBI made a surprising discovery: the $10 gold certificates were being passed in the
same sequence as their serial numbers appeared on the J. P. Morgan list. That meant, in all likelihood, that the same individual was
passing the $10 bills one at a time. If their reasoning was correct,
it was an indication that the ransom money still outstanding was
probably all in one place and had not been split up among kidnappers or spread around to money dealers.[2]

The FBI's Lindbergh squad now made an important decision. Taking into account that the passer of the ransom money was now spending gold certificates (instead of the $5 federal notes that made up almost half of all the ransom bills) and that the $10 and $20 gold certificates with their distinctive, bright yellow seals had become much rarer since President Roosevelt withdrew them from circulation, they decided to ignore the $5 ransom bills altogether and to concentrate on focusing the attention of the neighborhood banks and tellers on looking only for ransom gold certificates. In late August they began visiting all banks in the New York area in person and asking them to check every gold certificate they received against the list of Lindbergh serial numbers and to contact the FBI immediately if they received any ransom bill. To stimulate interest they mentioned confidentially that ransom gold certificates had started turning up in New York, a fact that most New York newspapers had voluntarily agreed not to report so as not to alert the passer.[3]

The strategy worked beautifully. Almost immediately tellers in neighborhood banks began noticing ransom gold certificates, and their banks began reporting them directly to the FBI. On August 29 Angelo DeFelice, the proprietor of a produce store on First Avenue near East 103rd Street in East Harlem, deposited a $20 ransom gold certificate at the East Harlem branch of the Chase National Bank. A bank employee spotted it and detained him until the FBI arrived. DeFelice said a stranger had come into his store that morning and bought some beans, then took his pile of change and left.

A week later, on September 6, the National Bank of Yorkville discovered a $10 ransom gold certificate in a deposit by Raphael Boccanfuso & Company, operators of a fruit store on the corner of Third Avenue and East 89th Street in the Upper East Side's Yorkville neighborhood (then commonly known as Germantown). A three-man team (one detective each from the FBI, NYPD, and NJSP) interviewed store clerk Salvatore Levatino, who recalled receiving the gold certificate because it was the first one he had seen in months. He remembered the man who gave it to him because it was unusual for anyone to pay for a six-cent head of cabbage with such a large bill. He described the man as Irish, German, or Scandinavian, slender, athletic, between thirty-eight and forty-two years old, five feet ten or eleven, with light brown hair. He was wearing a dark blue suit and a light gray fedora. Special Agent Sisk was encouraged; this was "the first worth-while description of the passer of the gold certificates since the inauguration of this investigation."[4]

Seven ransom gold certificates had now turned up in the seventeen days since they started appearing again in August. A definite pattern was emerging: the passer was making small purchases yielding large amounts of "clean" currency in change, often at fruit stands and produce stores where customers were in and out making small purchases throughout the day. He frequented East Harlem and Yorkville, so much so that the investigators began referring to him as the "Dutchman."[5]

At the suggestion of Jimmy Finn, back from vacation, the three organizations decided to put plainclothes squads into the East Harlem and Yorkville neighborhoods to try to catch the passer on sight. Each organization committed six men to work together in two-man teams with no two men from the same organization paired together. Beginning September 7 nine two-man teams took to the streets of the two neighborhoods, some on foot and some by car, every day from 9 a.m. to 7 p.m. Their instructions were to keep a close lookout in and near fruit and produce stands, especially corner stands, for the man fitting the descriptions provided by the produce store employees and the Berryman sketches.

The detectives looked not only for the passer himself, but for anything they came across that might lead them closer to their target. The unexpected discovery of bunches of fresh vegetables discarded in Yorkville garbage cans, for example, led them to hypothesize that the Dutchman either wasn't married or his wife was in the dark about where his cash was coming from.[6]

Hoover considered the pinpointing of recent ransom money trans-
actions to Yorkville and East Harlem the best development in the
case since the president had put him in charge of the federal effort.[7]
Sensing they were nearing the kidnappers, he wanted three-man
teams to replace the two-man teams that left the FBI without an
agent on a third of the teams. He was convinced Schwarzkopf
was "playing along with us just so they will be in on the kill"[8]
and that both the NJSP and NYPD would do everything they
could to "scoop us" on apprehending the passer of the gold certificates.[9] He ordered more men assigned to the joint patrols at
once so there would be a special agent on every team to keep an
eye on the others and make sure they didn't cut the FBI out of
any promising developments.[10]

"Put six more men on the case, twelve if necessary, or the whole
office force if advisable," Tamm told Sisk; use "men who will hang
right on when they try to shake us."[11] When Sisk announced to
the NYPD and NJSP that he was putting ten more FBI agents on
the patrols, they both responded by assigning another ten men of
their own. Forty-eight plainclothes detectives were now patrolling
the main streets of Yorkville and East Harlem ten hours a day.

On September 8 the Fordham Branch of the Chase National
Bank reported finding a $20 ransom gold certificate in a deposit
of the Exquisite Shoe store, located at 266 East Fordham Road
in the East Bronx. Thirteen customers had paid for shoes the day
before with $20 bills, but only four sales tickets contained the
customer's name and address. The four were interviewed, but
none appeared to be the passer of the ransom bill; the investigators were never able to determine who had passed it. But because
the store was in the East Bronx, where the Lindbergh squad had
long believed the kidnapper lived,[12] two more plainclothes teams
were added to patrol the vicinity of the shoe store.[13]

The FBI's in-person contacts with New York banks had borne
fruit: neighborhood banks were now spotting ransom gold certificates and contacting the FBI directly, sometimes days earlier

than the Federal Reserve could have discovered the certificates in bank deposits. In the most recent instances the investigators had been less than twenty-four hours behind the passer. They were now convinced that, as long as he kept spending, it was only a matter of time until they caught him.

Hoover was now confident the kidnapper would soon be caught and so distrustful of his rivals that he turned his attention to positioning the FBI to be the organization that captured him or, at the very least, was not left out when the arrest occurred. "The Director and I both feel that these fellows were born, raised and nourished on the double-cross," Tamm wrote to Sisk. "That is food and drink to them and it runs in their blood."[14]

Tamm instructed the Lindbergh squad to study carefully the eyewitness descriptions of the passer and the clothes he wore and to be prepared to pick him up on sight and take him directly to the FBI office on Lexington Avenue.[15] Sisk had to chuckle—he knew the NYPD had already ordered its men to take the suspect to the NYPD's Greenwich Street station, while the NJSP was struggling to figure out how to take the suspect to New Jersey without an extradition proceeding. Sisk fully expected a "free for all fight" when the time came.[16] He had already stationed an undercover agent near a telephone at the NYPD's Greenwich Street station with orders to let him know immediately of any development in the Lindbergh case.[17]

Hoover's next move was to draw a bright line between the three-way ransom money investigation conducted jointly with the NYPD and NJSP and every other aspect of the case the FBI was working on. Going forward he wanted everything the FBI was pursuing independently done in absolute secrecy from the NYPD and NJSP. Except for the agents involved in the three-way Yorkville and East Harlem patrols, all other Lindbergh work was to be FBI-only, using agents the NYPD and NJSP detectives didn't know by sight, transferred for that purpose to New York. The agents were ordered not to disclose what they were doing or share anything they learned with the other agencies. "Extreme care should be exercised in order that officials of the New Jersey State Police and New York City Police will not be advised of the identity of these agents or the fact that they are working on the Lindbergh case," Hoover instructed Sisk. "The agents . . . should not advise other agents in the New York Division Office of the nature or identity of the case . . . and they should be exceedingly discreet in contacting you concerning the case."[18] Hoover was explicit about his intention for the G-men to find and arrest the passer by themselves: "The leads we are going to work on jointly should be the ones that are the most remote; that is, anything we develop ourselves that looks good, we should work on ourselves."

Sisk already had in mind the operation he wanted the secret squad to tackle first. Analysis of the borough maps with the colored pins had shown that most of the ransom bills had been passed within one block of a subway station on the Lexington Avenue line, suggesting the passer traveled by subway.[19] He wanted to position FBI agents at the fourteen stations serving the Pelham Bay and East Mall sections of the Bronx, where many of the borough's German residents lived, to try and grab the passer entering or leaving one of those stations.[20] Hoover gave it the go-ahead; this was exactly the kind of investigation he had in mind for the secret squad to handle on its own.

Meanwhile ransom gold certificates continued appearing. On September 11 a $10 gold certificate turned up at an Upper East Side branch of the Manufacturers Trust Company in a deposit of Charles Aiello's fruit store in Yorkville. Aiello recalled that a man apparently of German extraction and fitting the same description provided by other recent recipients of ransom bills had used it to pay for a small purchase of vegetables or fruit. Three days later a $20 ransom gold certificate turned up at a Brooklyn bank; it was traced to a purchase made at Bloomberg's General Market in Yorkville. The Bloomberg's cashier recalled that the customer was "probably German" and gave a description similar to the others. Three more $10 ransom gold certificates turned up at banks in the Bronx between September 15 and September 18, including one passed at a grocery store and one at a lunchroom.[21]

Frederick Dingeldien was the assistant manager of the Corn Exchange Bank's branch located at Park Avenue and East 125th Street in Harlem. On the afternoon of Tuesday, September 18, he called the FBI to report that the bank had received a $10 ransom gold certificate. The teller who received it, M. J. Ozmec, had waited on nearly 150 customers the previous Saturday and neglected to check the serial number against the list of ransom bills when it was presented. Special Agent Seery, Lieutenant Finn, and Corporal Horn of the NJSP went immediately to the bank and examined the gold certificate. The bank's employees hadn't noticed it, but the notation "4 U 13-41 NY" was penciled in the margin on the back. The detectives thought the combination of numbers and letters might be an automobile license number. On a hunch, they asked Ozmec to look through his deposit tickets for Saturday to identify any deposits made by a gas station or garage. He found three, including a deposit by the Warner-Quinlan gas station located a few blocks away on Lexington Avenue at East 127th Street.

The manager of the station, Walter Lyle, identified the handwriting in the margin of the gold certificate as his and confirmed that it was an automobile license number. He had made the notation on Saturday, the fifteenth, around 10:00 a.m. when a customer (described as thirty-two years old, five feet eleven, 165 pounds, light complexion, "Scandinavian type") drove up in a Dodge sedan and bought five gallons of gasoline for ninety-eight cents, removed the $10 bill from an envelope in his pocket, and handed it to Lyle. Lyle noticed the gold seal and remarked, "You don't see many more of these."

"No," said the customer, "I have only about a hundred left."[22]

Lyle gave the customer his change, walked around behind

the car to check the license number, and wrote it on the back of the bill. He did that, he said, because he remembered the president had ordered gold certificates turned in, and he was afraid he would have to repay the company if the bank wouldn't accept it.[23] Later that day he included the gold certificate in the pay envelope he gave to his assistant, John Lyons, for his week's wages. When Lyons took the station's cash receipts to the Corn Exchange Bank for deposit, he also exchanged his gold certificate for two $5 bills.[24]

Jimmy Finn contacted the State Motor Vehicle License Division, which advised that license plate 4 U 13-41 NY had been issued earlier that year to Bruno Richard Hauptmann, of 1279 East 222nd Street, for a 1931 Dodge sedan. According to the division's records, Hauptmann was thirty-five years old, five feet ten, white, 180 pounds, with blue eyes and blond hair. With a little more digging the detectives learned that Hauptmann was an unemployed carpenter from Germany and that he and his wife, Anna, had lived at 1279 East 222nd Street in the Bronx since 1931. It all fit. They also learned that he had a son, Manfred, about a year old.

Investigators from the three agencies proceeded to the Hauptmann residence—a modest, two-story, three-family house—and began surveillance. They wanted to capture Hauptmann with ransom money in his possession, if possible, and figured their best chance of doing so would be to capture him away from home, perhaps on an errand, with money in his pocket. So they hid in the weeds and woods around the block and watched the house. Additional detectives arrived during the afternoon, causing some local storekeepers to report a possible stick-up; precinct police officers stopped by in squad cars to question them. At 1:00 a.m. the three agencies decided to discontinue the surveillance for the night. After the others had left the FBI doubled back to resume the watch alone.[25]

At 8:55 the following morning about seventy-five FBI agents, NYPD detectives, and New Jersey troopers concealed around the block watched as a man matching Hauptmann's description went down the front steps of his house, walked around to the garage in the rear, and drove away in a dark 1931 Dodge with license plate 4 U 13-41 NY. Three vehicles, each containing representatives of each of the three law enforcement agencies, followed the Dodge, keeping their distance. Hauptmann headed south on the Boston Post Road and continued in a southwesterly direction for about four miles until he appeared to spot the tail and took evasive action. NYPD detective William Wallace, on instructions from Finn, pulled Hauptmann over. Officers in the pursuit vehicles jumped out of their cars, surrounded the Dodge, and pulled Hauptmann from the car. Finn, Sisk, and Lieutenant Arthur Keaten (NJSP) frisked him. Keaten removed a wallet from his back pocket containing a single $20 gold certificate, which he handed to Special Agent Seery.

"What is this about, what are they doing, what is it?" asked Hauptmann. "We're looking for counterfeit money," replied Keaten.[26]

The detectives questioned him briefly, standing by the road. Hauptmann admitted buying gasoline on the 15th at a station on the corner of Lexington Avenue and 127th Street. When asked whether he told the attendant that he had "a hundred more just like" the $10 bill he used to pay for the gas, he admitted saying that; when asked whether it was true, he replied, "Yes, at home." Seery checked the serial number of the gold certificate from Hauptmann's wallet and confirmed that it was a ransom bill. Keaten, Finn, and Sisk all wrote their initials on it.[27]

The detectives took Hauptmann to the office of the NYPD's Police Undercover Squad at the old Greenwich Street station in Lower Manhattan—an out-of-the-way place where reporters rarely hung around looking for stories. There he was photographed and fingerprinted; copies of his fingerprints were rushed to the FBI in Washington. The Dodge was removed to the NYPD's Thirtieth Precinct station in Harlem, where it was stripped bare and searched for evidence.[28]

Sisk reported to Washington that there was "no possible question" Hauptmann was the man named John they had been looking for.[29] Hoover departed for New York.

Whether Hauptmann was the John they were looking for was precisely the question. Until his license plate number pointed to him, Hauptmann's name had never even come up in the two-and-a-half-year investigation. Aside from fitting fairly well the eyewitness descriptions of the passer of recent ransom bills and having a ransom bill in his wallet when he was stopped, the evidence that could prove Bruno Richard Hauptmann was Charlie Lindbergh's kidnapper and murderer—or one of them—had yet to be discovered or linked to him.

As soon as he was fingerprinted, detectives from the three agencies took turns firing questions at Hauptmann with hardly a break for the next forty-eight hours. He consistently denied any knowledge of the kidnapping except what he had read in the newspapers, and he denied ever having been in the vicinity of Hopewell. When questioned about the sources of his income since becoming unemployed in April 1932, he mentioned his wife Anna's waitress earnings, a fur trading business he sometimes conducted with his friend Isidor Fisch (now deceased), and playing the stock market.

Proving that Hauptmann had written the fourteen ransom notes sent to Lindbergh, Colonel Henry Breckinridge, and Jafsie was now an urgent priority. Several noted handwriting experts (then commonly referred to as "examiners of questioned documents") had examined the ransom notes earlier in the investigation. Based on the similarity of penmanship, writing style, and diction, as well as certain recurrent errors in spelling and phraseology, the experts agreed that all fourteen had been written by the same person.

One of the experts, Albert D. Osborn, had previously devised a handwriting "test" consisting of paragraphs of his own composition that were dictated to possible suspects to produce writing samples that were compared with the actual ransom notes.[30]

The test paragraphs were not verbatim excerpts from the ransom notes, but they incorporated many of the same words, including words that the writer of the notes had frequently misspelled: our ("ouer"), where ("were"), later ("latter"), not ("note"), anything ("anyding"), and something ("someding").[31] Over three hundred possible suspects, including David Bari, had taken the test in the past two years, but Osborn and his father had never considered any of the test samples a match with the handwriting of the ransom notes.

Hauptmann agreed to take the test. He was instructed to write from dictation one of the test paragraphs twice and a second paragraph seven times, the theory being that the more repetitive the exercise became, the more fatigued the suspect would become and the more likely it was that he would forget to disguise his handwriting, if he were trying to do so, and revert to his natural handwriting.[32]

Hauptmann's test paragraphs, together with other preexisting writings taken from his home, were delivered to the Osborns the night of September 19.[33] At 4:00 a.m. on the 20th, Albert D. called Schwarzkopf at the Greenwich Street station. Schwarzkopf asked for silence in the room so he could hear Osborn's conclusion. According to Sisk, who was present, Schwarzkopf listened to Osborn for several minutes and then asked whether additional handwriting specimens would be any help. Sisk's report continues:

> He then hung up the receiver and advised those present, "It doesn't look so good. He says that when he first looked at the specimens he thought they were the same, and that there were some striking similarities, but after examining them for a while he found a lot of dissimilarities, which outweighed the similarities, and is convinced he did not write the ransom notes. His father is coming to examine them in the morning, first thing. I told him we would give them more specimens to work with, but he doesn't think that would change his opinion."[34]

Additional handwriting samples were obtained from Hauptmann and delivered to the Osborns later that day.[35]

Searching Hauptmann's home for physical evidence linking him to the crime was another high priority. The initial, cursory search conducted the day he was arrested hadn't yielded anything of particular significance, though the detectives did find two pairs of expensive binoculars and observed that most of the furniture in the apartment was new and expensive, including a walnut bedroom suite and a $300 floor-model radio in a wooden cabinet.[36] Without informing the other detectives, Sisk removed notebooks, memorandum pads, and two fountain pens and shipped them to the FBI laboratory.[37]

The detectives returned the next day to give Hauptmann's garage a thorough going-over. One of them noticed that a board was nailed across two wall joists behind the workbench. He pried it away, uncovering a shelf holding two packages wrapped in newspaper. He unwrapped them and discovered one hundred $10 gold certificates in one package and eighty-three in the other, for a total of $1,830; a check of the serial numbers confirmed they were all Lindbergh ransom bills. Behind a second board nailed to the wall joists, they found a one-gallon shellac can containing another $11,930 of $10 and $20 ransom gold certificates in twelve bundles. The bills were damp as if the money had been soaked in water or buried underground for some time.[38]

At the direction of Inspector Lyons of the NYPD, the detectives rewrapped the ransom bills and put them back where they found them. Then they brought Anna Hauptmann to the garage to witness a reenactment of the discovery of the money that they pretended was the actual discovery, feigning surprise when they "found" the rewrapped bundles.[39] Anna denied knowing anything about the money or where it had come from. She told the detectives she was confident that Richard likewise knew nothing about it or would be able to explain everything.[40]

Confronted with the discovery of almost $14,000 of ransom money hidden in his garage,[41] Hauptmann said he could explain everything: when his friend and fur trading partner Isidor Fisch returned to Germany in December 1933, where he died of tuberculosis the following March, he left some of his belongings with Hauptmann for safekeeping, including a shoebox tied with string. Without knowing its contents Hauptmann stored the box in the kitchen closet and hadn't seen it again until a few weeks ago when a heavy rain had caused a leak in the closet. Only then did he open the box and find $40,000 worth of damp gold certificates (he later changed the amount to $14,000), which he wrapped in newspapers and hid in the garage.[42] In August he had started spending a bill here and a bill there, $380 altogether,[43] which he felt entitled to do, he said, because Fisch owed him $7,000.[44] It sounded like lies and more lies, though the detectives were beginning to think Hauptmann was a bit more clever than they had originally believed.

The discovery of the ransom money in his garage still didn't prove that Hauptmann had abducted Charlie Lindbergh or killed him, but it was momentous nonetheless. Finn called the Osborns to let them know that the suspect whose handwriting they were examining was now under arrest and that nearly $14,000 of ransom money had been found hidden in his garage: would they reconsider their opinion? An hour later Albert S., the father, called Schwarzkopf to say that the writer of the specimens was, indeed, the writer of the ransom notes! The reversal of the earlier opinion was greeted with laughter in the station house. "Those handwriting experts! Oh, boy!" said one detective.[45]

Later that night the FBI's handwriting expert Charles Appel indicated that he had "a number of mental reservations" about the identification of Hauptmann as the writer of the ransom notes, "which leaves the matter somewhat 'in the air.'"[46] Hoover was furious that Appel was hesitant to reach a final, positive conclusion, as the Osborns had finally done. He rewrote Appel's conclusions himself to delete Appel's reservations. Three days later he reported to the New York office that Appel was now certain that Hauptmann had written the ransom notes.[47]

By early afternoon on the 20th, the Greenwich Street station was teeming with reporters and photographers who had gotten wind that a suspect was in custody. After receiving the Osborns' opinion that Hauptmann had written the ransom notes, NYPD commissioner John O'Ryan, Schwarzkopf, and Hoover, up from Washington, decided to announce the arrest. Each of them thought his own agency deserved the most credit for the arrest, but they accepted Hoover's suggestion that they issue a joint announcement emphasizing the cooperative effort. At 4:00 p.m., after the preliminaries, O'Ryan read the announcement: "We have in custody a man who received the ransom money. His name is Bernard Richard Hauptman [*sic*], 1279 East 222 Street. He came to this Country as a stowaway 11 years ago, is an alien unlawfully in the Country.... What has been accomplished constitutes an outstanding example of the effectiveness of unified action and team work as displayed by the three Departments."[48]

Law enforcement officials almost always prefer confessions and guilty pleas to the uncertainty of trials. That was especially true in this case because the handwriting identification was a bit wobbly, and there still wasn't much else to tie Hauptmann to the Hopewell crime scene. According to Special Agent Leon Turrou of the Lindbergh squad, the time had come to play what he called "our main psychological card" in trying to get Hauptmann to confess: bringing Dr. Condon in to see whether he would identify Hauptmann as Cemetery John.[49] Turrou drove Condon from his home in the Bronx to the Greenwich Street station and led him upstairs to the second deputy commissioner's office. There Hoover, Schwarzkopf, O'Ryan, and a handful of edgy, sleep-deprived detectives and special agents waited anxiously to hear what Condon would say when he observed the lineup.

When he was shown into the room where the lineup took place, Condon quickly eliminated all but four of the men. He asked the remaining four to repeat certain words and phrases. Finally, he focused on Hauptmann: "Do you know me? Have you ever met me?" he asked. Hauptmann denied knowing or ever meeting him. After the lineup left the room Condon said he wasn't sure Hauptmann was Cemetery John.[50] Outside the room, however, he told Turrou that Hauptmann "is *not* the man. But he looks like his brother!"[51]

Condon's failure to pick Hauptmann out of the lineup frustrated everyone in the room. The NYPD had seemingly done everything possible to suggest that Hauptmann was Cemetery John by packing the lineup with four patrolmen and nine detectives from the NYPD and NJSP and avoiding jailed prisoners frequently used for the purpose. "The detectives were shaved, bright-eyed six-footers," recalled Turrou. "Hauptmann looked like a midget who had wandered into a Turkish bath for two sleepless days and nights."[52] How could Condon *not* have identified Hauptmann? Was the old man confused? Was he really the hero-worshipper who came out of nowhere to rescue a stolen child? Or was he in league with the kidnappers?

On the way back from the lineup to his cell, the detectives took Hauptmann on a detour to an empty room. Whether out of frustration that he still hadn't confessed despite the mounting circumstantial evidence against him or perhaps even baser motives, the NYPD and NJSP detectives gave him "a real going over and punched him in the back and twisted his arms and legs and 'gave him hell,'" reported Sisk.[53] The G-men, under orders from Sisk not to touch Hauptmann, stood by and watched the beating without attempting to intervene.

At least four other eyewitnesses did pick Hauptmann out of other lineups: Joseph Perrone, the taxi driver who delivered one of the ransom notes to Condon's home; Cecile Barr, a movie theater cashier who received a ransom bill from a man to whom she sold a ticket in November 1933; Salvatore Levatino, the Yorkville produce store clerk who received a $10 gold certificate from a man buying a six-cent head of cabbage; and Walter Lyle, the gas station operator who sold five gallons of gasoline to the man who gave him the $10 gold certificate on which he wrote the man's license plate number.[54]

Hoover returned angry from New York. He resented having had to take part in a joint announcement of the arrest, though practically any sort of joint appearance would have been more palatable than seeing Schwarzkopf emerge triumphant in the competition to catch the Lindbergh kidnapper.[55] Hoover told Tamm he had never been in "such a disagreeable situation in his life," and "everything had been against" the FBI in New York "one hundred per cent." He was convinced that if he hadn't gone to New York for the announcement, Schwarzkopf and O'Ryan wouldn't even have mentioned the FBI in connection with the investigation and arrest.[56] General O'Ryan had by now resigned from the NYPD, having delayed his previously announced departure until announcing the arrest. Hoover was already beginning to dread the prospect of continuing to wrestle Schwarzkopf, as resentful and uncooperative as ever, for a share of the limelight. The case was nowhere near concluded, though, and President Roosevelt expected him to *solve* it.

Catching Hauptmann was a major break, without question, but crucial questions were still unanswered. The NJSP investigators had always believed there was more than one kidnapper; arresting Hauptmann had not altered that belief. It was also the consensus within the FBI that others besides Hauptmann were involved; Fisch and Condon were regularly identified as potential suspects. *Was* Hauptmann one of the kidnappers? Were there others involved? Why hadn't Hauptmann's fingerprints been found *somewhere*—on the ransom demand notes, the ransom money, the ladder, or in the Lindbergh home? Reporters asked these and other questions; Hoover's response was that there was much work left to do.

Condon flip-flopped a few days after the lineup and said Hauptmann *was* Cemetery John, the man he met twice, once in Woodlawn Cemetery and once in St. Raymond's Cemetery, where he had delivered the ransom money to him. Nevertheless the Bronx County and New Jersey prosecutors were understandably nervous about relying on the enigmatic septuagenarian who never seemed to tell the same story twice to establish the critical link between Hauptmann and the kidnap-murder and extortion. But who else could establish that link?

Lindbergh had driven Condon to St. Raymond's to deliver the ransom but had remained in the car while Condon walked across the street to the cemetery to hand the money over. In a statement given to Inspector Harry Walsh of the Jersey City Police Department in May 1932, Lindbergh had said he heard a distant voice in a heavy accent say, "Ay, Doctor," while he was waiting. He hadn't claimed he could identify that voice if he heard it again, and apparently no one had tested his ability to do that after Hauptmann's arrest.[57]

On September 26 Lindbergh was called to testify before the Bronx County grand jury considering extortion charges against Hauptmann. District Attorney Samuel J. Foley asked him whether he had driven Dr. Condon to St. Raymond's to pay the ransom; Lindbergh said he had. A member of the grand jury followed up and asked him whether he could identify anyone in the vicinity of the cemetery that night. Lindbergh said he had heard the voice of a man at a distance while he waited in the car for Condon. The grand juror asked whether he would be able to recognize that voice.

"I can't say positively," replied Lindbergh. Though he said he had a clear memory of the voice, "it would be very difficult for me to sit here and say that I could pick a man by that voice." When he was asked whether the voice sounded foreign, he said, "It undoubt-edly was. It was a very distinct foreign accent, the voice simply called to Dr. Condon, saying 'hey doc' but there was a very distinct accent."[58]

The following morning two assistant distinct distinct attorneys drove Lindbergh to Foley's office in the Bronx, where Foley, at Lindbergh's request, had arranged for him to hear Hauptmann's voice. Wearing dark glasses and a hat pulled down over his face, Lindbergh took a seat among the lawyers and detectives crowded into Foley's office. Hauptmann was brought in and seated in a chair in the middle of the room not more than ten feet from Lindbergh. Foley told Hauptmann to say, "Hey, doc, over here!" several times, from softly to loudly, and to walk back and forth in the open space around the chair. After Hauptmann responded to several questions from Foley, including some suggested by Lindbergh, the guards returned him to his cell. Lindbergh walked over to Foley's desk.[59]

"That is the voice I heard that night," he said.

"Sir, are you perfectly sure?" asked Foley.

"Yes, I am sure," said Lindbergh.[60]

18

....

Verdict

New York and Flemington, September 26, 1934–April 3, 1936

After the joint announcement of Hauptmann's arrest, Hoover launched a publicity campaign to let it be known informally around the country that it was the FBI's planning and foundation work that had brought about Hauptmann's arrest, emphasizing the work of the FBI's crime laboratory and the ransom money trackers.[1] He invited reporters to interview him and members of the Lindbergh squad and welcomed reporters, photographers, and newsreel cameramen into the New York office to show off the borough maps with the colored pins the FBI had copied from Jimmy Finn's maps. The G-men explained how studying the pattern of the pins had led them to concentrate on Yorkville and East Harlem and how focusing the neighborhood banks on looking for gold certificates had helped them spot the ones that tightened the dragnet around Hauptmann. Attorney General Cummings released copies of the sketches of Cemetery John prepared for the FBI by James Berryman, noting the "amazingly striking resemblance to the man now held in connection with this hideous crime."[2]

Hoover's campaign was a great success. The Associated Press wrote that the FBI had "lifted the cover" on some of the federal government's efforts to catch the Lindbergh kidnapper, "showing that one of the largest details of men ever assigned to a single crime had been ordered by the government."[3] Headlines like "J. Edgar Hoover, Ace Kidnapping Solver, Never Gave Up Hope on Lindy Case" and "Hoover Stayed in Shadows to Lead Great Kidnap Hunt: Get Facts, Not Theories, Is Word to Men from Jinx of Gangsters" helped create the impression that Hoover and the G-men had revived a faltering investigation and finally caught the Lindbergh kidnapper.[4]

Hoover's emphasis on the FBI's relentless, groundbreaking pursuit of the ransom money, mostly ignoring the efforts of the NYPD, the NJSP, and the SIU, was deliberate. It was a new iteration of the narrative he had been constructing throughout the War against Kidnappers that it was futile for criminals to try to thwart the invincible G-men. Serial numbers of ransom bills had led to the identification of kidnappers and ransom money launderers like Boss McLaughlin before,[5] but for the first time the FBI was making a point of showing the public how the purchase of ninety-eight cents' worth of gasoline had doomed a kidnapper. The implications of Hauptmann's arrest were immediately clear to kidnappers and money dealers: they could now pass ransom money only at their peril. The FBI had the know-how and the resources to spot ransom money in circulation and trace it to the place where it was passed. The fact that it could be done in some cases within a matter of hours was a function of the FBI's nationwide footprint, something kidnappers and their money dealers had never had to contend with before the Lindbergh Law.

On September 26 the Bronx County grand jury indicted Hauptmann for extortion. The charge was enough to keep him in custody in New York until New Jersey could charge him with the more serious crimes of murder and kidnapping and seek extradition. New Jersey prosecutors wanted the death penalty, but New Jersey law did not authorize the death penalty for kidnapping, though it did authorize the death penalty for death occurring during commission of a felony. On October 8 the grand jury of Hunterdon County indicted Hauptmann for the murder of Charles Augustus Lindbergh Jr. in the course of a burglary of the Lindbergh home for the purpose of stealing him and committing a battery upon him.[6] The governor of New York signed the extradition order the following day, and Hauptmann was taken to New Jersey to await trial.

Identification of Hauptmann's accomplices, if any, remained a high priority. There were many reasons why investigators had never believed the kidnapping was a one-man job, beginning with the apparent difficulty any single individual would have had in taking Charlie from his crib and removing him from the home without alerting five adults and a dog. Two distinct sets of footprints had been found leading from below the nursery window away from the home. Condon had reported seeing a stoop-shouldered man with a handkerchief over his face giving signals outside both cemeteries when he met with Cemetery John; Lindbergh had reported seeing a man of similar description outside St. Raymond's Cemetery.[7] "J. J. Faulkner" had never been located, and the experts agreed that the handwriting on the Faulkner deposit ticket was not Hauptmann's.[8]

Hauptmann's arrest opened new lines of inquiry and suggested new reasons why he might not have acted alone. There was speculation that the 180-pound Hauptmann was large enough to have had difficulty climbing through the nursery window.[9] Hauptmann's claim that Isidor Fisch had given him the box of ransom money raised the possibility that Fisch was an accomplice or perhaps even the actual kidnapper. The FBI sent samples of his handwriting to Washington for analysis and obtained immigration files relating to Fisch from the Labor Department.[10]

Within days of the arrest, Hoover began to fidget. There was still plenty of investigating to do and a trial to prepare for, but the case was now on its way from New York back to New Jersey. In Hoover's mind, that meant the FBI would be returning to the role of Schwarzkopf's "office boy"—once again having to beg the NJSP for information and wait around at Trenton to pick up menial assignments.

Hoover sent Assistant Director Hugh Clegg to New York to keep an eye on postarrest developments. Like many of Hoover's close associates through the years, Clegg usually tried to find a way to tell Hoover what he thought Hoover wanted to hear. In his reports from New York, he criticized what he considered the sloppiness, bordering on incompetence, of the NYPD and NJSP. He told Hoover "it would be a splendid thing if we could gain control of the investigation." He realized that wasn't going to happen, but suggested that Hoover consider either reducing the number of men assigned to the case or withdrawing altogether before the other agencies embarrassed the FBI.[11] Tamm chimed in, too, referring to the situation as "a three-ring circus and no ring master."[12]

Hoover was concerned he would be criticized if the FBI withdrew before the investigation was completed and all the coconspirators brought to trial. But he was also beginning to worry that the case against Hauptmann was weak, because of the absence of direct evidence of his participation in the kidnapping, and that Schwarzkopf and the New Jersey authorities might not obtain a conviction. He fretted that the FBI's reputation would be tarnished by continued participation in a losing case.

Hoover was not the only one who wasn't confident New Jersey was up to the challenge of convicting Hauptmann. On October 4 a friendly reporter told Hoover that Lindbergh, supported by Schwarzkopf and New Jersey governor Harry Moore, had asked Treasury secretary Henry Morgenthau Jr. to reassign Frank Wilson to help New Jersey prepare for trial and that Morgenthau had approved the reassignment.[13] Hoover immediately asked Cummings to order the FBI's withdrawal from the case, citing both Wilson's return to the investigation and Schwarzkopf's "past attitude of hostility."[14] Without waiting for a response from the attorney general, he ordered the New York office to deny Wilson access to the office and to the FBI's Lindbergh investigation files.[15]

On October 9 Hoover again requested the attorney general to order the FBI to withdraw from the case. This time he asserted that New Jersey prosecutors had presented evidence to the Hunterdon County grand jury the day before that was either "phoney" or "they have not given us the information heretofore."[16] He was referring to expert evidence as to the source of the materials used in the homemade ladder the kidnappers used to enter the Lindbergh nursery, which had come as a surprise to Hoover. The following day Cummings announced that the active participation of the FBI in the investigation "has been brought to a conclusion" and that FBI facilities and information would continue to be made available to the State of New Jersey.[17] Schwarzkopf and the New Jersey prosecutors were completely blindsided by the announcement.

Hoover thought that the FBI's withdrawal would put the New Jersey authorities in "a situation which they cannot handle" and that they would have to come to the FBI for help. "I intend to limit this assistance to the facilities of our laboratory," he told Clegg and Tamm. "If they desire someone interviewed, or the like, in say San Francisco, we will do that."[18]

The FBI was now all but finished with the Lindbergh case. The search for accomplices was effectively over, too.

On January 2, 1935, the outside world descended upon the one-hotel town of Flemington, New Jersey, county seat of Hunterdon County, population three thousand. The trial of The State of New Jersey v. Bruno Richard Hauptmann was set to begin in the 106-year-old Greek Revival courthouse on Main Street. It was gray and cold that morning, with the remnants of Christmas snow still about, but nothing, not even knowing they couldn't all fit into the courtroom, deterred spectators from as far away as Minnesota and Mississippi, including some who had slept in their cars, from queuing for hours in the cold.[19]

Major newspapers and wire services sent reporters for the entire trial; other news outlets hired noted commentators and novelists like Edna Ferber, Alexander Woollcott, Ford Maddox Ford, and Fannie Hurst to drop in and record their observations and impressions of the event H. L. Mencken, with his usual irony, referred to as the "biggest story since the Resurrection." (It had been just three months since the sensational custody trial of little Gloria Vanderbilt, which the newspapers called "the trial of the century.")[20] Over a million words per day would stream from Flemington to newspapers around the world via temporary telegraph facilities sufficient to handle the normal traffic for a city of a million.[21]

William Randolph Hearst, in particular, poured resources into bringing the story to readers of the Hearst newspapers. In exchange for exclusive interviews with Hauptmann and his wife, Anna, Hearst paid the fees of Hauptmann's lead defense counsel and Anna's board and lodging during the trial.[22] He sent reporters Damon Runyon, Arthur Brisbane, Jack Clements, Jeannette Smits, Dorothy Kilgallen, Jimmy Cannon, and Adela Rogers St. Johns to cover the trial.[23] Hearst's interest was personal as well as business. In July 1933, a plot had been uncovered to kidnap one of his own children, who were then put under guard by Pinkertons detectives.[24] When Hearst asked St. Johns to cover the trial, he told her, "We cannot endure the kidnapping of our children. In this trial I am sure we can produce a flame of nationwide indignation that will deter other criminals. . . . We must not allow this to become a *wave*."[25]

By 10:00 a.m. 150 prospective jurors were assembled in the courtroom, and a like number of ticketed reporters had claimed their seats at long, narrow plank tables that filled every available spot around the room and in the balcony above.[26] The trial lawyers huddled together at small tables inside the bar. The lead prosecutor, New Jersey attorney general David T. Wilentz, was surrounded by four assistants. The Latvian-born Wilentz, forty, had been attorney general for less than a year; the Hauptmann case was the first criminal case he ever tried.[27] When it was over he would vow never again to prosecute a murder case.[28]

The "Bull of Brooklyn," well-known New York criminal lawyer Edward Reilly, headed Hauptmann's four-man defense team. Reilly, fifty-two, and his cocounsel Frederick Pope stood out in the packed courtroom in their dark gray morning coats and gray-striped trousers, not customary attire for lawyers in this rural New Jersey courtroom.[29]

Anne Lindbergh, Anna Hauptmann, members of the lawyers' families, and various dignitaries sat behind the bar in rows of camp chairs that one observer likened to "an American audience listening to a Chautauqua lecture."[30] Behind them, spectators with their thermoses and bags of sandwiches squeezed into rows of hard, wooden benches. As many more as could be fitted in were allowed to stand wherever they could. Five hundred people reportedly squeezed into the courtroom built to accommodate 150 that day.[31]

A hush suddenly descended upon the lively courtroom as a small door opened behind the bench. A deputy sheriff and two state troopers in their light blue tunics, dark blue trousers with gold stripes, and Sam Browne belts stepped through, leading the short, stocky Hauptmann, without handcuffs, to the defense table. Damon Runyon, known for his usually colorful writing and vivid characters, was subdued in his description of the thirty-six-year-old Hauptmann as "pasty-faced, hollow-eyed, but clean and neat in appearance."[32] Others would see Hauptmann differently as the trial progressed. "I was astonished to see that this Bruno Hauptmann is a distinguished-looking man—distinguished and graceful," wrote Edna Ferber.[33] Lindbergh would later tell British author

Harold Nicolson that Hauptmann was "a magnificent-looking man. Splendidly built. But that his little eyes were like the eyes of a wild boar. Mean, shifty, small and cruel."[34]

Moments later the thirty-three-year-old Lindbergh—tall, blond, not as boyish as the world remembered—quietly made his way to his seat behind the prosecution table between Colonel Schwarz-kopf and a Hunterdon County detective, four seats away from Hauptmann. Under the coat of his light gray suit, he carried a .38 caliber revolver in a shoulder holster, at Schwarzkopf's sugges-tion, visible when he leaned forward to consult with prosecutors.[35]

At 10:10 the court crier summoned all those having business with the court to draw nigh with the familiar "Oyez! Oyez! Oyez!" from old English court procedure. It was the signal for all to rise and for New Jersey Supreme Court justice Thomas W. Trenchard to emerge from his chambers and take his seat on the bench over-looking the assembly.[36] In his thirty-five years as a judge (the last twenty-nine on the Supreme Court), the tall, dignified seventy-three-year-old had never had a murder case reversed.[37]

In less than a day and a half, twelve jurors, four of them women, were seated and sworn in. New Jersey law didn't authorize alter-nate jurors; these twelve women and men would decide Haupt-mann's fate. If any one of them had to stop serving during the trial, a mistrial would occur.[38] As Lindbergh historian Mark Fal-zini has noted, the jurors soon found themselves thrust into "their own little world and they quickly realized that they had to create their own civilization to go with it." They set up a makeshift gym in the hotel hallway and exercised every evening; they celebrated each other's birthdays. One of the women served as the beauti-cian for the others, and one of the men cut the other men's hair; another female juror volunteered to launder the jurors' clothes.[39]

Charles Lindbergh took the stand on the second day of the trial, following Anne to the witness chair. His unequivocal identifica-tion of Hauptmann's voice as the voice of the man who had called out, "Hey, Doctor" to Dr. Condon in a foreign accent at St. Raymond's Cemetery was the high point of his direct testimony.[40] On cross-examination, Reilly tried several times in different ways to challenge Lindbergh, put him on the defensive. Yet, inexplicably, Reilly never probed Lindbergh's testimony that the voice he heard say those two words that night was Hauptmann's voice. We now know that Lindbergh had given a statement to New Jersey police in May 1932 in which he said that he had heard a foreign voice say, "Ay, Doctor"—not, "Hey, Doctor," as he testified at trial.[41] Had his prior statement been provided to defense counsel, perhaps Reilly might at least have tried to probe Lindbergh's voice identification. We will never know.

Skeptics questioned, and still question, Lindbergh's ability to make a positive voice identification on the basis of two words, uttered once, almost three years earlier, but Lindbergh convinced many of those present in the courtroom, including veteran United Press reporter Sidney Whipple. He believed the jurors were convinced, too—"unhesitatingly," another reporter observed.[42] Whipple pointed out that Hauptmann's voice was peculiar: a "rather shrill, metallic voice—a voice that seemed to be drained through a metal funnel"—one that those who heard it would not be likely to forget.[43] Special Agent Turrou of the Lindbergh squad believed Lindbergh's "cold unhesitating [identification] with stark drama convinced the jury more than anything else."[44]

"The problem for the defense now," wrote *Boston Globe* reporter Louis Lyons, "is whether anything this jury hears after this will make much difference. One has to be on the ground to appreciate the weight of Lindbergh's personality, as felt in the courtroom where his slow, level voice carried each individual along with him on all the tragic journeys that grew out of that awful night of three years ago."[45]

"Under fire," wrote St. Johns, Lindbergh was "the best witness I ever saw. Even the sympathy of the neutral press box went out to him."[46]

Frank Wilson, the man Hoover had twice removed from the investigation only to see him twice reinstated by Lindbergh's efforts, took the witness stand to tell the thrilling, now familiar, story of preparing the ransom money, listing the serial numbers, and tracking the gold certificates that set the trap that snared Hauptmann. The tall, taut Wilson, looking like "the crack human bloodhound he is,"[47] described how he oversaw twenty-five J. P. Morgan employees preparing the ransom bills "with a view to presenting it in court someday as evidence."[48] Two people worked on each bill, listing its serial number and series, and noting whether it was a gold certificate, a United States note, or a Federal Reserve note. Wilson identified the handwritten yellow sheets listing the serial numbers and types of the 4,750 ransom bills, now bound between cardboard covers, the size of a telephone book. He told how the Treasury Department ordered the printing of 250,000 circulars containing those serial numbers and distributed them to banks in the United States and around the world.[49]

Wilson identified a brown manila envelope the size of a briefcase, sealed shut with two white seals and tied with heavy cord. It contained the 966 $10 and $20 gold certificates, a total of $14,600, found in Hauptmann's garage. Before affixing the seals to the envelope, he had checked each one of the bills against the J. P. Morgan list and verified that each one had been part of the ransom paid by Lindbergh. In response to the prosecutor's question, he stated that no ransom bill, to his knowledge, had turned up since Hauptmann's indictment.[50] In response to a defense question, he testified that, despite diligent search, he had never located "J. J. Faulkner" and that handwriting experts had concluded that Hauptmann had not written the "J. J. Faulkner" deposit ticket.[51]

Special Agent Whitley, who monitored the trial for Hoover, reported that Wilson "made a rather poor witness, but he did make several good points."[52] Adela Rogers St. Johns couldn't have disagreed more:

The Federal boys moved into the Hauptmann trial today and with awe we saw the United States Government, cold, relentless, infinitely patient, following the trail of the Lindbergh kidnapper.... Frank J. Wilson, a big, slow-moving, slow-speaking man, with a round, kindly face, and round, moonlike glasses, and a slow smile. A Special Agent of the United States Treasury Department. He wasn't a movie conception of the part—he didn't measure up to any fiction detective. But before he was through with his slow, thorough answers, I felt I would rather have Philo Vance or Anthony Abbott after me—oh, a whole lot rather. They may get tired, Mr. Wilson never would. A year—ten years—twenty years—you would never be safe, never be out of reach of that relentless glacier.... He knew his job. He did it. You could no more shake him nor reflect upon his honesty or his sureness of his facts than you could melt a glacier with a blow torch.[53]

Another of Elmer Irey's Special Intelligence Unit investigators, Special Agent William E. Frank, testified about his examination of Hauptmann's assets, income, and expenses. Using techniques the SIU used to prove income tax evasion from a target's own records and account statements, as in the case of Al Capone, plus information Hauptmann himself provided about his expenditures, Frank demonstrated that during the period between the day the ransom was paid and the day Hauptmann was arrested, $44,486 of "new money" had come into his possession that was not accounted for—all but $5,514 of the ransom money.[54] The SIU's final report on Hauptmann's finances for that period, issued in 1936, accounted for $49,950.44—or all but $49.56 of the ransom money. In issuing the report, the SIU said the investigation proved conclusively that "Hauptmann had no partner, either dumb or silent," because he shared no part of the ransom money with anyone else.[55]

On January 11, the eighth day of the trial, handwriting expert Albert S. Osborn gave his opinion that Hauptmann had written all fourteen ransom notes.[56] His opinion was based on analysis of the ransom notes, writings obtained from Hauptmann in jail, and other conceded writings found at his home. His conclusion logically implicated Hauptmann not only in the extortion, but also in the kidnapping and murder. By identifying Hauptmann as the writer of the first ransom note left on the windowsill of the nursery, he placed him (or someone with whom he was in contact) in the nursery that night. By identifying Hauptmann as the writer of the address label on the package containing the baby's sleeping suit, he placed him in direct contact with the child and/or his kidnapper on or after that night.

Seven additional handwriting experts, including Albert D. Osborn, testified for the State, each adding or amplifying points, but all to the same effect as the senior Osborn.[57] The defense attempted to counter the State's experts by calling John M. Trendley of East St. Louis, Illinois, an "imitator" who imitated other people's handwriting to try to trick handwriting experts. (Eight other handwriting experts invited by the defense to compare Hauptmann's writings with the ransom notes were either unacceptable to the defense or unwilling to testify for the defense after examining the writings.)[58] On the basis of his two-and-a-half-hour study of Hauptmann's writings and the ransom notes, Trendley opined that Hauptmann had not written the ransom notes.[59]

"Where are you getting these witnesses?" Hauptmann reportedly asked defense counsel Lloyd Fisher the following day. "They are killing me."[60]

Mild-mannered, middle-aged Arthur Koehler was the head of the Forest Products Laboratory of the U.S. Department of Agriculture in Madison, Wisconsin. He was the U.S. government's expert on the identification of wood; some said he was the world's leading expert in that field. For almost two years Koehler had studied the kidnapper's homemade ladder at Schwarzkopf's request, mostly on his own time and at his own expense.[61] He was there to testify about where the wood used in the ladder and the tools used in its construction had come from. Schwarzkopf had not previously revealed to the FBI or the NYPD the work Koehler was doing.[62]

No single piece of evidence was as critical to the determination of Hauptmann's guilt or innocence as the kidnapper's ladder. Whether it could be shown to have a nexus to Hauptmann sufficient for admission into evidence would depend on Koehler's expert testimony. The defense objected strenuously to his qualifications as an expert on the ground that "there is no such animal known among men as an expert on wood." Justice Trenchard overruled the objection, permitted Koehler to offer his opinions, and ultimately admitted the ladder into evidence.[63]

In plain language readily understood by laymen and aided by well-chosen photographs, magnifications, and demonstrations, Koehler testified that the ladder was made of several different varieties of wood, including one-by-four boards of North Carolina pine used in the two bottom rails. He explained how he had traced those pieces of North Carolina pine to the particular planing mill that had dressed the wood (the M. G. and J. J. Dorn Company in McCormick, South Carolina) by the unique markings the planer machine at that mill had made in the wood.[64] From a study of the Dorn Company's shipments of one-by-four boards of North Carolina pine prior to the kidnapping, he determined that the boards used in the two bottom rails had been shipped to a lumberyard in the Bronx (the National Lumber & Millwork Company) in November 1931.[65] This much Koehler had learned by November 1933. Further investigation by the NJSP after Hauptmann's arrest revealed that Hauptmann had been an occasional employee of the National Lumber & Millwork Company and had purchased pieces of lumber costing $9.32 on December 29, 1931, two months prior to the kidnapping.[66]

After Hauptmann's arrest Koehler investigated possible direct links between Hauptmann and the wood and tools used in the ladder. He accompanied NJSP detectives to Hauptmann's house and garage to search for evidence. In the garage they found Hauptmann's tool chest and, in the tool chest, a wood plane. By comparing the size and spacing of ridges in the ladder rails to the size and spacing of ridges Koehler produced using Hauptmann's plane on a similar piece of wood, Koehler concluded that Hauptmann's plane had been used to plane the ladder rails in the kidnapper's ladder.[67]

In Hauptmann's tool chest Koehler also found a set of graduated chisels manufactured by Buck Brothers; the set was missing the three-quarter-inch chisel. Shown the chisel found near the ladder outside the Lindbergh home on the night of the kidnapping, he identified it as a three-quarter-inch Buck Brothers chisel of the same make and pattern and with a handle of the same kind of wood as the set in Hauptmann's tool chest that was missing that particular size.[68]

Finally Koehler testified that the lumber used to create one of the ladder's side rails (referred to as "Rail 16") had come from a piece of flooring in Hauptmann's attic. It was his opinion that Rail 16 had been cut from a shortened floorboard remaining in the attic—that is, that Rail 16 and the shortened floorboard were previously the same piece of wood, now cut in two.[69] His opinion was based on many factors: four nail holes in Rail 16 matched perfectly four nail holes in joists in the attic beneath where Rail 16 would have been situated; the grain of the wood in Rail 16 matched the grain in the floorboard; and the annual rings present in Rail 16 and in the shortened floorboard were identical.[70] Due to questions about the circumstances surrounding the discovery of the shortened floorboard in Hauptmann's attic, the Rail 16 analysis was the most controversial part of Koehler's testimony.

Special Agent Whitley reported back to Hoover that Koehler had made an excellent witness, the "most convincing testimony of this sort that he has ever heard," and that he was the State's most damaging witness.[71] Martin Sommers, writing for the *New York*

Daily News, called Koehler the "one and only great detective of the Lindbergh case," observing how he had taken Hauptmann's own tools and "turned this courtroom into a carpenter's workshop" as he painstakingly told, and demonstrated, "perhaps the greatest true scientific detective story of these times." When he was finished, wrote Sommers, "Hauptmann appeared betrayed as the builder of the fatal kidnap ladder by his own tools."[72]

After twenty-nine days of trial, 160 witnesses, and 1.5 million words of evidence, Justice Trenchard sent the case to the jury on the morning of February 13. Eleven hours and twenty-three minutes later the jurors returned with their verdict: guilty of murder in the first degree. Upon motion of Attorney General Wilentz, Trenchard immediately sentenced Hauptmann to death "at the time and place and in the manner provided by law," which in New Jersey meant in the electric chair. Trenchard had no discretion in sentencing: upon conviction of murder in the first degree, the death sentence was mandatory if, as in this case, the jury didn't recommend life imprisonment.[73] He signed the death warrant that night before leaving the bench.[74]

Hauptmann exhausted all appeals without success. The U.S. Supreme Court declined to review the case, and the New Jersey Court of Pardons denied his petition for clemency.[75] Despite considerable pressure to save his own life by confessing and identifying any accomplices, Hauptmann steadfastly maintained his innocence and never confessed. He died in New Jersey's electric chair on April 3, 1936.

Most people were satisfied with the verdict and were relieved by the prospect that it might bring welcome closure after almost three years of grief and anxiety. The outspoken First Lady, Eleanor Roosevelt, however, was not convinced the verdict was correct. From what she had read in the newspapers, she said, it seemed the verdict had been based entirely on circumstantial evidence, adding, "While not in sympathy with Hauptmann, I was a little perturbed at the thought of what might happen to any innocent person in a similar situation. The entire trial left me with a question in my mind and I certainly was glad that I did not have to sit on that jury."[76]

Four months after the verdict, jury foreman Charles P. Walton, a fifty-one-year-old machinist from High Bridge, New Jersey, responded to those who criticized the jury for convicting Hauptmann on the circumstantial evidence presented. "Had these people been in our chairs, they would have got a great respect for circumstances," he wrote. Then he explained, step by step, how the jury reached the conclusion Hauptmann was guilty:

> A ransom note had been left on the windowsill of the stolen baby's bedroom. The person or persons who left that note got the baby. How they entered the room and left, by ladder, stairs or balloon, made no difference—he or they got that baby!
>
> The person or persons who got the baby got the sleeping garment.
>
> Some person, a man, gave Dr. J.F. Condon (Jafsie) the sleeping garment, in exchange for $50,000.
>
> That money was recorded by bill numbers and all the bills were on record.
>
> Hauptmann was caught with $14,000 of those bills.
>
> A million-and-a-half words did not bury those simple facts. Every circumstance brought out made them clearer.
>
> We 12 did only what you millions of readers would have done.[77]

Eighty-five years later, questions about Hauptmann's role in the kidnapping and murder and whether others were involved have never been eliminated. Few, if any, students of the case have the slightest doubt that Hauptmann possessed and spent large amounts of Lindbergh ransom money, but views still diverge on whether he was the person, or one of those, who kidnapped Charlie Lindbergh.

The most serious questions, going to the heart of Haupt-mann's guilt, concern Condon's and Lindbergh's identifications of Hauptmann as Cemetery John and whether the NJSP somehow planted or otherwise altered the shortened floorboard, allegedly from Hauptmann's attic, from which Koehler testified that Rail 16 had been cut. Suspicions that the NJSP may have mishandled or destroyed fingerprints not matching Hauptmann's are also disturbing, especially in light of the NJSP's previous failures to secure and protect evidence in the infamous Hall-Mills and Siege at Jutland cases, but they are less likely to have affected the out-come of the case.

Another factor making it difficult to resolve all doubts in favor of Hauptmann's sole responsibility for the kidnapping and murder is the great disparity in resources available to the State and those that were available to Hauptmann. That disparity explains, among other things, the enormous imbalance in the number and quality of expert witnesses each side called at trial. That is not unusual in criminal trials in the United States. In cases with plenty of direct evidence of guilt such as confessions, eyewitnesses, photographic evidence, and the like, such disparities may not have much impact on the outcome and don't necessarily affect the fundamental fair-ness of the trial. But the same cannot be said for cases such as Hauptmann's, in which circumstantial evidence, and expert evi-dence in particular, was the crux of the case.

19

Ocklawaha and Beyond

Chicago, Ocklawaha, and New Orleans, December 1934–May 1936

For over eight months the Barker-Karpis gang, suspected kidnappers of Bill Hamm and Edward Bremer, had eluded the FBI. The investigation had made little progress since Boss McLaughlin's arrest in April 1934 for exchanging Bremer ransom money. With the killing of Dillinger and the arrest of Hauptmann, Hoover elevated the hunt for the Barker-Karpis gang to a top priority. In December he sent Earl Connelley to Chicago to assume command of the FBI's secret "flying squad," established earlier that year to round up gangsters and kidnappers all around the Midwest. Connelley, forty-two, was a veteran of the Lindbergh investigation. He replaced the flying squad's first head, Inspector Sam Cowley, who had been gunned down in a shootout with Baby Face Nelson in November.

Connelley's orders were to bring in the Barker-Karpis gang as soon as possible.[1] When he took over, there was solid evidence against Doc Barker and Alvin Karpis: Doc's fingerprint had been found on a gas can used in refueling the Bremer kidnappers' cars, and a St. Paul store clerk had identified Karpis as the purchaser

of flashlights the kidnappers used in collecting the ransom. There
was plenty of evidence of others' participation in the kidnappings,
but still not enough to implicate particular individuals. Connelley decided to focus on the basics: follow the women and concentrate on the money.

As one of his first efforts to put the investigation back on track,
Connelley summoned agents working on the case to Chicago
to strategize about finding the wives and girlfriends of the gang
members and putting them to use.[2] The notable example of Ana
Sage's delivering Dillinger into the death trap at the Biograph Theater was still fresh in everyone's mind.

Karpis liked to consider himself a thief rather than a murderer or
kidnapper. He had a benign, if naive, view of the kinds of women
available to men like him:

> A thief has to select his girls from the world he moves in, and
> the broads you find there are likely to be making their own liv-
> ings in some kind of underworld activity. I took up with a lot of
> whores in my time, but I never had any complaints about the
> personalities or morals or brains of any of them. And if my girl-
> friends weren't engaged in something criminal, then they were
> the daughters or sisters or cousins of burglars or holdup men or
> killers. I had plenty of them, too, and like the whores, you could
> trust them. . . . I could always rely on them to play it smart with
> cops and other outsiders. We were all in the same general busi-
> ness and looked out for one another.[3]

Hoover, on the other hand, believed all women who consorted
with gangsters were despicable, deceitful lowlifes. And, by his own
admission, they thoroughly fascinated him: "This blissful type of
ignorance, as displayed by the average gun moll, always has interested me strangely. The one quality which woman is supposed to
possess is that of curiosity. Yet the gun moll always seems able
to convince the world in general—especially those sentimental

moo-cows of scant knowledge but loud voices who are forever interfering with businesslike law enforcement by their turn-the-other-cheek theories of crime eradication—that she was born entirely without the quality which made Eve eat the apple."[4]

Notwithstanding Hoover's contempt, the FBI had at least two uses for molls: as honeypots to attract gangsters and as sources of information. To use them as attractions, the FBI had only to locate them and put them under surveillance—watching, wire-tapping, and covering their mail—until their men showed up or they moved on to the next place. Getting information from them, though, required their cooperation. Sometimes the FBI obtained their cooperation by offering something valuable, like a fresh change of clothes in jail or reduced charges; at other times the FBI held them incommunicado until their mental resistance broke down.[5]

At the last minute Connelley's moll conference had to be post-poned when three Barker-Karpis gang members showed up in Chicago in January. For over a month the flying squad had been watching and wiretapping the Pine Grove Avenue apartment of Clara Gibson, wife of gang member Russell Gibson, and the Surf Street apartment of Mildred Kuhlman, a young prostitute Doc Barker had met in Toledo.[6] The surveillance indicated that Gibson and Doc were in Chicago. On the evening of January 8 nine heavily armed special agents proceeded to Kuhlman's apartment and another seventeen to Gibson's apartment.[7]

Around 6:30 p.m. Kuhlman and Doc left her apartment to hail a taxi. As the G-men closed in and ordered them to surrender, Doc, who was unarmed, started to run and slipped on the ice. The G-men surrounded him and drew their guns. Doc offered no resistance. "This is a helluva time to be caught without a gun," he muttered, as he and Kuhlman were led away to the Chicago office.[8] A search of Kuhlman's apartment yielded a Thompson .45 caliber submachine gun and a .38 caliber Colt automatic pistol.[9] More importantly agents also found a letter addressed to Doc from his mother, Ma Barker, postmarked Ocala, Florida, and two Florida maps with circles drawn around Ocala and nearby Lake Weir in central Florida.[10]

Assistant Director Harold Nathan tried to get a confession from Doc that night, but Doc refused to talk. When Nathan reported that Doc was "a tough one and is not going to talk,"[11] Assistant Director Ed Tamm in Washington ordered Connelley to take over the interrogation and "make vigorous physical efforts" to get a complete confession concerning the Bremer kidnapping. It was the "impression" in Washington, Tamm said, that "men assigned to the Chicago office"—meaning Nathan—"had a preconceived idea that Barker would not talk and accordingly would not attempt to secure a statement with the vigor which should be displayed."[12] There was no mistaking what "vigorous physical efforts" meant.

Meanwhile, around 10:45 that same night, the other contingent of FBI agents observed Gibson, his wife, Clara, gang member Byron Bolton, and another woman entering the Gibson apartment building. Connelley picked up a speaking tube and announced that the FBI had the building surrounded and would use tear gas to force them out if they didn't surrender immediately. There was no response. Three tear gas shells were fired into the building, one landing in the apartment next to the Gibson apartment, before Bolton and the two women surrendered.[13] At the same time Gibson, in a bulletproof vest, emerged from the rear entrance where twelve G-men were waiting. He fired his Browning automatic rifle. The agents returned fire, mortally wounding him in the head and chest.[14]

Three more rifles (two automatic), a sawed-off shotgun, two automatic pistols, a police revolver, and an Ithaca auto-burglar handgun were found in the Gibson apartment; a .32 caliber Colt automatic pistol was found in the alley near Gibson's body.[15] The coroner's jury returned a verdict of justifiable homicide, but recommended that when the FBI in the future went out armed with high-powered weapons to capture a suspect, they should "observe reasonable caution in order to prevent the killing or wounding of innocent citizens in the building occupied by the suspects."[16]

Doc never talked, but Byron Bolton (alias Monty Carter) did. He had been recruited for the Hamm and Bremer kidnappings by Shotgun George Ziegler, who had mentored him since they had both taken part in the St. Valentine's Day Massacre. After Ziegler's gangland-style murder in Cicero in March 1934, Bolton had begun to drift from the Barker-Karpis gang. Now in custody, he decided to tell what he knew in hopes of getting a reduced sentence at a federal prison where he could obtain treatment for his chronic tuberculosis. He started by divulging the location of the hideout where Bremer was held in Bensenville, Illinois, and directions to the rental cottage in Florida where Fred and Ma Barker were spending the winter, hosting Karpis and other gang members and their girlfriends.[17] Though Bolton couldn't remember the name of the lake, he described the shady lawn that sloped down from the cottage to a boathouse and fishing dock. He also told the FBI the name of every person who had participated in both kidnappings and what each had done.[18]

Connelley had to move fast. The newspapers had reported the killing of Russell Gibson and the arrests of Bolton and the two women at the Gibson apartment, but the FBI hadn't announced Doc's arrest and was trying to keep the news from getting out. Once the gang members still at large learned that the FBI had caught Doc, they would hit the road again, and Bolton's directions and Doc's maps would be worthless. Connelley and three special agents chartered a plane for Ocala, where they met up with ten more agents, including the flying squad's sharpshooters, who arrived by train with an arsenal of rifles, machine guns, ammunition, and tear gas to outlast an unknown number of shooters holed up inside the cottage.

There are several lakes near Ocala, but with the circle drawn around Lake Weir on Doc's map, the G-men concentrated their search there. After a couple of days sniffing around undercover, they located a two-story, white frame cottage fitting Bolton's description. It was on Highway 41 in the town of Ocklawaha (population two hundred) and fronted on the north shore of Lake Weir. They learned that the president of the Biscayne Kennel Club in Miami, Carson Bradford, owned the house and that a man named Blackburn (the townspeople called him "Shorty")[19] and his mother had rented it for the winter.[20] According to the postmaster of Ocklawaha, the Blackburns had been receiving lots of out-of-town newspapers.[21]

On January 15 Connelley drove by the Bradford house and observed a short man (Fred was five feet four) and a stout, older woman matching the Barkers' descriptions in the yard.[22] He set the raid for sunup the next morning. Later that evening, while parked in his car keeping an eye on the house, he saw Fred and Ma leave the house and drive away. According to a *Tampa Times* reporter, he followed them to Ocala and saw them buy movie tickets and enter the theater, but he made no attempt to arrest them that night.[23]

By 6:00 the next morning, fifteen G-men were positioned around the cottage, behind tall oak trees covered in Spanish moss, peering around outbuildings, and crouching in a grapefruit grove. Guns, ammunition, and tear gas shells were distributed. Just before 7:00 two special agents began diverting Highway 41 traffic away from the Bradford property.

When it was light enough to see anyone leaving the house, Connelley called out that the FBI had the house surrounded and if those inside came out one at a time, no one would be hurt. Getting no response, he tried again. Still no answer. Agents fired a tear gas shell into the house, and more warnings were shouted. Finally Connelley heard a voice inside say something like, "All right, go ahead," or, "Let's go." He took that to mean that those inside were coming out; he told them to come ahead, Freddie first. Instead of coming out, someone fired a machine gun at Connelley from an upstairs window but missed him. From four different directions the G-men returned fire. The gun battle was on.

By mid-morning, when Hoover hadn't heard how the raid was going, he became nervous and began imagining all sorts of disasters. Worried the battle would last into the night, he ordered more planeloads of G-men rushed to Ocklawaha, with high-powered Monitor rifles and lots more ammunition, including tracer bullets and flares for nighttime shooting.[24]

The shooting continued for nearly four hours, though after the first half hour or so most of the firing came from outside, while the shots from inside tapered off. When the smoke cleared enough for a good look around, the G-men surveyed the broken windows, bullet holes all over the outside of the cottage, and bricks blasted loose from the chimney.[25] FBI reports estimated the G-men had fired approximately five hundred rounds and the Barkers perhaps half that many.[26]

During the lull Special Agent J. C. White entered the small guesthouse on the property. There he discovered a terrified Willie Woodbury, twenty-five, and his wife, Annie Bell, hiding under the bed. The "Blackburns" had hired them to be their cook and handyman, and they were living in the guesthouse. Woodbury confirmed that the only people in the main house that morning were Mr. Blackburn and his mother.[27] Connelley told him to go to the main house to see whether the Blackburns were alive. The front and back doors were both locked, but Woodbury forced the front door open and entered.[28] When he called out to the Blackburns, there was no response. He climbed the stairs, his eyes burning from tear gas. A few minutes later he stuck his head out the window of the southwest corner bedroom and reported that the Blackburns were both in the bedroom, dead.[29] Connelley and his men then entered the cottage and confirmed that no one else was there. Shortly after noon he telephoned Tamm to report: Ma and Fred were dead, the FBI had suffered no casualties, and the coroner would rule the FBI had shot the Barkers in self-defense while they were resisting arrest.[30]

The FBI seized four bulletproof vests, three Thompson machine guns, two .45 caliber Colt automatic pistols, one .38 caliber Colt automatic pistol, one Browning automatic shotgun, one Remington pump shotgun, one Winchester rifle, several 50- and 100-shot drums, and fourteen automatic pistol clips from the cottage.[31] In addition they found four $1,000 bills tucked inside Fred's belt and ten $1,000 bills, four $50s, one $20, one $10, and one $5 bill in Ma's purse.[32] The large bills were a big disappointment. The Bremer ransom had been paid all in $5 and $10 bills; even the $5 and $10 bills in Ma's purse weren't Bremer ransom bills.

Another disappointment was that Alvin Karpis and Harry Campbell, the last two principal members of the Barker-Karpis gang still alive and at liberty, weren't at Ocklawaha that morning.

Hoover knew there were no kidnapping or other federal charges outstanding against Fred and Ma before the shootout. His long-time intimate associate, Assistant Director Clyde Tolson, reported to him that afternoon that the FBI had never even issued an identification order (the customary way of advising the FBI and other law enforcement agencies that an individual was wanted for questioning) for either of them because there wasn't enough evidence of their participation in any kidnapping. As far as Tolson could determine, "Maw" Barker had never been arrested or charged with a crime anywhere.[33]

It did not look good for fifteen G-men, armed with machine guns and high-powered rifles but without arrest warrants, to be shooting it out with a sixty-one-year-old woman and her son, even if their names were Barker. Hoover decided to try to improve that picture somewhat by persuading the U.S. attorney in St. Paul to charge Fred and Ma, as well as Russell Gibson and Shotgun George Ziegler, all dead, with Bremer's kidnapping.[34] Criminal charges can't be brought against dead people, though. The U.S.

attorney refused to do it, but he agreed to name them as unindicted coconspirators in future indictments in the Bremer case.

When he failed to get the cover of indictments, Hoover began creating a persona for Ma Barker to provide a justification for the shootout. In doing so he was benefitted by the dearth of actual information about her. A few things, of course, were known. She was born Arizona Clark in Ash Grove, Missouri, in 1873, and was known as "Kate" Barker. Her fingerprints weren't on file at the FBI; law enforcement agencies had few, perhaps only one, authentic photographs of her. She was so short that she sat on a wooden crate to look out a car window, and she entertained herself for hours at a time working jigsaw puzzles and listening to country music on the radio. She often strolled around singing the hymns she had learned growing up in the Ozarks.

Her four boys—Herman (deceased), Lloyd (incarcerated), Doc (incarcerated), and Fred—had been her passion. She treated Karpis almost as another son. She barely tolerated her husband, George, and hadn't lived with him for several years. He seemed to lack ambition and never held a job for long, though he apparently never tried crime either. It may have been his disapproval of the boys' wrongdoing that set Ma against him.

The boys were all hardened criminals from their teens, but there is no evidence it bothered Ma or that she tried to steer them in another direction. On the contrary, she made excuses for them, bought their way out of jails and prisons whenever she could, and lived off their ill-gotten gains. She could look respectable and grandmotherly when she wanted to, which made her useful when the boys were on the run, serving as the front person to rent apartments and houses, shopping for groceries, and cooking for the boys and their friends. Ma may have been brighter than any of the Barker boys, but she didn't plan their crimes or take part in them, as Hoover claimed from the day she died. Bank robber Harvey Bailey, who had sometimes worked with Karpis and Fred before the kidnappings started, ridiculed the idea that Ma was a mastermind. "The old woman couldn't plan breakfast," he said.[35]

"She was just an old-fashioned homebody from the Ozarks," wrote Karpis, whose word on this must be taken with caution. "Ma was superstitious, gullible, simple, cantankerous and, well, generally law-abiding."[36] Her single function as far as the gang was concerned, he said, was to travel with them as a widowed mother and her three sons. "What could look more innocent?"[37]

The other Ma Barker, the one Hoover conjured up, was "the brains of the gang, a domineering woman of about 60 years, so clever that she never had been arrested . . . a domineering old battle-ax."[38] He created the fiction that she was "the hub of the Bremer kidnapping. During the moving about necessary to the sending of ransom notes and quick trips to and from the kidnap hideout, there might have been a lack of contact had it not been for Ma. They all reported to her, like telephone lines to a central switchboard."[39] With her death, Hoover told reporters, the gang's "backbone is shattered."[40] Later he would write that she was the "most vicious, dangerous, and resourceful criminal brain of the last decade . . . an animal mother of the she-wolf type . . . a veritable beast of prey."[41]

It was all made up. There's not a shred of supporting evidence for the story in more than five hundred surviving FBI files on the Bremer kidnapping and the Barker-Karpis gang. Even the FBI's 126-page, single-spaced summary of the Bremer kidnapping doesn't mention anything Ma did to bring about or take part in the kidnapping.[42] Hoover's well-documented vitriol toward female criminals and molls doesn't fully explain his attacks on Ma Barker. It is possible that concern that the G-men had finally crossed the line in their zeal to overpower and eradicate the "public enemies" led him to exaggerate her dangerousness and culpability. Or perhaps he thought he could make Ma Barker into another symbolic target for the War against Kidnappers, like the machine gun–toting desperadoes Machine Gun Kelly, Albert Bates, and Harvey Bailey, who had captured the public's attention at the outset of the war.

Whatever the point of it, Hoover's demonization of Ma seemed to work. "Congratulations to the Department of Justice on the knocking off of Ma Barker and her son Fred," wrote the *New York Daily News* on its editorial page. "It looks as if this is the only way to make sure that kidnappers will get what is coming to them in this country. . . . The utter ruthlessness of the Department of Justice in tracking kidnappers down and then shooting them down gets better and quicker results."[43]

While the flying squad was hunting down the last members of the gang, it was also looking for the rest of the Bremer ransom money and those involved in converting it. Not much had turned up, aside from the money changed by Boss McLaughlin and his helpers in Chicago. More than $100,000 was still not accounted for.

When the gang split up into smaller groups after the McLaughlin debacle, most of the hot Bremer money remained with Fred and Karpis for safekeeping until it could be exchanged. They put it into a couple of leather Gladstone bags and buried them under Karpis's garage in Cleveland while they tried to come up with a plan. Everyone was impatient waiting for their cuts, including St. Paul fixer Harry Sawyer, who had been responsible for getting them into the Bremer snatch in the first place.

Finally, in August 1934, Sawyer made contact with a "rich hood" in Grosse Point, Michigan, named Cassius McDonald, who said he could exchange the money in Havana for a 15 percent fee; he guaranteed that the "hot bills wouldn't turn up in Havana but in safer places like Caracas and Mexico City."[44] To Sawyer and the cash-poor kidnappers, McDonald seemed like the real deal: a big-time gambler and former Detroit racetrack owner who lived in a Grosse Point mansion and spent his winters in Havana. He claimed he controlled gambling in Havana and held the Cuban government's concession for the Havana racetrack and for prize-fights, tennis tournaments, and other Cuban sporting events.[45]

When Karpis and Fred dug up the ransom money to deliver to McDonald, they found the bags submerged in water and the bills damp and soggy. Spinning the money around in a washing machine didn't help, so they bought electric fans and tried to blow the bills dry as they floated around inside the house. Finally, when they had done the best they could, they wrapped the bundles of money in newspaper and took them to McDonald, who left for Havana in early September.

There, over the course of several days, McDonald found a broker to exchange $18,000 of ransom money for $14,000 in gold, which he then exchanged for fourteen $1,000 bills at the National City Bank of Havana. He took another $72,000 of the $5 and $10 ransom bills to the broker a few days later and swapped them for bills in larger denominations; he then exchanged those bills for seventy-two $1,000 bills at the Havana branch of the Chase National Bank.[46] Sawyer and the gang were delighted. McDonald had come through: the Bremer ransom money was spendable at last. Or so they thought.

Now, with money to spend and the G-men knocking themselves out to find him, Karpis decided to lay low on a quiet beach in Cuba with his girlfriend Dolores Delaney. Or maybe he wanted to see for himself whether the rich hood was really as good as he seemed. Through contacts of Joe Adams, manager of the El Commodoro Hotel in Miami—the same Joe Adams who rented the Ocklawaha house to Fred and Ma—Karpis rented a place in the resort town of Varadero, where Al Capone and American businessman Irénée Du Pont had built mansions.

According to Karpis, he went to Havana one day and exchanged one of the $1,000 bills from McDonald at the Royal Bank of Canada for $750 in $10s and $250 in $5s. As soon as he saw that some of the bills he received were discolored, he realized McDonald had lied about the Bremer money going to Caracas and Mexico

City. He figured the FBI would be in Havana soon, hot on his trail. He and Dolores hastily fled Cuba and headed to Miami, where Adams found him a nice house and car. In late December he and Dolores spent some time around the holidays with Fred and Ma at the Ocklawaha cottage.[47]

In late January the Federal Reserve Bank's branch in Havana notified the FBI that it had located several thousand dollars of $5 and $10 bills with serial numbers of Bremer ransom money.[48] The fourteen $1,000 bills found in the cottage at Ocklawaha were determined to be part of the clean money McDonald had obtained in Havana in exchange for the Bremer ransom money.

After Doc's capture and the deaths of Fred and Ma, Karpis managed to remain at liberty for another sixteen months. He and gang member Harry Campbell stuck together for several months, joining up with an Ohio ex-con named Freddie Hunter and three others to rob the mail car of an Erie train stopping at Garrettsville, Ohio, on November 8, 1935. Armed with machine guns, they robbed passengers and picked through mailbags until they found what they were looking for: the Youngstown Sheet & Tube payroll, a haul of about $32,000.[49] Thereafter both the flying squad and the U.S. Postal Inspection Service were after them.

Karpis and Campbell split, and Karpis and Hunter stayed together, mostly in Hot Springs, Arkansas, a good town like St. Paul, where law enforcement turned a blind eye. There Karpis lived with Grace Goldstein, operator of Hot Springs's finest brothel. Goldstein claimed to have married the already-married Karpis in New York in September 1935, "during the Baer-Louis fight."[50]

In April 1936 word got out that the G-men were on their way to Hot Springs. Karpis and Hunter left town. The FBI picked up Goldstein and tried to get her to tell them where Karpis and Hunter were, but she refused to talk until Special Agent Connelley promised that if she cooperated she and her family would not be prosecuted for harboring Karpis.[51] With that assurance Goldstein gave up the address of an apartment on Canal Street in New Orleans, where Karpis often visited Hunter and Connie Morris, one of Goldstein's prostitutes.[52]

On the afternoon of May 2, fifteen heavily armed FBI agents had the Canal Street apartment house surrounded, preparing to raid, when Karpis and Hunter walked out to a parked car, on their way to get strawberries for dinner. The agents identified themselves; Karpis and Hunter surrendered without any shots fired. Hoover was at the scene, having chartered a plane to take him from New York to New Orleans for Karpis's arrest, with a stop in Washington on the way to pick up his pearl handle revolver.[53]

Bail was set for Karpis at $500,000, the highest ever at the time.[54] He agreed to plead guilty to kidnapping Hamm, which enabled the FBI to erase the blot of the Touhy gang's acquittal and record the case as solved. Karpis arrived at Alcatraz in August 1936 at the age of twenty-nine to serve a life sentence.

By late 1938, when the Bremer kidnapping case was finally closed, eighteen people had been convicted of kidnapping or conspiracy and seven of harboring members of the Barker-Karpis gang. Three others were killed resisting arrest, while another three were murdered by associates. Alvin Karpis was never brought to trial for the Bremer kidnapping.[55]

In 1959 an FBI agent investigating a prison murder met Karpis at Alcatraz. "If it's any consolation to you, Karpis," he said, "your arrest has made the FBI what it is today. Anytime we've needed appropriations over the years, we bring up your name and case."[56]

On May 7, five days after the capture of Karpis, the FBI arrested Harry Campbell in a dawn raid at Toledo.[57] He was the last member of the Barker-Karpis gang still at large.

Six hours later the FBI picked up William Dainard (also known as William Mahan) in San Francisco. He was charged with the May 24, 1935, kidnapping of nine-year-old George Weyerhaeuser, heir to a large timber fortune, in Tacoma, Washington. George had been released after eight days in captivity, when his parents paid a $200,000 ransom (over $3.7 million in 2020).

On May 11 the FBI arrested Thomas H. Robinson Jr. in Glendale, California, for the October 10, 1934, kidnapping of Louisville socialite Alice Speed Stoll, twenty-six. After six days of captivity and payment of a $50,000 ransom (over $950,000 in 2020), Stoll had been freed by Robinson's wife, but Robinson remained at liberty for nineteen months. He was the last major target of the War against Kidnappers still sought by the FBI.

Campbell, Dainard, and Robinson were all convicted of kidnapping and sent to Alcatraz.

It was a spectacular ten days for Hoover and the FBI. Congratulatory letters poured into Washington from grateful citizens, including John D. Rockefeller Jr., who had, along with family members, been the target of a number of kidnap plots. The country feels safer, he wrote, because "a man of your courage, determination and high technical training is at the head of the Federal Bureau of Investigation."[58]

Newspapers across the country praised the FBI's accomplishment. The G-men "have shown the difference between going out with an ancient revolver to capture a desperado armed with a machine gun, and the calculating rounding up of lawbreakers with weapons better than the outlaws have and strategy which outmatches theirs," observed one.[59]

President Roosevelt was as dazzled as anyone by Hoover's success in catching kidnappers.[60] There is every reason to believe it was that success that led the president to invite Hoover to the White House in August 1936 and direct him to begin investigating "subversive activities" of American communists and fascists, in secret and without legislative authorization. That investigation launched Hoover and the FBI on the path that would lead to some of their gravest missteps.[61]

Epilogue

Not quite three years after it started, the War against Kidnappers was over, and the snatch racket was a thing of the past. Hoover had made kidnapping the FBI's signature crime, and American families now knew where to turn if their loved ones were kidnapped. The G-men had shown they were, on the whole, up to the task. Widespread fear of ransom kidnapping had subsided and would never return, though those who lived through the dark days of the snatch racket and the terrifying kidnappings of Dee Kelley, Nell Donnelly, Charlie Lindbergh, Charles Urschel, Peggy McMath, Bill Hamm, Brooke Hart, Edward Bremer, and so many hundreds more would never forget what it was like to be afraid their children, their parents, their friends, or they themselves might be kidnapped.

The lack of reliable kidnapping statistics makes it impossible to confirm the estimate of three thousand kidnappings in 1931 that proponents of the antikidnapping legislation that became the Lindbergh Law used. Whether there were three thousand kidnappings, or some smaller or larger number, kidnapping was increasing dramatically. This was due in large part to the rise of organized crime and the lawlessness, corruption, and disrespect for law enforcement that flourished during Prohibition and that undermined confidence in government at all levels. In the interest of restoring confidence in government, the Roosevelt administration confronted the kidnap epidemic head-on and with guns blazing.

Hoover's fledgling Bureau of Investigation was inexperienced and amateurish in many respects when charged with enforcing the Lindbergh Law, but he made the most of the colossal advantage the FBI enjoyed over kidnappers and state and local law enforcement agencies alike: the ability to operate from coast to coast and border to border, in an increasingly mobile society. The FBI demonstrated that the crime-fighting resources at its command were superior to the resources available to state and local police, though mobile forces and sophisticated tools could never render local policing obsolete.

The FBI constantly improved its tools and techniques. None was more important in the War against Kidnappers than methods for efficiently and speedily tracking ransom money to the spot where it left the kidnappers' possession. Once the professional kidnappers—the instigators of the kidnap epidemic—realized they could no longer be confident they could exchange or spend ransom money without getting caught, they gave up on kidnapping as a business, and the magnitude of the threat rapidly diminished. Amateurs and petty criminals still attempted kidnappings for ransom for a while after the professionals quit, but they were no match for the FBI.

By the end of the War against Kidnappers, the once-derided Bureau of Investigation had become *the* Federal Bureau of Investigation—a major victory for Hoover, but a painful slight to the Secret Service, the U.S. Postal Inspection Service, the Special Intelligence Unit, and all other investigatory agencies of the federal government. The FBI no longer worked under the official seal and insignia of the Department of Justice. It had its own seal with its own insignia and its own motto—"Fidelity, Bravery, Integrity"—authorized by President Roosevelt. It had 623 special agents, 76 percent more than it started the war with, and its annual appropriation from Congress had grown by 113 percent, from less than $2.8 million to more than $5.9 million.[1]

When Hoover's constant critic, Tennessee senator Kenneth McKellar, member of the Senate Appropriations Committee, tried to cut $225,000 from the FBI's budget in 1936, Michigan senator Arthur Vandenberg denounced him on the Senate floor as "a miser whose parsimony would cause the threat of kidnapping to hang once more over every cradle in America."[2]

The victory over ransom kidnapping doesn't explain by itself the evolution of the FBI or the ascendancy of Hoover. With the expansion of the FBI's jurisdiction to new federal crimes in 1934, Hoover embarked on an aggressive, "take no prisoners" style of campaign against violent criminals like John Dillinger, Pretty Boy Floyd, and Baby Face Nelson that also helped define the FBI for decades to come. But that style of law enforcement was not the reason the public threw its support behind the FBI and Hoover personally. Hoover had appreciated that the public's fear of kidnapping could be leveraged into wide popular support for the FBI and for himself, for the simple reason that American families felt threatened by ransom kidnapping to a degree never approached by the threat of any other crime, at least until 9/11.

Despite its many ups and downs the American people supported with enthusiasm the effort to eradicate ransom kidnapping. They believed that Hoover's dedication and the G-men's invincibility had won the War against Kidnappers and that their families were safer because of it. With their support and the political influence that came with it, Hoover was, by 1936, the face of law enforcement in America. He would ultimately serve as director of the FBI for forty-eight years, until his death on May 2, 1972—thirty-six years longer than any other FBI director in history.

The Survivors

Two years after she and George Blair were kidnapped outside her home in Kansas City, Nell Donnelly married Senator Jim

Reed. As head of the Donnelly Garment Company, she continued to design and manufacture the stylish "Nelly Don" fashions coveted by millions of American women. She was just as innovative in providing benefits to the company's employees—life and health insurance, a pension plan, tuition assistance for employees attending college, and a scholarship fund for their children.[3] Nell died in 1991 at the age of 102. Her home, site of the kidnappings, is now the National Museum of Toys and Miniatures.

Charles and Berenice Urschel moved to San Antonio in 1945, where they continued their active philanthropy. Through confidential arrangements made by trial judge Edgar Vaught, Urschel anonymously paid all fees and expenses for Kathryn Kelly's daughter Pauline Fry, who was fourteen when Kathryn went to prison, to attend college.[4] He died in 1970 at the age of eighty, four months after Berenice's death. He never divulged his gift to Pauline.

Eleven-year-old James DeJute Jr., kidnapped the morning after Charlie Lindbergh was kidnapped, was rescued by police acting on an informant's tip. He had spent four days concealed behind a false wall in a deserted farmhouse. He was still wearing the Lindbergh cap and goggles he had been wearing when he was abducted. Jimmy graduated from Kent State University and received a medical degree from the University of Buffalo. He served in the Korean War, practiced medicine in Toledo, Ohio, and died in 1989 at the age of sixty-eight.

Peggy McMath graduated from Vassar College and joined the navy as a meteorologist's mate during World War II. Speaking out for the first time about her kidnapping experience seventy-seven years later, Peg McMath Herring said she didn't recall having been afraid and didn't believe the experience had changed her very much, though "it certainly changed the family. Mother and dad became very protective. And mother hated the press; she wouldn't let the press anywhere near me."[5] Peg's daughter, Frances Herring Rich, recalled that when she was growing up, "my mother could never let me out of her sight. She never ever got over it—just pretended that she had a happy childhood and that was it."[6] Peg died in 2014 at the age of ninety-one.

Nine-year-old George Weyerhaeuser Jr. was kidnapped on his way home from school in Tacoma, Washington, in 1935. One of his kidnappers, William Dainard, was the next to last high-profile kidnapper the FBI arrested at the end of the War against Kidnappers in May 1936. For eight days his kidnappers had hidden George in holes dug in the ground and in the trunk of a car. After his parents paid a $200,000 ransom, the kidnappers left him alone in a deserted shack in the middle of the night. George got away and walked to a nearby farmhouse. He identified himself to the couple in the house, and they fed him and drove him home. George went on to graduate from Yale University with honors, serve in the navy in World War II, and become chairman of the Weyerhaeuser Company, one of the world's largest forest products companies. "A 9-year-old boy is a pretty adaptable organism," he said of the kidnapping in later life. "He can adjust himself to conditions in a way no adult could. It didn't affect me personally as much as anyone looking back on it might think. But a family—I think a kidnapping is one of the worst things that can happen to a family."[7]

Kidnappers and Accomplices

Joseph "Legs" Laman, whose System stoked America's ransom kidnapping epidemic, helped put sixteen of his fellow gang members in prison by testifying about their participation in notorious Detroit-area kidnappings. For his cooperation, the governor of Michigan commuted his sentence. After his release from prison Laman went to work for Harry Bennett, head of Ford Motor Company's Service Department, the three-thousand-man private police force that protected Henry Ford and his children and grandchildren, enforced the company's workplace rules, and provided muscle in opposition to union organizing activities.[8]

Machine Gun Kelly was one of the small handful of gangsters always mentioned by name as examples of why Alcatraz was necessary. As a prisoner on the Rock, he was congenial and quiet; he spent much of his free time reading and playing dominoes and bridge. Kelly died at Leavenworth penitentiary in 1954, at the age of fifty-nine.

Kelly's partner Albert Bates spent much of his time in his early years at Alcatraz being interviewed by FBI agents about the whereabouts of his share of the unrecovered portion of the Urschel ransom money. His wife, Clara Feldman, pleaded guilty in 1934 to conspiracy for receiving $90,000 of ransom money from Bates. She led Charles Urschel and officials to the Oregon burial site of six jars full of ransom money and directed them to places where ransom money was stashed in California and Washington. For her cooperation in recovering about $44,000 of the ransom money, her five-year sentence was suspended. About $60,000 of the Urschel money was never recovered.[9] Bates died at Alcatraz in 1948 at the age of fifty-four.

Harvey Bailey spent twenty-eight years in federal custody, twelve of them at Alcatraz, for the Urschel kidnapping. He was released on parole in 1965, at the age of seventy-six. It had been almost a decade since Urschel, trial judge Edgar Vaught, and prosecutor Herbert Hyde all supported his first application for parole. Hyde wrote to the Board of Parole that Bailey had had nothing to do with the kidnapping.[10] Bailey died in 1979 at the age of ninety-one.

Doc Barker arrived at Alcatraz in October 1935 to serve a life sentence for the kidnapping of Edward Bremer. On January 12, 1939, under the cover of heavy fog, he and four other inmates escaped from the cell house and made their way out into San Francisco Bay before the tide swept them back onto the island. A guard standing on the cliff above the shore shot Doc and another escapee with a submachine gun; the others surrendered. Doc died the following day from a bullet wound to the head.

Alvin Karpis went to Alcatraz in August 1936 for the kidnapping of William Hamm. Depending on who was evaluating his behavior, he was either a good worker or an evil influence, a respected leader or unpopular with the other inmates.[11] In 1958 he was transferred to Leavenworth; seven months later he was shipped back to Alcatraz as an "instigator" and a "menace." He remained at the Rock until 1962—twenty-six years in all, longer than any other inmate in Alcatraz history. He was next sent to the federal prison at McNeil Island, Washington, where he lived in "model prisoner" housing off the prison grounds; one of his jobs was conducting prison tours for visitors.[12] In 1969, over the objection of J. Edgar Hoover, Karpis was released on parole and deported to his native Canada. According to his nephew Albert Grooms, while Karpis was on the run from the FBI and postal inspectors, he had arranged for relatives to deposit what was left of his ransom and robbery proceeds in savings accounts in several banks in the Midwest. After Karpis's release from prison, Grooms took a large check to him in Canada—or so he claimed. Karpis moved to Torremolinos on the Costa del Sol in Spain, where he died in 1979 at the age of seventy-two.[13]

The St. Paul Police Department dismissed detective "Big Tom" Brown in 1936 for conspiring with the Barker-Karpis gang and their accomplices to kidnap William Hamm and Edward Bremer and for tipping them off during those investigations. He lost his appeal of the dismissal, but criminal charges were never brought against him.

Nellie Muench was tried in 1935 for her part in fingering Dr. Dee Kelley for his kidnappers. Nellie won a change of venue and went to trial in Mexico, Missouri, where her father had preached for forty years. Her brother, the Missouri Supreme Court justice, sat beside her during the trial; twenty-two of his fellow members of the Missouri bar provided free legal services for her. She was acquitted, but her legal problems were only beginning. In an effort to win the sympathy of jurors, the forty-four-year-old Nellie, childless after twenty-three years of marriage, had conspired with her scofflaw lawyer in an elaborate hoax pretending to give birth to a "gift of God" child just before her trial. In reality she had paid an unwed teenager fifty dollars for her newborn son, but the child soon died of natural causes. Nellie's lawyer then found her another newborn and tricked the baby's nineteen-year-old mother into parting with the child temporarily. Reading about Nellie's trial in the newspapers, the mother realized that Nellie's "gift of God" was her own child, and she went to court to get him back. This time Nellie was convicted of mail fraud and extortion (she had also tricked a physician colleague of her husband's into believing he was the father of her baby to extort money from him) and was sentenced to ten years in prison. Her husband, Dr. Ludwig Muench, was sentenced to eight years in prison for signing the false birth certificate stating that he had delivered Nellie's "gift of God" baby. After his release from prison Ludwig divorced Nellie, got his medical license reinstated, and resumed practicing medicine before his death in 1967. Nellie was released on parole in 1944. She remarried, went into the real estate business in Kansas City, and declared bankruptcy (again) in 1962. She died twenty years later at the age of ninety-one.

Government and Law Enforcement

Attorney General Cummings authored President Roosevelt's ill-fated "court-packing" plan in 1937, to enable the president to add new Supreme Court justices more favorably disposed toward his New Deal programs. In the face of strong, bipartisan opposition, the proposal was abandoned; Cummings's standing with the president never recovered. He resigned in 1939 and returned to practicing law. He died in 1956 at the age of eighty-six.

Cummings's successor, Attorney General Frank Murphy, had an entirely different view of Alcatraz than Cummings. After touring the prison in 1939, Murphy called it "sinister and vicious" and a "place of horror."[14] "The whole psychology of Alcatraz seems bad," he said, and tends to make inmates more "stir crazy" than at other facilities.[15] Attorney General Robert F. Kennedy finally ordered the closure of Alcatraz in 1962.

Frank Wilson became chief of the U.S. Secret Service in 1936, a post he held until his retirement in 1947. He died in 1970 at the age of eighty-three.

Elmer Irey became chief coordinator of all six enforcement agencies of the Treasury Department in 1937. In addition to the Special Intelligence Unit he had headed since 1919, he took charge of the Secret Service, the U.S. Customs Service, the Bureau of Narcotics, the Alcohol Tax Unit, and the U.S. Coast Guard Intelligence Service. At his death in 1948 it was reported that 64 percent of all peacetime criminals then in federal prisons were there on account of Irey and his "T-men."[16]

Assistant Attorney General Joseph B. Keenan became the chief prosecutor for the International Military Tribunal for the Far East in 1945. Known as the "Tokyo War Crimes Tribunal," it prosecuted Japanese leaders for war crimes after World War II.

The day after Bruno Richard Hauptmann was convicted, Colonel Norman Schwarzkopf Sr. unwittingly handed critics of the verdict another argument. Speaking to the press, he said, "There is nothing I wouldn't do for Colonel Lindbergh—there is no oath that I wouldn't break if it would materially help his well-being. There is not a single man in my outfit who would not lay down his life for Colonel Lindbergh."[17] When his third term as superintendent of the New Jersey State Police expired in 1936, Governor Harold G. Hoffman did not reappoint him, citing Schwarzkopf's failure to cooperate fully with Hoffman's personal reinvestigation of the Lindbergh case, which he called "the most bungled [investigation] in police history."[18] Schwarzkopf returned to active duty with the army in World War II and commanded a mission to Iran to train its national police force in 1942, for which he was awarded the Distinguished Service Medal. Before retiring as a major general in 1953, he returned to Iran in connection with the UK- and U.S.-backed coup that deposed the elected prime minister, Mohammad Mosaddegh, and put the exiled monarch Mohammad Reza Shah in power. Schwarzkopf died in 1958, thirty-two years before his son, General Norman Schwarzkopf Jr., commanded the Allied forces in the Gulf War.

Morris "Mickey" Rosner, Charles Lindbergh's emissary to the underworld, was appointed chief of police of Long Beach, New York, in September 1934. He was forced to resign for unspecified reasons in January 1936.

The Lindberghs

Anne and Charles Lindbergh had five children after Charlie's death. Jon (b. 1932) became an underwater diver and U.S. Navy demolition expert. Land (b. 1937) became a rancher in Montana. Anne (b. 1940) became an author of children's books. Scott (b. 1942) moved to France, where he and his wife operated a primate center. Reeve (b. 1945) became an author and teacher.

Anne won the National Book Award for Most Distinguished General Nonfiction in 1935, the first awarded, for *North to the Orient*, her account of her 1931 flight to the Orient with Charles via the Great Circle Route. She won the same award again in 1938 for *Listen! The Wind*, an account of their flight over the Atlantic from Africa to South America in 1933. She continued to write and publish and died in 2001 at the age of ninety-four.

The perfusion pump Charles developed in collaboration with Dr. Alexis Carrel performed well in perfusing animal organs and made a significant contribution to the future development of perfusion systems that made transplantation of human organs possible. Charles opposed American intervention into World War II on isolationist grounds and because he believed the United States was unprepared to meet the challenge of German air superiority. He became a spokesperson for the America First Committee in 1940. When Japan bombed Pearl Harbor in December 1941, he supported the United States' entry into the war and tried to serve on active duty as a pilot, but his request for reinstatement of his commission was denied by order of President Roosevelt on account of his opposition to American intervention in the war before Pearl

Harbor. Instead Lindbergh tested planes and trained pilots to maneuver aircraft during combat as a consultant to manufacturers of military aircraft. In 1944 the forty-two-year-old Lindbergh persuaded United Aircraft and the U.S. Marines to allow him to go to the South Pacific to train combat pilots. There he flew fifty combat missions as a civilian.[19] In 1954 he won the Pulitzer Prize for *The Spirit of St. Louis*, his most detailed account of the flight to Paris. He died of cancer in 1974 at the age of seventy-two. In 2003 it was revealed that Lindbergh had been involved in secret, long-term relationships with two women in Germany and one in Switzerland, with whom he had a total of seven children born between 1958 and 1967.

ACKNOWLEDGMENTS

Many people have helped me along the way to this book. Without the benefit of their knowledge, experience, support, and encouragement, it would not have happened.

I am indebted to the many individuals and agencies that facilitated my access to the government records that enabled me to tell the story of *The Snatch Racket*. I thank the FBI's Freedom of Information and Privacy Act staff in Winchester, Virginia, for responding to my numerous FOIA/PA requests and the staff of the National Archives and Records Administration in College Park, Maryland, for making the actual records available. Broad public access to government records is vital to democracy; it must be secured, expanded, and adequately funded.

Thanks to the reference librarians at public libraries and universities across the country, too many to mention individually, who enthusiastically and promptly responded to my many requests. They found not only what I was looking for but usually went beyond my request and searched for additional useful information.

Mark Falzini, archivist of the New Jersey State Police Museum, gave generously of his time and knowledge as I delved ever deeper into the Lindbergh kidnapping investigation. His considerable scholarship and encyclopedic knowledge of the museum's Lindbergh collection are extraordinary. Thank you, Mark.

Thanks to Wyatt Bouma, who sifted through boxes of original papers at the University of Wyoming on a very tight schedule.

My long-time law partner and good friend John Harwood read very early pieces of the book and graciously introduced me to literary agents Peter and Amy Bernstein. Peter and Amy believed in the book from the beginning, found a good home for it, and guided me through the publishing process. I am deeply grateful for all their efforts and support.

Many thanks to the dedicated, professional team at Potomac Books and the University of Nebraska Press. Special thanks to copyeditor Vicki Low, whose careful, thoughtful efforts greatly improved the book.

Many friends and family members have shared their own memories of kidnap stories and have otherwise by their interest and discussions helped me better understand—and hopefully better tell—my story. I am especially grateful to Ann and Chris Colmo, David Perkins, John and Ingola Hodges, Abby Stoll, Joel Rosenberg, Michael Grosso, and Thomas Traill.

I am so fortunate to have a family that has always supported me and taken an interest in everything I do. To Frank and Anita Cox, Marion Cox and Dave Oboler, and Charlie Cox and Tal Howell, your love and kindness all my life have been a source of strength and an inspiration. To Leni Perkins, Will Perkins and Stephanie Hodges, and Ingola, Philip, and Flora Perkins, thank you for putting up with me during the book years and for enriching my life beyond anything I could have imagined.

All along the way, Sam has been with me: reading countless drafts, gently suggesting ways to improve the telling of the story or the structure of a sentence, helping hunt through old files for photographs and documents, and patiently providing the IT skills I've never mastered. Thank you for everything.

NOTES

Prologue

1. "Cass Relates Giving Ransom," *Detroit Free Press*, October 2, 1929.

2. "Detroit Police Smash Kidnap Ring Whose Crimes Terrorize City," *Alton Evening Telegraph*, December 20, 1929.

3. Kavieff, *Violent Years*, 83.

4. Scott Burnstein, "Prohibition & the Detroit Underworld," *Gangster Report*, July 2, 2014, https://gangsterreport.com/prohibition-the-detroit-underworld/.

5. Burnstein, "Prohibition & the Detroit Underworld."

1. The Good Samaritans

1. "Dr. Kelley's Story of Experience in Kidnapers' Hands," *St. Louis Post-Dispatch*, April 28, 1931. In the 1920s and early 1930s the word *kidnaper* was spelled either with one *p* or two *p*'s. The same was true for *kidnaping* and *kidnaped*. By the mid-1930s, the single-*p* spelling rarely appeared. For simplicity, the later, now more familiar double-*p* spelling is used hereinafter in all quotations and citations.

2. "Eyewitness Says Captors Seized Physician in Davis Place," *St. Louis Post-Dispatch*, April 22, 1931.

3. "Dr. Kelley's Story."

4. "Dr. Kelley on Cross-Examination Identifies McDonald Fourth Time," *St. Louis Post-Dispatch*, January 26, 1935.

5. "Police Captain Tells of Kelley Kidnapping Inquiry," *St. Louis Post-Dispatch*, August 21, 1934.

6. "Dr. Kelley's Story."

7. "Dr. Kelley's Story."

8. Stevens, *Centennial History of Missouri*, https://accessgenealogy.com/missouri/biography-of-ludwig-o-muench-m-d.htm.

9. Florence Shinkle, "'The Strangest Personality' of a St. Louis Era," *St. Louis Post-Dispatch*, January 23, 1983.

10. Kirschten, *Catfish and Crystal*, 380–81.

11. Shinkle, "'The Strangest Personality.'"

12. "Mrs. Kelley's Testimony; Says Mrs. Muench Asked Her about Doctor's Night Calls," *St. Louis Post-Dispatch*, September 29, 1934.

13. "Every Effort Will Be Made for Doctor's Safe Return," *St. Louis Post-Dispatch*, April 22, 1931; "Family Has No Word Yet of Kidnapped Dr. Kelley," *St. Louis Post-Dispatch*, April 23, 1931.

14. "Dr. Kelley Spends 3 Hours Telling Story to Police," *St. Louis Post-Dispatch*, May 2, 1931.

15. "Details of Yesterday's Testimony; Newspaper Men Questioned about Dr. Kelley's Return from Captivity," *St. Louis Post-Dispatch*, October 2, 1934.

16. "Attorney Tells of His Service in Dr. Kelley Case," *St. Louis Post-Dispatch*, May 6, 1931.

17. "Dr. Kelley Ends Testimony Naming Davit as Third Kidnapper He Recognized," *St. Louis Post-Dispatch*, September 30, 1934.

18. "Interesting Incidents in the Career of John T. Rogers, Reporter; Many Testimonials to His Public Service," *St. Louis Post-Dispatch*, March 4, 1937.

19. "Lawyer Hired by Family of St. L. Physician," *Daily Free Press* (Carbondale IL) (AP), May 6, 1931.

20. John T. Rogers, "John T. Rogers Tells How He Followed Orders and Found Dr. Kelley," *St. Louis Post-Dispatch*, April 28, 1931.

21. "Details of Yesterday's Testimony."

22. Rogers, "John T. Rogers Tells How He Followed Orders."

23. "Dr. Kelley Unable to Explain Release," *New York Times*, April 30, 1931.

24. "Interesting Incidents."

25. "Attorney Tells of His Service."

26. "Not a Dime Paid in Ransom, Says W.D. Orthwein II," *St. Louis Post-Dispatch*, April 28, 1931.

27. "Police Wonder Why P-D Man Didn't Tell of His Rendezvous," *St. Louis Star and Times*, May 4, 1931.

28. "Fighting in the Dark," *St. Louis Star and Times*, May 7, 1931.

29. Pfaff, *Joseph Pulitzer II*, 158; "Dr. Kelley Spends 3 Hours Telling Story."

30. "$18,000 'Legal Fees' Paid by Kelley Family," *St. Louis Star and Times*, September 4, 1934.

31. "Interesting Incidents"; "Ira Wilzer Says He Was Caller Several Times a Day at Home," *St. Louis Post-Dispatch*, October 3, 1935.

32. "Fights Off Two Thugs Who Try to Kidnap Him," *New York Times*, August 4, 1931.

33. "Adolph Fiedler Names Eight Men and Woman as Kidnappers of Dr. Kelley," *St. Louis Post-Dispatch*, February 7, 1934.

34. "Indicted Negro's Confession Had Been Kept Secret," *St. Louis Post-Dispatch*, May 13, 1934; "Kidnap Confessor Slain," *New York Times*, May 13, 1934.

2. *"This . . . Is Not Manchuria"*

1. "Kidnappers Have Taken Heavy Toll in Middlewest in Recent Months," *St. Louis Star and Times*, May 8, 1931.

2. "St. Louis' Contribution to Chicago Crime," *Chicago Tribune*, May 5, 1931.

3. "Driver of Blue Auto Is Sought in Johnson Case," *St. Louis Star and Times*, August 5, 1931.

4. "How Kidnapping Is Being Fought in Kansas City," *St. Louis Star and Times*, May 5, 1931.

5. Hernon and Ganey, *Under the Influence*, 159.

6. "Busch, Sr., in Constant Fear of Abduction," *Belvedere Daily Republican*, December 5, 1932.

7. Kirkendall, *History of Missouri*, 43.

8. "Agency Formed Here to Combat Kidnapping Quits," *St. Louis Post-Dispatch*, August 4, 1934.

9. "How Kidnapping Is Being Fought in Kansas City."

10. "Bunsen Picked to Head Drive against Gangs," *Southeast Missourian*, July 2, 1931.

11. "Secret Six (Chicago)," Wikipedia, https://en.wikipedia.org/wiki/Secret _Six_(Chicago).

12. "Racketeer Bill Offered to Congress," *Tampa Times* (AP), December 1, 1930.

13. "Arthur J. Freund Agitating for U.S. Law on Kidnapping," *St. Louis Star and Times*, December 31, 1931.

14. "Nell Reed, Women's Clothing Pioneer," *Chicago Tribune*, September 12, 1991.

15. Larsen and Hulston, *Pendergast!*, 34.

16. Oswald Garrison Villard, "James A. Reed," *Nation*, March 28, 1928, 343, quoted in Pomerantz, *Devil's Tickets*, 73.

17. McMillen and Roberson, *Called to Courage*, 110.

18. McCullough, *Truman*, 200.

19. Pomerantz, *Devil's Tickets*, 206.

20. "Counter Kidnap 'Plot' Revealed," *Detroit Free Press* (AP), December 21, 1931.

21. "Free Mrs. Donnelly without a Ransom," *New York Times*, December 19, 1931.

22. "K.C. Woman Is Released, No Ransom to Kidnapper," *Jefferson City Post-Tribune*, December 18, 1931.

23. "Participants in K.C. Kidnapping under Arrest," *Jefferson City Post-Tribune* (AP), December 22, 1931; "Two Confess Aiding Donnelly Abduction," *New York Times* (AP), December 23, 1931.

24. "Plot to Kidnap General Dawes Reported Today," *Dixon Evening Telegraph*, January 23, 1932.

25. William K. Hutchinson, "Dawes 'Plot' Spurs Action by Congress," *Coshocton Tribune* (INS), January 24, 1932.

26. "'Plot' to Kidnap Him Amuses Gen. Dawes," *New York Times*, January 24, 1932; Hutchinson, "Dawes 'Plot' Spurs Action by Congress."

27. "Congressmen Are Told of St. Louis Kidnapping Menace," *St. Louis Star and Times*, February 25, 1932; "St. Louisans Urge Approval of U.S. Kidnapper Bills," *St. Louis Post-Dispatch*, February 25, 1932.

28. "Headhunters Bare Crime Tales," *Cincinnati Enquirer*, February 26, 1932; "Ace Detective Describes New Kidnap Racket," *Jacksonville Daily Journal*, February 27, 1932.

29. "Kidnapping Ring's Tortures Bared at House Probe," *Morning News* (Wilmington DE), February 27, 1932.

30. "Congressmen Are Told of St. Louis Kidnapping Menace."

31. Raymond P. Brandt, "Police Chief Gerk Asks for Federal Kidnapping Law," *St. Louis Post-Dispatch*, February 26, 1932.

32. "Ohio Second in Total of Kidnappings," *Cincinnati Enquirer*, January 27, 1932.

33. Based on a total population of 124 million and a murder rate of 10.7 per year per 100,000 population. *Statistical Abstract of the United States 1931*, https://www2 .census.gov/library/publications/1933/compendia/statab/55ed/1933-02.pdf?#; National Center for Health Statistics, Vital Statistics, https://www2.census.gov /library/publications/1933/compendia/statab/55ed/1933-03.pdf?#.

34. "Committee Acts to Curb Kidnapping," *Boston Globe*, March 2, 1932.

3. *The Snatch of the Eaglet*

1. Dr. Carrel won the Nobel Prize in Physiology or Medicine in 1912 for his pioneering work in developing techniques of vascular suturing and grafting. His later work concentrated on human organ transplantation and eugenics, which would also become a field of great interest to Lindbergh.

2. Fisher, *Lindbergh Case*, 7, 431.

3. The Bureau of Investigation was renamed the United States Bureau of Investigation on July 1, 1932; then the Division of Investigation on June 10, 1933; and, finally, the Federal Bureau of Investigation on July 1, 1935. For simplicity, unless the context otherwise requires, "FBI" is used throughout to refer to the same organization.

4. R. L. Duffus, "Kidnapping: A Rising Menace to the Nation," *New York Times*, March 6, 1932.

5. Thomas Payone, "Stories from Inside the *Spirit of St. Louis*," Smithsonian National Air and Space Museum website, November 8, 2016, https://airandspace.si.edu/stories /editorial/stories-inside-spirit-st-louis.

6. Kauffman, *Pan Am Pioneer*, 196.

7. Yagoda, *Will Rogers*, 250.

8. Smallwood, *Will Rogers' Daily Telegrams*, 90.

9. Berg, *Lindbergh*, 146.

10. "Brussels Burghers Honor Lindbergh," *New York Times* (AP), May 30, 1927.

11. "Brussels Burghers."

12. Mosley, *Lindbergh*, 116, 406.

13. Berg, *Lindbergh*, 149.

14. "Lindbergh Leaves Brussels in Flight to Croydon, England," *St. Louis Globe-Democrat* (AP), May 30, 1927.

15. Berg, *Lindbergh*, 167, 170.

16. Jennings and Brewster, *Century*, 137.

17. "The Birth of Commercial Aviation," *Birth of Aviation*, December 12, 2014, www.birthofaviation.org/birth-of-commercial-aviation.

18. C. A. Lindbergh, *Autobiography of Values*, 310.

19. C. A. Lindbergh, *Autobiography of Values*, 123.

20. A. M. Lindbergh to Elizabeth Cutter Morrow, letter, October 13, 1929, in A. M. Lindbergh, *Hour of Gold*, 103, 104.

21. Heywood Broun, "It Seems to Me," *Pittsburgh Press*, June 30, 1930.

22. "Is Lindbergh Still Famous?" *St. Louis Post-Dispatch*, November 22, 1930.

23. Scaduto, *Scapegoat*, 34.

24. Vitray, *Great Lindbergh Hullabaloo*, 21.

25. Whipple, *Lindbergh Crime*, 17.

26. Cahill, *Hauptmann's Ladder*, 14.

27. "Abductor Is Trailed 2 Miles by Trappers," *New York Times*, March 3, 1932.

28. "Vigilantes to Fight Kidnappers Hinted," *Morning Post* (INS), March 3, 1932.

29. "Entire City Force Hunts Kidnappers," *New York Times*, March 3, 1932.

30. "100,000 in the Man Hunt," *New York Times*, March 3, 1932.

31. A. M. Lindbergh to Evangeline Lodge Land Lindbergh ("E.L.L.L."), letter, March 5, 1932, in A. M. Lindbergh, *Hour of Gold*, 229.

32. A. M. Lindbergh to E.L.L.L., letter, March 2, 1932, in A. M. Lindbergh, *Hour of Gold*, 224.

33. A. M. Lindbergh to E.L.L.L., letter, March 3, 1932, in A. M. Lindbergh, *Hour of Gold*, 227.

34. A. M. Lindbergh to E.L.L.L., March 5, 1932.

35. "Noted Pilots Take to Air in Search," *New York Times*, March 3, 1932.

36. "Sleepless Father Persists in Search," *New York Times*, March 3, 1932.

37. Cpl. Joseph A. Wolf, NJSP, major initial report, March 1, 1932, New Jersey State Police Museum.

38. Whipple, *Lindbergh Crime*, 18.

39. "Demand Ransom for Lindy Baby; Niles Schoolboy Is Kidnapped; Contractor's Son Driven Off in Auto," *East Liverpool Review* (AP), March 2, 1932; "DeJute Boy Found Concealed in Wall," *New York Times*, March 6, 1932.

4. The Colonel's Mission

1. Berg, *Lindbergh*, 240–41.

2. Milton, *Loss of Eden*, 215; Falzini, *Their Fifteen Minutes*, 69.

3. "Henry Breckinridge Youngest of Men Now in High Places," *Washington Herald*, November 23, 1913.

4. Falzini, *Their Fifteen Minutes*, 72.

5. C. A. Lindbergh, *Autobiography of Values*, 97.

6. "Thomas Lanphier, Aviation Pioneer; Colonel Who Helped Chart First Passenger Route Dies," *New York Times*, October 10, 1972.

7. "Lindy Pledges Safety of Kidnappers for Baby," *New York Daily News*, March 5, 1932.

8. "Lindy Pledges Safety."

9. "Failure of Police Arouses Lindbergh to Ask Withdrawal," *Philadelphia Inquirer*, March 6, 1932.

10. Memorandum re telephone call to Mr. Keith, March 4, 1932, FBI File #62-26664-67.

11. Memorandum re telephone conversation with Mr. Connelley, March 4, 1932, FBI File #62-26664-73.

12. "J. Edgar Hoover's Career," *New York Times*, March 5, 1932.

13. "Wire Tapping by Dry Agents to Be Probed," *Pittsburgh Post-Gazette*, January 16, 1931.

14. J. Edgar Hoover to Files, memorandum, March 9, 1932, FBI File #62-26664-108.

15. "Police Heads Meet with Moore Today," *New York Times*, March 5, 1932.

16. Colonel Schwarzkopf was the father of General H. Norman Schwarzkopf Jr. ("Stormin' Norman"), the commander-in-chief of the U.S. Central Command and leader of coalition forces in the 1990–91 Gulf War. General Schwarzkopf Jr. was born in Trenton, New Jersey, on August 22, 1934, during the Lindbergh investigation.

17. "Police of East Confer," *New York Times*, March 6, 1932.

18. "Failure of Police."

19. H. I. Phillips, "The Once Over," *Philadelphia Inquirer*, March 17, 1932.

20. J. Edgar Hoover, marginalia, March 17, 1932, on copy of Phillips, "The Once Over."

21. "New Jersey State Police: History," New Jersey State Police website, http/njsp .org/about/history/index.shtml.

22. "An Opportunity to Serve," *Trenton Evening Times*, June 9, 1921.

23. Falzini, *Siege at Jutland*, 126n28, quoting Leo Coakley, *Jersey Troopers: A Fifty Year History of the New Jersey State Police* (New Brunswick NJ: Rutgers University Press, 1971), 46–47.

24. "Governor Edwards Demands Arrest of Hall Murderer," *New York Times*, October 8, 1922.

25. "Arrest of Youth Fails to Halt Hunt for Hall's Slayer," *New York Times*, October 11, 1922; "The New Brunswick Mystery," *New York Times*, October 11, 1922.

26. "Dickman Tells Jury of $2,500 Bribe from Beekman to Quit Hall Case," *New York Times*, November 7, 1926.

27. Peter Levins, "When Justice Triumphed: The 'Siege of Jutland' Added No Lustre to Jersey State Troopers," *Atlanta Constitution*, June 12, 1932.

28. "Killing in New Jersey Siege Defended," *Brooklyn Daily Eagle*, December 27, 1926.

29. "Another Battle of Jutland," *New York Times*, December 24, 1926.

30. "Disciplining a State Police," *New York Times*, February 1, 1927.

31. Levins, "When Justice Triumphed."

32. Memorandum re telephone call to Mr. Connelley, March 2, 1932, FBI File #62-26664.

33. Memorandum re telephone call from Keith, March 4, 1932.

34. Memorandum re telephone call to Connelley, March 4, 1932.

35. Joseph Kraft, "FBI's Hoover—'Larger than Life,'" *Star Tribune*, November 24, 1966.

5. Lifting the Veil

1. "Prove Immunity and Get Baby, Lindbergh Told on Phone," *New York Daily News*, March 11, 1932.

2. Robert Thayer, statement, March 3, 1932, Robert Helyer Thayer Papers, Manuscript Division, Library of Congress, Washington DC, Box 7; Fensch, *FBI Files*, 191.

3. Behn, *Lindbergh*, 82.

4. Westbrook Pegler, "Fair Enough," *Bridgeport Post*, October 30, 1947.

5. "Kidnap Trail Now in Detroit," *Minneapolis Star*, March 11, 1932.

6. Fensch, *FBI Files*, 188.

7. "Kidnappers Still Fear Trap," *New York Daily News*, March 11, 1932.

8. Behn, *Lindbergh*, 83.

9. Fensch, *FBI Files*, 193.

10. Morris Rosner, unpublished memoir, April 1932, New Jersey State Police Museum, 6.

11. Rosner, memoir, 1.

12. Okrent, *Last Call*, 273; "Owen Vincent Madden (1891–1965)," *Encyclopedia of Arkansas History and Culture*, http://encyclopediaofarkansas.net/Owen-Vincent-Madden-1702.

13. Coll was gunned down in a telephone booth while talking with Owney Madden in February 1932, less than a month before Charlie Lindbergh's kidnapping. Though Coll's assassins were never charged, Madden was a prime suspect.

14. Gardner, *Case That Never Dies*, 38.

15. Fensch, *FBI Files*, 189.

16. "Spitale Vanishes on Secret Mission," *New York Times*, March 7, 1932.

17. Rosner, memoir, 12.

18. "Text of Announcement Made by the Lindberghs Authorizing Negotiations with the Abductors," *New York Times*, March 6, 1932.

19. Letter to President Hoover, March 7, 1932, A1-COR 109, NARA File #109 Sub I, Department of Justice Files.

20. A. M. Lindbergh to E.L.L.L., March 5, 1932.

21. A. M. Lindbergh to E.L.L.L., March 6, 1932, in Lindbergh, *Hour of Gold*, 229, 230.

22. "Hatchet Buried by Underworld to Help Lindy," *Greenville News*, May 20, 1932.

23. "Hunt for Baby Ends Gang War," *Arizona Daily Star*, May 20, 1932.

24. Katz, *Uncle Frank*, 76, 255.

25. "Capone Offers $10,000 Reward for Kidnappers," *Richmond Item*, March 3, 1932.

26. Frank Wilson, report to Elmer Irey, November 11, 1933, FBI File #62-3057-29.

27. Irey, *Tax Dodgers*, 68.

28. Irey, *Tax Dodgers*, 68.

29. Irey, *Tax Dodgers*, 69.

30. Irey, *Tax Dodgers*, 67.

31. "Offered Capone Aid in Lindbergh Search," *New York Times*, February 25, 1935.

32. "Lindbergh Reward of $25,000 Voted," *New York Times*, May 24, 1932.

33. Fensch, FBI *Files*, 384–88.

34. "Capone Would Aid Hunt," *New York Times*, March 11, 1932.

35. Gus T. Jones to Director, memorandum, March 17, 1932, FBI File #62-26664-396.

36. "Ralph Capone Ordered Taken to Distant Prison," *Milwaukee Journal*, December 2, 1931.

37. Jones to Director, March 17, 1932.

38. Jones to Director, March 17, 1932.

39. Gus T. Jones to Director, telegram, March 15, 1932, FBI File #62-26664-331.

40. J. Edgar Hoover to File, memorandum, March 14, 1932, FBI File #62-26664-384.

41. Hoover to File, March 14, 1932.

42. E. J. Connelley to File, memorandum, June 3, 1932, FBI File #62-3057-19-51.

43. Wilson, report, November 11, 1933.

44. Connelley to File, June 3, 1932.

45. J. M. Keith to Director, memorandum, April 6, 1932, FBI File #62-3057-19-17.

46. "Capone Aid Weighed," *Los Angeles Times*, April 26, 1932.

47. Rudensky, *Gonif*, 56.

6. "Ay, Doctor"

1. Telegram, March 3, 1932, A1-COR 109, NARA File #109 Sub I (3/2/32–3/6/32), Department of Justice Files.

2. "Says Kidnappers Have Not Talked: Urge Baby Be Returned to Mrs. Evangeline Lindbergh," *Times Herald* (Port Huron MI) (AP), March 7, 1932.

3. Waller, *Kidnap*, 30; Mark W. Falzini, "Enter: Jafsie," *Archival Ramblings*, March 1, 2010, www.njspmuseum.blogspot.com/2010/02/enter-jafsie.html.

4. Falzini, "Enter: Jafsie."

5. Condon, *Jafsie Tells All*, 20.

6. Fisher, *Ghosts of Hopewell*, 10.

7. Gardner, *Case That Never Dies*, 61.

8. Fisher, *Ghosts of Hopewell*, 11.

9. Fisher, *Lindbergh Case*, 44.

10. Mark W. Falzini, "The Ransom Notes: An Analysis of Their Content & 'Signature,'" *Archival Ramblings*, September 2008, http://njspmuseum.blogspot.com/2008/02/one-of-most-fascinating-areas-of-study.html.

11. Falzini, *Their Fifteen Minutes*, 30.

12. Irey, *Tax Dodgers*, 70; Fensch, FBI *Files*, 216.

13. Rosner, memoir, 63.

14. A. M. Lindbergh to E.L.L.L., letter, March 10, 1932, in A. M. Lindbergh, *Hour of Gold*, 232.

15. L. G. Turrou to Connelley, memorandum, April 8, 1932, FBI File #62-26664-602. Three kidnapper notes preceded Condon's entry into the case, including the Nursery Note and a March 4 note scolding Lindbergh for contacting the police and press and raising the ransom demand from $50,000 to $70,000.

16. Falzini, *Their Fifteen Minutes*, 48.

17. Condon, *Jafsie Tells All*, 87.

18. Whipple, *Trial*, Testimony of Dr. John F. Condon, 215.

19. Whipple, *Trial*, Testimony of Dr. John F. Condon, 219.

20. Doctor Denton blanket sleepers were the most popular brand of sleeping suits in the country.

21. Fisher, *Ghosts of Hopewell*, 13, 14.

22. Turrou to Connelley, April 8, 1932.

23. Fisher, *Ghosts of Hopewell*, 14–15.

24. Turrou to Connelley, April 8, 1932.

25. Irey, *Tax Dodgers*, 74.

26. Condon, *Jafsie Tells All*, 141.

27. Wilson, report, November 11, 1933.

28. Irey, *Tax Dodgers*, 74.

29. Irey, *Tax Dodgers*, 75.

30. Fensch, FBI *Files*, 340.

31. "State Forges Many New Links as Trial Proceeds Swiftly," *Boston Globe*, January 18, 1935.

32. Turrou to Connelley, April 8, 1932.

33. Fisher, *Ghosts of Hopewell*, 16.

34. Turrou to Connelley, April 8, 1932.

35. Fisher, *Ghosts of Hopewell*, 17.

36. Fisher, *Ghosts of Hopewell*, 18.

37. Condon, *Jafsie Tells All*, 146.

38. Fisher, *Ghosts of Hopewell*, 18.

39. Statement of Charles A. Lindbergh to Inspector Harry Walsh, Jersey City Police Department, May 20, 1932, files of New Jersey State Police Museum.

40. Condon, *Jafsie Tells All*, 155, 156.

41. Condon, *Jafsie Tells All*, 156.

42. Fisher, *Ghosts of Hopewell*, 20.

43. Irey, *Tax Dodgers*, 78.

44. Irey, *Tax Dodgers*, 78.

45. Irey, *Tax Dodgers*, 78.

46. Irey, *Tax Dodgers*, 79.

47. Turrou to Connelley, April 8, 1932.

48. Charles A. Lindbergh to Hon. Ogden L. Mills, letter, April 4, 1932.

49. "Fire Threatens Lindbergh Home," *Hopewell Herald*, April 6, 1932.

50. A. M. Lindbergh to E.L.L.L., letter, April 6, 1932, in A. M. Lindbergh, *Hour of Gold*, 236.

51. A. M. Lindbergh to E.L.L.L., letter, April 8, 1932, in A. M. Lindbergh, *Hour of Gold*, 237.

52. Draft statement of Charles A. Lindbergh, April 9, 1932, edits in Lindbergh's handwriting, files of New Jersey State Police Museum; Delos Smith, "Lindbergh Pays Kidnappers $50,000 But Fails to Get Back His Baby," *Minneapolis Star Tribune*

(AP), April 10, 1932; "Lindbergh Ransom Paid? Banks Are Tracing Bills," *Herald-News* (Passaic NJ), April 9, 1932.

53. "Pastors Aroused by Kidnap Trickery," *New York Times*, April 11, 1932.

54. A. M. Lindbergh, diary, May 11, 1932, in A. M. Lindbergh, *Hour of Gold*, 246.

7. Competing Investigations

1. Statement of William Allen to Inspector Harry Walsh, May 12, 1932, files of New Jersey State Police Museum.

2. Whipple, *Trial*, Testimony of Bessie Mowat Gow, 166.

3. C. A. Lindbergh, *Autobiography of Values*, 140.

4. A. M. Lindbergh to E.L.L.L., letter, May 22, 1932, in A. M. Lindbergh, *Hour of Gold*, 257.

5. A. M. Lindbergh to E.L.L.L., letter, June 10, 1932, in A. M. Lindbergh, *Hour of Gold*, 269.

6. Herbert Hoover, statement on the Lindbergh kidnapping, May 13, 1932.

7. J. Edgar Hoover to Hon. A. Harry Moore, letter, May 14, 1932, FBI File #62-26664-935.

8. Connelley to File, June 3, 1932.

9. J. M. Keith to Director, memorandum, April 6, 1932, FBI File #62-26664-612.

10. J. Edgar Hoover to Special Agent in Charge, New York, letter, April 11, 1932, FBI File #67-3052-19-19; H. Nathan to Director, memorandum, April 28, 1932, FBI File #62-2664-849.

11. Nathan to Director, April 28, 1932.

12. John E. Brennan, memorandum, May 3, 1932, FBI File #62-26664-878.

13. J. Edgar Hoover to Mr. Nathan, memorandum, May 16, 1932, FBI File #62-26664-998.

14. Hoover to Nathan, May 16, 1932.

15. E. J. Connelley to File, memorandum, May 17, 1932, FBI File #62-3057-19-36.

16. Transcript of conference regarding the Lindbergh case held in office of Colonel H. Norman Schwarzkopf, May 18, 1932, FBI File #62-3057-18-38.

17. F. X. Fay to J. Edgar Hoover, letter, May 18, 1932, FBI File #62-26664-1030.

18. Wilson, report, November 11, 1933.

19. Demaris, *Director*, 63.

20. Irey, *Tax Dodgers*, 36.

21. Spiering, *Man Who Got Capone*, 46, 47.

22. J. Edgar Hoover to Mr. Nathan, memorandum, May 24, 1932, FBI File #62-26664-1316.

23. J. Edgar Hoover to Mr. Nathan, memorandum, May 25, 1932, FBI File #62-26664-1299.

24. J. Edgar Hoover to Mr. Nathan, memorandum, June 13, 1932, FBI File #62-26664-1466.

25. "Inquiry Looms on Bungling by Jersey Police," *Brooklyn Daily Eagle*, May 13, 1932.

26. "Was Colonel Schwarzkopf's Training Equal to Handling Biggest Criminal Hunt of Age?" *Brooklyn Daily Eagle*, June 19, 1932.

27. "Inquiry Looms."

28. "Schwarzkopf Is Denounced as a Bungler," *El Paso Times* (AP), May 20, 1932.

8. Call NAtional 8-7117

1. "Girl, 10, Kidnapped in Cape Cod Town," *New York Times*, May 3, 1933.

2. Alex Kingsbury, "Kidnapped on Old Cape Cod," *Boston Globe*, August 28, 2016.

3. "Kidnap Victim Found Captivity like Nightmare," *Salt Lake Tribune* (AP), May 7, 1933; Statement of Kenneth Buck, *Syracuse American*, May 7, 1933, quoted in Jack Major, "Peggy McMath," http://major-smolinski.com/KIDNAP/MCMATH.html.

4. Kingsbury, "Kidnapped on Old Cape Cod."

5. "Buck Collapses at Kidnap Trial," *New York Times*, June 22, 1933.

6. "Girl, 10, Kidnapped."

7. "Kidnappers Urged to Answer Pleas," *New York Times*, May 5, 1933.

8. "Kidnap Hunt Spurred by Search for Fleeing Car," *Philadelphia Inquirer* (AP), May 5, 1933.

9. "Girl, 10, Kidnapped."

10. "Kidnap Hunt Spurred."

11. J. Edgar Hoover, memorandum, May 4, 1933, FBI File #7-61-7-71.

12. V. W. Hughes to Director, memorandum, May 3, 1933, FBI File #7-61-7-71.

13. "Plenty of Rope Promised for Gang," *Pittsburgh Press* (UP), May 5, 1933.

14. Kingsbury, "Kidnapped on Old Cape Cod."

15. Neil McMath to J. Edgar Hoover, letter, May 25, 1933, FBI File #7-61-7-71.

16. Annual Report of Division of Investigation for FY 1933, FBI File #66-3700, Section 2.

17. Howard P. Locke to Director, memorandum, July 20, 1933, FBI File #66-3700-63.

18. According to Police Chief Gerk's 1932 study in connection with the St. Louis proposal for federal antikidnapping legislation.

19. V. W. Hughes to Director, memorandum, June 24, 1932.

20. Turrou, *Where My Shadow Falls*, 15.

21. Theoharis, *FBI: A Comprehensive Reference Guide*, 4.

22. E. A. Tamm to Director, memorandum, October 12, 1934, FBI File #7-HQ-1128 (the "Director wants to be sure we dominate the situation. . . . The Director wants to outnumber the police on that detail; in other words, if we can't outnumber them, at least we want to have an equal number").

23. J. Edgar Hoover to Attorney General, memorandum, July 13, 1933.

9. Epidemic

1. Arthur Krock, "100,000 at Inauguration," *New York Times*, March 5, 1933.

2. Krock, "100,000 at Inauguration."

3. Franklin D. Roosevelt, "Inaugural Address," *The American Presidency Project*, University of California Santa Barbara, www.presidency.ucsb.edu/documents /inaugural-address-7.

4. Walter Lippman, "Today and Tomorrow: The National Policy," *Boston Globe*, March 11, 1933.

5. Walter Lippman, "The Second Marne," *Cincinnati Enquirer*, March 17, 1933.

6. "Will Reorganize Department," *New York Times*, March 1, 1933.

7. Lowenthal, *Federal Bureau of Investigation*, 187.

8. Lowenthal, *Federal Bureau of Investigation*, 197–98; Colyer v. Skeffington, 265 F. 17 (D.Mass. 1920).

9. Whitehead, FBI *Story*, 107.

10. Rappleye, *Herbert Hoover*, 451.

11. Black, *Franklin Delano Roosevelt*, 270.

12. Theoharis and Cox, *Boss*, 114.

13. Moley, *After Seven Years*, 274n2.

14. "Roosevelt's Search Finds Boy in Atlanta," *Atlanta Constitution*, April 25, 1933.

15. Elton C. Fay, "Government Aroused by K.C. Murder," *Ogden Standard-Examiner* (AP), June 18, 1933.

16. For example, "Roosevelt Family Guards against Kidnapping Peril: Children," *Cincinnati Enquirer* (AP), July 14, 1933.

17. "Lloyd's Is Writing Kidnap Insurance," *New York Times*, August 5, 1933.

18. Chernow, *House of Morgan*, 301.

19. "Kidnap Alarm Emits Wail if Crib Touched," *Los Angeles Times*, February 22, 1934.

20. "Lindbergh Ransom Note Chief Hope for Solution," *Pittsburgh Press*, February 1, 1934.

21. Toland, *Dillinger Days*, 59.

22. "U.S. Decrees 'Real' War on Gangsters," *Pittsburgh Press* (UP), June 23, 1933.

23. "Cummings Asks All Details," *Wilkes-Barre Record* (AP), July 14, 1933.

24. "Will Aid Cummings in War on Gangs," *New York Times*, July 4, 1933.

25. "Cummings Offers Kidnapping Advice," *New York Times*, July 14, 1933; "How to Obtain Federal Aid in Kidnapping Cases," *Chicago Tribune*, July 14, 1933.

26. "Cummings Offers Kidnapping Advice."

27. "Federal Men Organize for Kidnapper War," *Middletown Times Herald*, July 14, 1933.

28. "Roosevelt Family Guards."

29. "Grandchildren of Chief Executive under Guard: Protective Measures Are Taken as Kidnap Epidemic Spreads," *Tribune* (Coshocton OH), July 13, 1933.

30. "40 Chicagoans Guarded from Kidnappers; Hertz, Cutten and Warren Wright on List," *New York Times*, July 15, 1933.

31. "Federal Officers Active in Raids," *New York Times*, July 21, 1933.

32. Summers, *Official and Confidential*, 65.

33. Homer S. Cummings to Joseph Keenan, memorandum, August 1, 1933, Selected Papers of Homer Cummings, Library of Congress.

34. Fensch, FBI *Files*, 278.

35. L. G. Turrou to File, memorandum, October 12, 1933, FBI File #62-3057-8-55.

10. The Road to Paradise

1. "Kidnappers Hold Urschel: Mrs. Urschel's Story," *Daily Oklahoman*, July 23, 1933; R. H. Colvin, report, February 23, 1934, FBI File #7-115-1111.

2. Kirkpatrick, *Voices from Alcatraz*, 6; "Kidnappers Hold Urschel."

3. The fact that Jarrett was freed was one of several factors leading the FBI to suspect Jarrett was the finger man in the kidnapping: he and Urschel rode together in the back seat of the kidnappers' car; Jarrett's difficult financial circumstances at the time; and the Kellys' later claims that he was the finger person. The suspicions were never proved, however. Colvin, report, February 23, 1934.

4. Ellis, *Man Named Jones*, 106.

5. Kirkpatrick, *Voices from Alcatraz*, 6.

6. R. H. Colvin, report, August 5, 1933, FBI File #7-115-62.

7. Colvin, report, February 23, 1934.

8. Ellis, *Man Named Jones*, 137.

9. Colvin, report, February 23, 1934.

10. "No Changes Expected for Slick Force," *Daily Oklahoman*, August 27, 1930.

11. "Oklahoma's 'King of the Wildcatters,'" America's Oil & Gas Historical Society website, https://aoghs.org/petroleum-pioneers/wildcatter-tom-slick.

12. Miles, *King of the Wildcatters*, xii.

13. Frates, *Oklahoma's Most Notorious Cases*, 13.

14. "Kidnappers Hold Urschel."

15. This request was unusual. In subsequent cases, the FBI encouraged families to let them monitor all contacts.

16. Colvin, report, February 23, 1934.

17. Colvin, report, February 23, 1934.

18. Hamilton, *Machine Gun Kelly's Last Stand*, 25.

19. Colvin, report, February 23, 1934.

20. Kirkpatrick, *Voices from Alcatraz*, 16.

21. Colvin, report, February 23, 1934.

22. Hamilton, *Machine Gun Kelly's Last Stand*, 28.

23. Ellis, *Man Named Jones*, 91.

24. Kirkpatrick, *Voices from Alcatraz*, 17.

25. Hamilton, *Machine Gun Kelly's Last Stand*, 30.

26. Experienced kidnappers usually specified used bills because new bills would typically contain sequential serial numbers that would be easier to record.

27. Hamilton, *Machine Gun Kelly's Last Stand*, 34.

28. Kirkpatrick, *Crimes' Paradise*, 53.

29. Kirkpatrick, *Voices from Alcatraz*, 31–32.

30. Kirkpatrick, *Voices from Alcatraz*, 35.

31. Kirkpatrick, *Voices from Alcatraz*, 36.

32. D. L. McCormack, report, August 7, 1933, FBI File #7-115-99.

33. Gus T. Jones to J. Edgar Hoover, letter, August 19, 1936, FBI File #7-115.

34. F. J. Blake to Special Agent in Charge of Kansas City office, letter, July 7, 1933, FBI File #62-28915-221.

35. Winstead, *Memoir*, 33.

36. McCormack to F. J. Blake, telegram, July 25, 1933, FBI File #7-115.

37. McCormack, report, August 7, 1933.

38. The Treasury Department's Bureau of Prohibition (later part of the Justice Department separate from the Bureau of Investigation) handled most Prohibition violations; bank robbery was not a federal crime.

39. Hamilton, *Machine Gun Kelly's Last Stand*, 158.

40. Hamilton, *Machine Gun Kelly's Last Stand*, 70.

41. Jones to Hoover, August 19, 1936.

42. Frates, *Oklahoma's Most Notorious Cases*, 15.

43. Maccabee, *John Dillinger Slept Here*, 125.

44. Ellis, *Man Named Jones*, 81.

45. Gary Cartwright, "Showdown at Waggoner Ranch," *Texas Monthly*, January 2004.

46. Hoover, *Persons in Hiding*, 152.

47. Ellis, *Man Named Jones*, 82.

48. Ellis, *Man Named Jones*, 105.

49. Ellis, *Man Named Jones*, 109–10.

50. Ellis, *Man Named Jones*, 110, 111; Colvin, report, August 5, 1933.

51. Ellis, *Man Called Jones*, 112.

52. J. Edgar Hoover to William Stanley, memorandum, August 12, 1933, FBI File #7-115-125.

53. The escape of Bailey and his fellow convicts was covered by newspapers across the country. In an editorial, the *New York Times* treated the fugitives as romantic figures of a bygone era: "It is almost in Jesse James's country that the adventure of the eleven fugitive Kansas convicts is working itself out. The professors say that the American frontier passed away in the year 1890, but the spirit of the 'Wild West' is in this entire episode—the amazing boldness of the escape from prison, the capture of the hostages, the flight across country, down to the disappearance of the fugitives in the Ozarks." Editorial, "Frontier Life Revived," *New York Times*, June 2, 1933.

54. "Plot Depicted; Stress Put on Cruel Methods," *Miami Daily News-Record*, September 19, 1933; Hamilton, *Machine Gun Kelly's Last Stand*, 42–43.

55. Robert Talley, "America's No. 1 'Bad Man,'" *Alton Evening Telegraph*, September 16, 1933.

56. "Urschel Case Solved with Arrest in Texas of Harvey Bailey, Also Machine Gunner in K.C. Massacre," *Miami Daily News-Record*, August 14, 1933; "Paradise, Wise County, Hilltop Farmhouse Gives Up Head of K.C. Massacre and Leader of Urschel Kidnap Outrage," *Waco News-Tribune*, August 15, 1933.

57. "Urschel Abductor Captured in Texas on a Lonely Ranch," *New York Times*, August 15, 1933.

58. "A Triumph for Uncle Sam," *Courier-Journal*, August 16, 1933.

59. CEK, memorandum, September 4, 1933, FBI File #7-115-470.

60. Hamilton, *Machine Gun Kelly's Last Stand*, 84.

61. Hamilton, *Machine Gun Kelly's Last Stand*, 84.

62. Telephone call from Mr. Nathan, August 10, 1933, FBI File #7-115-207.

63. Winstead, *Memoir*, 35.

64. "Nation's Attorneys Set About to Solve Racket Problems," *Ludington Daily News*, August 29, 1933.

65. "Anti-Crime Army Urged before Bar," *New York Times*, August 31, 1933.

66. "U.S. Legal Chief Talks to Law Body," *Great Falls Tribune*, September 1, 1933.

67. "Cummings Bars Federal Police," *New York Times*, September 1, 1933.

68. "Cummings Tells Crime War Plans," *Reading Times*, September 1, 1933.

69. Homer S. Cummings, "Predatory Crime," radio address broadcast by the National Broadcasting Company, September 11, 1933.

70. "Tax-Dodging Case Not Prosecuted So Official Quits," *St. Louis Post-Dispatch*, October 5, 1933.

71. Address of Homer Cummings, January 10, 1934, National Broadcasting Company.

72. Special Agent [name redacted] to J. Edgar Hoover, letter, October 4, 1933, FBI File #7-115-712.

11. The Symbol of the Crusade

1. The tower was heavily damaged during the April 1995 bombing of the nearby Alfred P. Murrah Federal Building by Timothy McVeigh. It has since been restored and is still in use.

2. Kirkpatrick, *Voices from Alcatraz*, 80.

3. "Urschel Defies Death Threats: 'See You in Hell,' Kelly Tells Victim," *Daily Oklahoman*, September 21, 1933.

4. "Gang Warning Says His Life in Danger Now," *Daily Oklahoman*, September 21, 1933.

5. "Principals in Kidnap Case Threatened," *Tampa Times* (AP), September 20, 1933.

6. Hamilton, *Machine Gun Kelly's Last Stand*, 97.

7. Kirkpatrick, *Voices from Alcatraz*, 93.

8. Hamilton, *Machine Gun Kelly's Last Stand*, 109.

9. "Kidnapping Victim Points Out Bates as Gang's Leader," *Waco News-Tribune*, September 20, 1933; Hamilton, *Machine Gun Kelly's Last Stand*, 108.

10. "Jury Reaches Verdict in Kidnapping Case after an Hour's Debate," *Abilene Reporter-News* (AP), October 12, 1933.

11. "U.S. Views Kelly Letter as Plot to Frighten Shannons," *Daily Oklahoman*, September 20, 1933.

12. Hamilton, *Machine Gun Kelly's Last Stand*, 164.

13. Charles A. Appel, laboratory report, September 23, 1933, FBI File #7-115-557.

14. Turner, *Hoover's F.B.I.*, 23–24.

15. Hoover, *Persons in Hiding*, 142–43.

16. "Capture of Kelly Called Underworld Ultimatum," *Pittsburgh Post-Gazette*, September 27, 1933.

17. Homer S. Cummings, address broadcast by Columbia Broadcasting Service, April 19, 1934.

18. "Cummings Orders Halt in Crime Glorification," *Spokane Chronicle* (AP), August 17, 1934.

19. "Keenan, U.S. Prosecutor Defies Gangs with Threat of Noose, Electric Chair," *Daily Oklahoman*, August 24, 1933.

20. Jack Alexander, "Profiles: The Director—I," *New Yorker*, September 25, 1937, 24, 25.

21. "Liquor Racket to Be Tougher," *Los Angeles Times*, September 13, 1933.

22. "George 'Machine Gun' Kelly," FBI website, https:/www.fbi.gov/history /famous-cases/machine-gun-kelly.

23. Turner, *Hoover's F.B.I.*, 80.

12. The All-American Boy

1. "Brooke L. Hart Made Executive in Father's Firm," *San Jose Mercury Herald*, September 19, 1933.

2. "Panic Held Reason for Hart Murder," *Oakland Tribune*, November 16, 1933.

3. Farrell, *Swift Justice*, 19.

4. Farrell, *Swift Justice*, 13.

5. Farrell, *Swift Justice*, 55.

6. "Panic Held Reason for Hart Murder."

7. "Hart Ready to Meet Kidnappers' Demands," *Press Democrat* (Santa Rosa) (UP), November 14, 1933.

8. Farrell, *Swift Justice*, 60, 63.

9. Farrell, *Swift Justice*, 109.

10. Farrell, *Swift Justice*, 111.

11. Farrell, *Swift Justice*, 86.

12. R. E. Vetterli, report, December 19, 1933, FBI File #7-375.

13. Report, February 27, 1934, FBI File #7-375, Box 87.

14. Farrell, *Swift Justice*, 44.

15. "Hart Shot While Struggling in Bay, Kidnapper Quoted," *Fresno Bee the Republican* (UP), November 17, 1933.

16. Farrell, *Swift Justice*, 58.

17. "Woman Questioned in Hart Murder," *New York Times* (AP), November 19, 1933.

18. Farrell, *Swift Justice*, 128, 135.

19. V. W. Hughes to Director, memorandum, November 20, 1933, FBI File #7-375.

20. "Woman Questioned in Hart Murder."

21. Hughes to Director, November 20, 1933.

22. "Kidnappers Lynched!: Kidnap Victim's Body Found in Bay by Hunters," *San Francisco Chronicle*, November 27, 1933.

23. Farrell, *Swift Justice*, 139.

24. Farrell, *Swift Justice*, 147.

25. Farrell, *Swift Justice*, 139.

26. "Vigilante Group Being Formed at San Jose, Claim," *Reno Gazette-Journal* (AP), November 25, 1933.

27. Farrell, *Swift Justice*, 193.

28. "Body of Brooke Hart, Kidnap Victim Is Found," *Press Democrat*, November 28, 1933.

29. "Identity of Hart's Body Established at Autopsy," *Oakland Tribune*, November 27, 1933.

30. R. E. Vetterli, report, November 27, 1933, FBI File #7-375.

31. Farrell, *Swift Justice*, 203.

32. "Rolph Promises to Pardon Members of Lynching Mob," *Salt Lake Telegram*, November 27, 1933.

33. "Rolph Promises."

34. Young, *Hot Type*, 54.

35. Young, *Hot Type*, 55.

36. Farrell, *Swift Justice*, 202.

37. "Hart's Parent Satisfied for Law to Reign," *San Bernardino County Sun*, November 30, 1933.

38. "Rolph Statement Stirs Storm Here," *New York Times*, November 28, 1933.

39. "Gov. Rolph Backs San Jose Lynching as Kidnap Warning," *New York Times*, November 28, 1933.

40. "Will Rogers Says," *Lansing State Journal*, November 28, 1933.

41. "Rolph Statement Stirs Storm Here."

42. "Churchmen Launch Fight on Lynching," *New York Times*, December 4, 1933.

43. "Trial by Lynching," *Harvard Crimson*, November 28, 1933.

44. "Jean Harlow Says Lynching 'Eased' Film Colony Folks," *Star Press* (Muncie IN) (AP), December 3, 1933.

45. William Allison, "Mob Violence Shows Big Gain during Year," *Pittsburgh Press*, December 31, 1933.

46. "Rolph Statement Stirs Storm Here."

47. "Southern Woman Calls Rolph Stand Astounding," *New York Times*, November 29, 1933.

48. "Rebuke to Rolph Is Seen," *New York Times*, December 7, 1933; "A Timely Lead," *New York Times*, December 8, 1933.

13. Framing God's Bagman

1. Karpis, *Alvin Karpis Story*, 9.

2. Fred's brother Lloyd was in the federal penitentiary at Leavenworth, Kansas, and brother Arthur ("Doc") was in the Oklahoma State Prison. Brother Herman committed suicide in 1927 to escape prosecution after killing a policeman during a robbery.

3. Karpis, *Alvin Karpis Story*, 41–42.

4. Karpis, *Alvin Karpis Story*, 56, 61.

5. Kazanjian and Enss, *Ma Barker*, 69.

6. Karpis, *Alvin Karpis Story*, 42.

7. Karpis, *Alvin Karpis Story*, 43.

8. Reprinted in "Bandits Rob Peoples Bank of Mountain View," *Houston Herald* (MO), October 15, 1931.

9. Mahoney, *Secret Partners*, 39–41.

10. "Sheriff C.R. Kelly Killed by Bandits," *Journal-Gazette* (West Plains MO), December 24, 1931; "West Plains Sheriff Is Shot Down," *Moberly Monitor-Index*, December 19, 1931.

11. "Identify Slayers of Sheriff Kelly," *Journal-Gazette* (West Plains MO), December 31, 1931.

12. Westbrook Pegler, "Fair Enough," *El Paso Herald-Post*, February 20, 1934.

13. John Lauritsen, "Notorious St. Paul Gangster Kidnapping Turns 80," CBS Minnesota website, January 18, 2014, https://minnesota.cbslocal.com/2014/01/18/notorious-st-paul-gangster-kidnapping-turns-80.

14. Karpis, *Alvin Karpis Story*, 98, 100.

15. Maccabee, *John Dillinger Slept Here*, 24; Karpis, *Alvin Karpis Story*, 100.

16. Maccabee, *John Dillinger Slept Here*, 138; Karpis *Alvin Karpis Story*, 101.

17. Maccabee, *John Dillinger Slept Here*, 135.

18. John William Tuohy, "The St. Paul Incident," *Rick Porrello's American Mafia*, July 2001, www.americanmafia.com/Feature_Articles_152.html.

19. Karpis, *Alvin Karpis Story*, 127, 130, 132.

20. Breuer, *Hoover and His G-Men*, 36.

21. Karpis, *Alvin Karpis Story*, 134.

22. Karpis, *Alvin Karpis Story*, 135–36.

23. Karpis, *Alvin Karpis Story*, 142.

24. Karpis, *Alvin Karpis Story*, 144.

25. Gilbert reportedly had so many sources of illicit income that he was known as "America's richest cop." Ron Grossman, "Who Was Chicago's Dan Gilbert? 'The World's Richest Cop,'" *Chicago Tribune*, February 25, 2016, https://www.chicagotribune.com/history/ct-daniel-gilbert-richest-cop-flashback-20160224-story.html.

26. Tuohy, *Capone's Mob*, 55.

27. "Hamm Failure to Make Positive Identifications Brings Touhy Acquittal," *Minneapolis Star*, November 29, 1933.

28. "Verdict to Spur U.S. Activities, Keenan Avers," *Minneapolis Star*, November 29, 1993.

29. "Jury Acquits Touhy Mob in Hamm Case," *Decatur Herald* (AP), November 29, 1933.

30. "Verdict Flayed as 'Terrible' by Some Citizens," *Minneapolis Star*, November 29, 1933.

31. "Great for the Touhys, but How about the Public?" *Minneapolis Star*, November 29, 1933.

32. "Barker/Karpis Gang: The Hamm Kidnapping," FBI website, https://www.fbi.gov/history/famous-cases/barker-karpis-gang.

14. *"Like a Damned Albatross around My Neck"*

1. John H. Harvey, "Six Abductions in Three Years, and St. Paul Is Dubbed 'Kidnapping Capital of America,'" *News Journal* (Wilmington DE), January 26, 1934.

2. Karpis, *Alvin Karpis Story*, 101–2.

3. Karpis, *Alvin Karpis Story*, 163.

4. S. P. Cowley to Director, memorandum, February 16, 1934, FBI File #7-576-845.

5. "Bremer Sees Vast Changes among Banks," *Brainerd Daily Dispatch*, September 28, 1929.

6. "Kidnappers Hold St. Paul Banker; Note Asks $200,000," *New York Times*, January 19, 1934.

7. "Roosevelt Hailed by Minnesota Democrats," *Journal Gazette*, April 23, 1932.

8. Karpis, *Alvin Karpis Story*, 164.

9. Ward, *Alcatraz*, 92.

10. "Kidnappers Hold St. Paul Banker"; Mahoney, *Secret Partners*, 114.

11. Karpis, *Alvin Karpis Story*, 166.

12. H. Nathan, memorandum, January 31, 1934, FBI File #7-576-711.

13. Maccabee, *John Dillinger Slept Here*, 194.

14. Hanni to J. Edgar Hoover, telegram, January 19, 1934, FBI File #7-576-11.

15. C. A. Appel, laboratory report #265, January 19, 1934, FBI File #7-576-6.

16. C. A. Appel, laboratory report #271, January 23, 1934, FBI File #7-576-49.

17. Charles B. Cheney, "Twin Cities Resent Crime Hub Charge," *New York Times*, February 25, 1934.

18. Maccabee, *John Dillinger Slept Here*, 188.

19. Mahoney, *Secret Partners*, 18.

20. Karpis, *Alvin Karpis Story*, 163.

21. Karpis, *Alvin Karpis Story*, 167.

22. "Bremer Is Released: Banker Freed by Kidnappers at Rochester, Minn., after $200,000 Ransom Payment," *Stevens Point Daily Journal*, February 8, 1934.

23. H. H. Clegg to Director, memorandum, February 8, 1934, FBI File #7-576-207.

24. H. H. Clegg to Director, memorandum, February 12, 1934, BKF Sec. 5, #419, quoted in Mahoney, *Secret Partners*, 55.

25. Harold Nathan to Director, letter, February 20, 1934, FBI File #7-576.

26. H. H. Clegg to Director, memorandum, February 12, 1934, FBI File #7-576-295.

27. H. H. Clegg to Director, memorandum, February 13, 1934, FBI File #7-576-491.

28. Karpis, *Alvin Karpis Story*, 19.

29. J. Edgar Hoover to Attorney General, memorandum, February 20, 1934, FBI File #7-576-594.

30. Hoover to Attorney General, February 20, 1934; Maccabee, *John Dillinger Slept Here*, 200; Mahoney, *Secret Partners*, 125, 174.

31. J. Edgar Hoover to SAIC Birmingham, letter, February 21, 1934, FBI File #7-756-711; J. Edgar Hoover to William Stanley, memorandum, February 21, 1934, FBI File #7-576-702.

32. S. P. Cowley to Director, memorandum, J. Edgar Hoover marginalia, March 9, 1934, FBI File #7-576-1184.

33. "The Kidnapping of Edward George Bremer, St. Paul Minnesota," November 19, 1936, FBI File #7-576, 27.

34. John J. Edwards to Mr. Tolson, memorandum, January 24, 1934, FBI File #7-576-112.

35. Karpis, *Alvin Karpis Story*, 170.

36. Karpis, *Alvin Karpis Story*, 170–71.

37. "Klutas' Fingertips Reported Changed: Illinois Kidnapper Has Also Altered Face; Blow to Nation's Police," *Rutland Daily Herald* (AP), November 20, 1933.

38. S. P. Cowley to Director, memorandum, April 23, 1934, FBI File #7-576-1760.

39. "Kidnapping of Edward George Bremer," November 19, 1936.

40. J. Edgar Hoover to Attorney General, memorandum, April 30, 1934, FBI File #7-576-1791.

15. Fifty-Three Crates of Furniture

1. David C. Wheelock, "Changing the Rules: State Mortgage Moratoria during the Great Depression," Federal Reserve Bank of St. Louis, *Review*, May/June 2008, 90 (3, Part 1), 133–48.

2. Karpis, *Alvin Karpis Story*, 50; "Tells of Bank Bandit Chase," *Star Tribune*, October 2, 1932.

3. Jennifer Latson, "Hero or Villain? Why Thousands Mourned a Bank Robber," *Time*, October 22, 2014, https://time.com/3518207/pretty-boy-floyd/.

4. Remarks of Homer S. Cummings, broadcast over Columbia Broadcasting System network, April 19, 1934.

5. "Anti-Gangster Action Is Plea of Roosevelt," *Rhinelander Daily News*, April 24, 1934.

6. "New Carlisle Bank Is Robbed of $10,800: Bandits Bind Cashier, Clerk and Assistant," *Dayton Daily News*, June 21, 1933; "Bandits Grab $10,000 in Holdup of New Carlisle Bank, Escape in Auto: Three Robbers Wait at Institution All Night for Employees," *Dayton Herald*, June 21, 1933.

7. Baby Face Nelson, John "Red" Hamilton, Homer Van Meter, Harry "Pete" Pierpont, Charles Makley, Russell Clark, Ed Shouse, Henry Copeland, Tommy Carroll, Eddie Green, and John Paul Chase.

8. Maccabee, *John Dillinger Slept Here*, 218.

9. Purvis and Tresniowski, *Vendetta*, 90.

10. "Has Dillinger a Hideout in This County?" *Noblesville Ledger*, April 19, 1934.

11. Cromie and Pinkston, *Dillinger*, 192.

12. Borne, *Troutmouth*, 97; Purvis and Tresniowski, *Vendetta*, 98.

13. "Demand Probe about Outlaw Gang's Flight," *Green Bay Press-Gazette*, April 25, 1934.

14. "Will Rogers Says," *Lansing State Journal*, April 24, 1934.

15. "Anti-Gangster Action."

16. Larry Wack, "Perpetuating a Myth: The 1934 Crime Bills & FBI Weaponry," *Faded Glory*, http://ticklethewire.com/2014/01/13/history-perpetuating-a-myth-the-1934-crime-bills-fbi-weaponry/.

17. Franklin D. Roosevelt, statement on signing crime bill, May 18, 1934; "Roosevelt Opens Attack on Crime, Signing Six Bills as 'Challenge,'" *New York Times*, May 19, 1934.

18. Clyde Tolson to Director, memorandum, July 13, 1933, FBI File #66-3760-73.

19. R. H. Colvin to J. Edgar Hoover, letter, June 25, 1933.

20. "How the Government Battles Organized Lawlessness," radio address by Homer Cummings, broadcast over National Broadcasting Company network, May 12, 1934.

21. "Federal Men Open Crime War Today," *New York Times*, May 18, 1934.

22. "U.S. Offers $10,000 to Get Dillinger," *New York Times*, June 24, 1934; "Cummings Puts $10,000 Price on Dillinger," *Baltimore Sun*, June 24, 1934.

23. Theoharis, *FBI: A Comprehensive Reference Guide*, 55; Kessler, *Bureau*, 34.

24. Terry Wolkerstorfer, "Dillinger's Shoot-out," *Minneapolis Star*, April 1, 1974.

25. J. Edgar Hoover, memorandum, July 22, 1934, FBI File #62-29777.

26. S. P. Cowley to Director, letter, July 24, 1934, FBI File #62-29777-1-1.

27. Purvis and Tresniowski, *Vendetta*, 167.

28. Cowley to Director, July 24, 1934.

29. Carl F. Ogle, "Double Doesn't Believe Slain Man Is Dillinger," *Indianapolis Star*, July 24, 1934.

30. Rudensky, *Gonif*, 61

31. "Capone Put on Alcatraz," *Oakland Tribune*, August 22, 1934.

32. Johnston, *Alcatraz Island Prison*, 19.

33. Jackson McQuigg, "Capone Rides the Rails to Alcatraz," *Train*, April 2012.

34. Ward, *Alcatraz*, 76.

35. J. A. Johnston to Sanford Bates, letter, August 22, 1934; Johnston, *Alcatraz Island Prison*, 21.

36. Homer Cummings to Warden Robert Hudspeth, letter, October 17, 1933, quoted in Ward, *Alcatraz*, 40.

37. "Two Girls Brave Alcatraz Swim," *Petaluma Argus-Courier*, October 19, 1933.

38. "Attorney General Defends 'Devil's Isle' on Alcatraz," *Petaluma Argus-Courier*, January 31, 1934.

39. According to the Bureau of Prisons, during Alcatraz's twenty-nine years as a federal prison (1934–63), there were fourteen separate escape attempts involving thirty-six inmates (including two who tried to escape twice). Twenty-three were caught, six were shot and killed during the attempt, and two drowned. "The Rock: Alcatraz Origins: Escape Attempts," Bureau of Prisons website, https://www.bop.gov/about/history/alcatraz.jsp.

40. "The Rock: Alcatraz Origins: Life at the Prison," Bureau of Prisons website, https://bop.gov/about/history/alcatraz.jsp.

41. An undercover investigation by the FBI in 1929, for example, had revealed that federal prisoners at Atlanta and Leavenworth were able to continue running criminal businesses from their cells and to order meals from their favorite restaurants. They were even able to bribe officials to transfer them for the summer months from their stifling cells to cooler army camps in the north. Ward, *Alcatraz*, 42–44.

42. Ward, *Alcatraz*, 79–82.

43. Ward, *Alcatraz*, 70.

44. Sanford Bates to Attorney General, January 8, 1933, quoted in Ward, *Alcatraz*, 61.

45. Those conditions also encouraged inmates to become informants in order to win transfers to more hospitable federal prisons.

16. "Solve That Lindbergh Case"

1. Fensch, *FBI Files*, 288–89, 324–25.

2. Wilson, report, November 11, 1933.

3. Whipple, *Lindbergh Crime*, 170–71.

4. Fensch, *FBI Files*, 296.

5. T. D. Quinn to File, memorandum, October 12, 1932, FBI File #62-3057-19-68.

6. Quinn to File, October 12, 1932.

7. Quinn to File, October 12, 1932.

8. L. G. Turrou, report, October 13, 1932, FBI File #7-1-1723.

9. Executive Order 6102, April 5, 1933. The rationale for the order was that the private hoarding of gold limited the government's authority to increase the money supply (by reducing its gold supply) during the Great Depression, which limited economic growth and deepened the depression.

10. Fensch, *FBI Files*, 334.

11. Unnamed author, "Changes in Administrative Policy in the Investigation of the Kidnapping of Charles A. Lindbergh, Jr., Due to Variations in Conditions Encountered," January 3, 1935, FBI File #7-1-5903.

12. J. Edgar Hoover to T. F. Cullen, letter, July 21, 1933, FBI File #62-3057-5-122.

13. J. Edgar Hoover to T. F. Cullen, letter, August 12, 1933, FBI File #62-3057-5.

14. J. Edgar Hoover to Attorney General, memorandum, September 13, 1933, FBI File #7-1-2333.

15. "Oral History with Mr. Hugh H. Clegg, Native Mississippian, Former Assistant Director of the FBI and Educator," University of Southern Mississippi Center for Oral History and Cultural Heritage, Hattiesburg, 1977, p. 111.

16. "Open Fresh Inquiry in Lindbergh Case," *New York Times*, October 20, 1933.

17. "Department of Justice Takes over Full Probe of Lindbergh Kidnapping: Action Sanctioned by Roosevelt—Lone Income Tax Division Investigator Is Withdrawn—J. Edgar Hoover to Assume Charge of U.S. Search for Kidnappers," *Courier-News* (Bridgewater NJ) (AP), October 20, 1933.

18. H. Nathan to Director, memorandum, November 2, 1933, FBI File #62-3057-19-90.

19. H. Nathan to Director, memorandum, December 2, 1933, FBI File #7-1-2697.

20. J. Edgar Hoover to Special Agent in Charge, New York, letter, December 15, 1933, FBI File #7-1-2697.

21. Fensch, *FBI Files*, 283.

22. Federal Reserve Bank of New York, Circular No. 1337, January 17, 1934.

23. Fensch, *FBI Files*, 284.

24. Fensch, *FBI Files*, 340.

25. Francis X. Fay to Special Agents in Charge, letter, February 26, 1934, FBI File #62-3057-5 Sub I.

26. F. X. Fay to Director, letter, February 28, 1934, FBI File #7-1-3060.

27. T. H. Sisk to J. Edgar Hoover, letter, May 29, 1934, FBI File #62-3057-5 sub IV.

28. S. P. Cowley to Director, memorandum, J. Edgar Hoover marginalia, March 7, 1934, FBI File #7-1-3191.

29. J. Edgar Hoover to T. H. Sisk, letter, March 13, 1934, FBI File #7-1-3192.

30. J. Edgar Hoover to Colonel H. Norman Schwarzkopf, letter, April 6, 1934, FBI File #62-3057.

31. H. Norman Schwarzkopf to J. Edgar Hoover, letter, April 11, 1934. FBI File #62-3057.

32. J. Edgar Hoover to Colonel H. Norman Schwarzkopf, letter, April 23, 1934, FBI File #62-3057-19-133.

33. H. Norman Schwarzkopf to J. Edgar Hoover, letter, May 1, 1934.

34. T. H. Sisk to J. Edgar Hoover, letter, May 16, 1934, FBI File #7-1-3811.

35. J. Edgar Hoover to Mr. Cowley, memorandum, June 4, 1934, FBI File #7-1-3936.

36. J. Edgar Hoover to Mr. Tamm, memorandum, June 19, 1934, FBI File #7-1-4017.

37. "Handwriting Study Made of 5,000 at Sing Sing," *New York Times*, September 24, 1934.

38. E. A. Tamm to Director, memorandum, August 3, 1934, FBI File #62-3057.

39. "Sketch from 'Jafsie's' Memory like Hauptmann," *St. Louis Post-Dispatch*, September 23, 1934.

40. E. A. Tamm to Director, memorandum, July 20, 1934.

17. Dragnet

1. T. H. Sisk, report, October 17, 1934, FBI File #62-3057-19-255.

2. Sisk, report, October 17, 1934.

3. Sisk, report, October 17, 1934.

4. Sisk, report, October 17, 1934.

5. Leon G. Turrou, "Was Hauptmann Really Guilty? Yes, Says Man Who Caught Him," *Pittsburgh Press*, July 27, 1941.

6. Turrou, *Where My Shadow Falls*, 126.

7. E. A. Tamm to Director, memorandum, September 8, 1934, FBI File #7-1-4529.

8. Tamm to Director, September 8, 1934.

9. E. A. Tamm to Director, memorandum, September 8, 1934, FBI File #7-1-5867.

10. E. A. Tamm to J. Edgar Hoover, memorandum, J. Edgar Hoover marginalia, September 7, 1934, FBI File #7-1-4518.

11. Tamm to Director, September 8, 1934, FBI File #7-1-4529.

12. Tamm to Director, September 8, 1934, FBI File #7-1-5867.

13. Sisk, report, October 17, 1934.

14. E. A. Tamm to Director, memorandum, September 11, 1934, FBI File #7-1-5869.

15. E. A. Tamm to Director, memorandum, September 10, 1934, FBI File #7-1-5868.

16. Tamm to Director, September 10, 1934.

17. E. A. Tamm to Director, memorandum, September 11, 1934, FBI File #7-1-4533.

18. J. Edgar Hoover to T. H. Sisk, letter, September 18, 1934, FBI File #62-3057-19-231.

19. "Science Used in Search," *New York Times*, September 22, 1934.

20. Tamm to Director, September 11, 1934; J. Edgar Hoover to Mr. Smith, memorandum, September 13, 1934, FBI File #7-1-5075.

21. Sisk, report, October 17, 1934.

22. Whipple, *Trial*, Testimony of Walter Lyle, 304.

23. Sisk, report, October 17, 1934.

24. Whipple, *Trial,* Testimony of John Joseph Lyons, 288; Falzini, *Their Fifteen Minutes,* 18.

25. Sisk, report, October 17, 1934.

26. "Science Used in Search."

27. Sisk, report, October 17, 1934.

28. Falzini, *Their Fifteen Minutes,* 18.

29. H. H. Clegg to File, memorandum, September 19, 1934, FBI File #62-3057-37-4.

30. Albert D. Osborn was the son of handwriting expert Albert S. Osborn, who has been called the "father of the science of questioned document examination in North America." Albert S. was the author of the seminal work in the field, *Questioned Documents,* first published in 1910 and revised in 1929. Father and son worked together on the Lindbergh case.

31. Whipple, *Trial,* 24.

32. Kennedy, *Airman and the Carpenter,* 174.

33. T. H. Sisk to J. Edgar Hoover, memorandum, September 20, 1934, FBI File #62-3057; T. H. Sisk to Assistant Special Agent in Charge R. Whitley, memorandum, November 28, 1934, FBI File #62-3057-19-309.

34. Kennedy, *Airman and the Carpenter,* 182; Sisk to Whitley, November 28, 1934.

35. Sisk to Hoover, September 20, 1934.

36. Sisk to Hoover, September 20, 1934; Fisher, *Lindbergh Case,* 187. Further investigation revealed that Hauptmann had purchased the radio on May 2, 1932, for $300 in gold certificates. J. Edgar Hoover to Mr. Tamm, memorandum, September 26, 1934, FBI File #7-1-5067.

37. J. Edgar Hoover to Mr. Tamm, memorandum, October 6, 1934, FBI File #7-1-5180.

38. L. G. Turrou to File, memorandum, September 21, 1934, FBI File #62-3057.

39. Turrou to File, September 21, 1934. A different version of this story, told many years later by Detective John Wallace of the NJSP, attributed to Schwarzkopf the direction to return the ransom money to the garage and stage a second "discovery" in Anna Hauptmann's presence. Fisher, *Lindbergh Case,* 202, 447n3.

40. Fisher, *Lindbergh Case,* 203.

41. Another $840 in ransom bills was later discovered rolled up and stuffed into holes bored into the rafters of Hauptmann's garage. Hoover to Tamm, September 26, 1934, FBI File #7-1-5067.

42. T. H. Sisk to J. Edgar Hoover, memorandum, September 21, 1934, FBI File #62-3057-19-234.

43. Sisk to Hoover, September 21, 1934.

44. Fisher, *Lindbergh Case,* 205.

45. This account of Finn's communication with the Osborns and their change of opinion about Hauptmann's handwriting matching that of the ransom notes' writer is based on the account by Ludovic Kennedy in *The Airman and the Carpenter,* 183.

46. Memorandum of telephone conversation of Mr. Hoover and Mr. Tamm, September 21, 1934, FBI File #7-1-4780.

47. J. Edgar Hoover to Special Agent in Charge, New York City, letter, September 23, 1934, FBI File #62-3057-37-62.

48. Statement for the press, 4 p.m., September 20, 1934, FBI File #7-1-4878.

49. Turrou, *Where My Shadow Falls*, 122.

50. Sisk to Hoover, September 21, 1934.

51. Turrou, *Where My Shadow Falls*, 124.

52. Turrou, *Where My Shadow Falls*, 123.

53. E. A. Tamm to Director, memorandum, September 24, 1934, FBI File #7-1-4739.

54. Behn, *Lindbergh*, 221.

55. Memorandum of telephone conversation of Hoover and Tamm, September 21, 1934.

56. Memorandum of telephone conversation of Hoover and Tamm, September 21, 1934; T. D. Quinn, memorandum, September 21, 1934, FBI File #7-1-4633.

57. Charles A. Lindbergh, statement, May 20, 1932, files of New Jersey State Troopers Museum. Walsh was assisting the NJSP in its investigation at Governor Moore's request.

58. Gardner, *Case That Never Dies*, 188–89.

59. "Hauptmann Bail $100,000; Col. Lindbergh, Disguised, Sees Suspect Questioned," *New York Times*, September 28, 1934; Gardner, *Case That Never Dies*, 191.

60. Fisher, *Lindbergh Case*, 249–50, 450n5.

18. Verdict

1. J. Edgar Hoover to Mr. Tamm, memorandum, September 23, 1934, FBI File #7-1-4899; J. Edgar Hoover to Mr. Tamm, memorandum, September 22, 1934, FBI File #7-1-4898.

2. "Resemblance Noted in Kidnapper Sketch," *Ogden Standard-Examiner* (AP), September 23, 1934.

3. "Department of Justice Lifted Cover on Some Efforts to Solve Kidnapping," *Standard-Sentinel* (Hazleton PA) (AP), September 22, 1934.

4. *Austin American*, September 21, 1934; *Pittsburgh Press*, September 21, 1934.

5. In September 1931, one of the kidnappers of Long Island stockbroker Charles M. Rosenthal was arrested when he went to a branch of the Harriman National Bank to change a $100 bill of ransom money. Nassau County police detectives had previously circulated to area banks lists of the serial numbers of the $50,000 ransom paid by Rosenthal's mother, and a bank teller spotted the ransom bill and contacted the police, who arrived before the kidnapper departed. "Seize 5 Kidnappers of Young Rosenthal," *New York Times*, September 2, 1931.

6. "Lindbergh Sure of Hauptmann," *Boston Globe*, October 9, 1934.

7. J. Edgar Hoover to Mr. Tamm, memorandum, September 26, 1934, FBI File #7-1-4880.

8. Whipple, *Trial*, Testimony of Frank J. Wilson, 262.

9. Hoover to Tamm, September 26, 1934, FBI File #7-1-4880.

10. E. A. Tamm to J. Edgar Hoover, memorandum, September 22, 1934, FBI File #7-1-5126.

11. Hoover to Tamm, September 26, 1934, FBI File #7-1-4880.

12. E. A. Tamm to Director, memorandum, September 27, 1934, FBI File #7-1-5112.

13. J. Edgar Hoover, memorandum, October 4, 1934, FBI File #7-1-5081.

14. J. Edgar Hoover to Attorney General, memorandum, October 4, 1934, FBI File #7-1-5111X.

15. Hoover, memorandum, October 4, 1934.

16. J. Edgar Hoover to Mr. Tamm, memorandum, October 9, 1934, FBI File #7-1-5228.

17. "Justice Department Ends Its Part in Inquiry," *Baltimore Sun*, October 11, 1934.

18. J. Edgar Hoover to Mr. Tamm, memorandum, October 11, 1934, FBI File #7-1-5335.

19. Mary Elizabeth Plummer, "Lindbergh Faces Hauptmann as Celebrated Trial Opens: Famous Flier within an Arm's Reach of Defendant in Little Flemington Courtroom as Tranquil Town Throbs with Activity," *Morning Call* (Paterson NJ) (AP), January 3, 1935.

20. Gillian Brockell, "'Poor Little Rich Girl': Gloria Vanderbilt Was Caught between a Neglectful Mother and an Oppressive Aunt," *Washington Post*, June 17, 2019, https://www.washingtonpost.com/history/2019/06/17/poor-little-rich-girl-gloria-vanderbilt-was-caught-between-neglectful-mother-an-oppressive-aunt/.

21. "Huge Wire Service Set Up for Trial," *New York Times*, January 2, 1935.

22. Kennedy, *Airman and the Carpenter*, 238.

23. St. Johns, a syndicated columnist for the Hearst newspapers, was the daughter of noted trial lawyer Earl Rogers, veteran of seventy-seven murder trials, who was said to have been Erle Stanley Gardner's inspiration for the fictional courtroom titan Perry Mason. As a child, St. Johns watched many of her father's trials and listened to his tales and critiques, which informed and enlivened her own courtroom reporting.

24. J. Edgar Hoover, memorandum, July 19, 1933, FBI File #7-104-Section I.

25. St. Johns, *Honeycomb*, 288.

26. Plummer, "Lindbergh Faces Hauptmann."

27. Glenn Fowler, "David Wilentz, 93, the Prosecutor in Lindbergh Kidnapping, Is Dead," *New York Times*, July 7, 1988.

28. Henry W. Levy, "First Murder Trial Catapulted Young Jewish Lawyer to Fame," *Jewish Daily Bulletin*, February 7, 1935.

29. Russell B. Porter, "10 Hauptmann Case Jurors, 4 Women, Quickly Chosen; Col. Lindbergh a Spectator," *New York Times*, January 3, 1935.

30. Plummer, "Lindbergh Faces Hauptmann."

31. Porter, "10 Hauptmann Case Jurors."

32. Damon Runyon, "10 Selected for Hauptmann Jury; Lindbergh May Take Stand Today," *Reading Times* (UP), January 3, 1935.

33. Edna Ferber, "Miss Ferber Views 'Vultures' at Trial," *New York Times*, January 28, 1935.

34. Nigel Nicolson, ed., *Diaries and Letters of Harold Nicolson*, Vol. 1 (New York: Atheneum, 1966), quoted in Scaduto, *Scapegoat*, 223.

35. Porter, "10 Hauptmann Case Jurors"; Frank Emery, "Dramatic Plea to Jury Brings Mistrial Move," *Brooklyn Daily Eagle*, January 3, 1935; "Lindbergh's Pistol Strapped under Arm," *Morning News* (Wilmington DE) (AP), January 4, 1935.

36. As the member of the New Jersey Supreme Court assigned to the Third Judicial Circuit, which included Hunterdon County, he was responsible under New Jersey court rules for presiding over Third Circuit murder cases. Though he could have elected to have the county judge of the Court of Common Pleas join him on the bench, Justice Trenchard exercised his prerogative to preside alone. Falzini, *Their Fifteen Minutes*, 135.

37. Falzini, *Their Fifteen Minutes*, 139.

38. Juror Liscom Case would suffer a mild heart attack over a weekend during the fifth week of the trial. He continued to serve, and the trial proceeded without delay. Anne Gordon Suydam, "Argument for Alternate Juror Plan Seen in Hauptmann Case," *Evening Star* (Washington), January 28, 1935.

39. Falzini, *Their Fifteen Minutes*, 142; "How Hauptmann Was Convicted," *Los Angeles Times Sunday Magazine*, July 7, 1935.

40. Trial of Bruno Richard Hauptmann, Testimony of Charles A. Lindbergh, January 4, 1935, *Lindbergh Kidnapping Hoax*, www.lindberghkidnappinghoax.com /witnesses.html, 109, 113; Whipple, *Trial*, Testimony of Charles A. Lindbergh, 123.

41. Statement of Charles A. Lindbergh to Inspector Harry Walsh, Jersey City Police Department, May 20, 1932, files of New Jersey State Police Museum.

42. Louis M. Lyons, "Swears Hauptmann Stole Baby: Jury Listens to Colonel as to an Idol—Hears Him Identify Voice," *Boston Globe*, January 5, 1935; St. Johns, *Honeycomb*, 321.

43. Whipple, *Trial*, 54.

44. Turrou, *Where My Shadow Falls*, 127–28.

45. Lyons, "Swears Hauptmann Stole Baby."

46. St. Johns, *Honeycomb*, 324.

47. "Hauptmann Trapped by Own Cunning," *New York Daily News*, January 12, 1935.

48. Louis M. Lyons, "Says Hauptmann Wrote Notes," *Boston Globe*, January 12, 1935.

49. Whipple, *Trial*, Testimony of Frank J. Wilson, 261.

50. Whipple, *Trial*, Testimony of Frank J. Wilson, 261.

51. Whipple, *Trial*, Testimony of Frank J. Wilson, 262; "Expert Says Hauptmann Wrote All Ransom Notes," *New York Times*, January 12, 1935.

52. E. A. Tamm to Director, memorandum, January 11, 1935, FBI File #7-1-5871.

53. Adela Rogers St. Johns, January 11, 1935, quoted in Wilson and Day, *Special Agent*, 71.

54. Whipple, *Trial*, Testimony of William E. Frank, 313.

55. "Hauptmann Funds Traced to Ransom," *New York Times*, April 29, 1936.

56. Whipple, *Trial*, Testimony of Albert S. Osborn, 263.

57. Russell B. Porter, "Week's Fight Due over Handwriting in Hauptmann Case," *New York Times*, January 14, 1935.

58. Fisher, *Lindbergh Case*, 346.

59. Whipple, *Trial*, Testimony of John M. Trendley, 467.

60. Cahill, *Hauptmann's Ladder*, 292.

61. Jeff Nilsson, "I Tracked the Lindbergh Kidnapper," *Saturday Evening Post Weekly Newsletter*, February 23, 2013, https://www.saturdayeveningpost.com/2013/02/lindbergh-kidnapping.

62. Schrager, *Sixteenth Rail*, 155.

63. Whipple, *Trial*, Testimony of Arthur Koehler, 338.

64. Whipple, *Trial*, Testimony of Arthur Koehler, 350.

65. Whipple, *Trial*, Testimony of Arthur Koehler, 349; Whipple, *Trial*, Testimony of J. J. Dorn, 330; Whipple, *Trial*, Testimony of William M. Schulter, 331.

66. Whipple, *Trial*, Testimony of David Hirsch, 331.

67. Whipple, *Trial*, Testimony of Arthur Koehler, 346.

68. Martin Sommers, "'Wood Detective' Pins Fatal Ladder on Bruno: U.S. Expert Takes 'Fingerprints' of Hauptmann's Own Tools," *New York Daily News*, January 24, 1935; Arthur Koehler to Gov. Harold G. Hoffman, letter, 1937, *Lindbergh Kidnapping Hoax*, www.lindberghkidnappinghoax.com/koehlerletter.html.

69. Whipple, *Trial*, Testimony of Arthur Koehler, 340.

70. Whipple, *Trial*, 340–44.

71. E. A. Tamm to Director, memorandum, January 23, 1935, FBI File #7-1-5991.

72. Sommers, "'Wood Detective' Pins Fatal Ladder on Bruno."

73. Russell B. Porter, "Hauptmann Guilty, Sentenced to Death for the Murder of the Lindbergh Baby," *New York Times*, February 14, 1935.

74. Sidney B. Whipple, "Death Verdict Breaks Bruno: Spirit Is Broken, Begins 'Thawing,'" *Wisconsin State Journal* (UP), February 14, 1935.

75. C. Harold Levy, "Hoffman Puzzles Jersey," *New York Times*, March 29, 1936.

76. "Hauptmann Verdict Worried First Lady," *St. Louis Globe-Democrat* (AP), February 23, 1935.

77. Charles P. Walton, "Unyielding Evidence Put 'Guilty' Stamp on Hauptmann, Juror Says," *Daily Oklahoman* (North American Newspaper Alliance), June 23, 1935.

19. Ocklawaha and Beyond

1. J. Edgar Hoover to Mr. Tamm, memorandum, December 20, 1934.

2. R. E. Newby to Director, memorandum, January 17, 1935, FBI File #7-576-4183.

3. Karpis, *Alvin Karpis Story*, 106.

4. Hoover, *Persons in Hiding*, 54.

5. R. E. Newby to Mr. Tamm, memorandum, September 17, 1934, FBI File #62-28915-2478.

6. Kazanjian and Enss, *Ma Barker*, 120.

7. E. J. Connelley to Director, telex, January 11, 1935, FBI File #7-675-3757.

8. R. E. Newby to Director, memorandum, January 31, 1935, FBI File #7-576-4991; Burrough, *Public Enemies*, 497.

9. Newby to Director, January 31, 1935.

10. E. A. Tamm to Director, memorandum, January 12, 1935, FBI File #7-576-3775.

11. E. A. Tamm to Director, memorandum, January 8, 1935, FBI File #7-576-3765.

12. E. A. Tamm to Director, memorandum, January 14, 1935, FBI File #7-576-3967.

13. Connelley to Director, January 11, 1935.

14. Newby to Director, January 31, 1935.

15. Newby to Director, January 31, 1935.

16. "Kidnapping Suspect Identified as Leader of Jewelry Thieves," *St. Louis Post-Dispatch* (AP), January 11, 1935.

17. R. D. Brown to E. J. Connelley, memorandum, January 11, 1935; E. A. Tamm to Director, memorandum, January 11, 1935, FBI File #7-576-3754.

18. Brown to Connelley, January 11, 1935.

19. John V. Watts, "Long Trail for Gangsters Ends At Ocklawaha," *Tampa Times*, January 17, 1935.

20. The Barkers' lease of the Ocklawaha house was arranged by Bradford's business partner Joe Adams, who managed both the Kennel Club (a greyhound racetrack) and the El Commodoro Hotel in Miami, known as a political and underworld gathering place. Adams was the Miami contact man for the Barker-Karpis gang and other underworld figures. Agnes Ash, "The Cross-Eyed Irish Hound Had the Last Laugh," *Miami News*, June 19, 1966.

21. E. J. Connelley, report, February 3, 1935, FBI File #7-576-4315.

22. Connelley, report, February 3, 1935.

23. Watts, "Long Trail for Gangsters."

24. J. Edgar Hoover to Mr. Tamm, memorandum, January 16, 1935 (11:10 AM), FBI File #7-576-3820; J. Edgar Hoover to Mr. Tamm, memorandum, January 16, 1935 (11:20 AM), FBI File #7-576-3782; J. Edgar Hoover to Mr. Tamm, memorandum, January 16, 1935 (11:25 AM), FBI File #7-576-3783.

25. Hoover later refused to reimburse the Bradfords for the damage to their house from the shootout and the subsequent tearing up of floors and walls looking for ransom money. In 1937 Congress passed a bill to reimburse them $2,500 for the damage. "$2,500 for Bullet Holes," *New York Times*, August 8, 1937.

26. R. E. Newby to Director, memorandum, February 8, 1935, FBI File #7-576-5072.

27. J. C. White to E. J. Connelley, memorandum, https://vault.fbi.gov/barker-karpis-gang/bremer-kidnapping/bremer-kidnapping-part-89-of-459/view, p. 36.

28. Newby to Director, February 8, 1935.

29. R. E. Newby to Mr. Tamm, memorandum, January 31, 1935 (4:30 PM), FBI File #7-576-4281; Newby to Director, February 8, 1935; Tom Harmon, "'Ma' Barker's Last Stand: Handyman Remembers Tumultuous Morning When Gangland Queen and Son Died in Ocklawaha Gun-Battle," *Tampa Tribune*, July 28, 1963.

30. E. A. Tamm to Director, memorandum, January 16, 1935 (12:40 PM), FBI File #7-576-3772; E. A. Tamm to Director, memorandum, January 16, 1935 (12:15 PM), FBI File #7-576-3872.

31. R. A. Alt to Director, letter, January 22, 1935, FBI File #7-576-3921; Newby to Director, February 8, 1935.

32. E. A. Tamm to Director, memorandum, January 16, 1935 (12:15 PM), FBI File #7-576-3872.

33. Clyde Tolson to Director, memorandum, January 16, 1935, FBI File #5-576-3822, https://vault.fbi.gov/barker-karpis-gang/bremer-kidnapping/bremer%20kidnapping %20part&2077%20of%20459/view.

34. J. Edgar Hoover to Mr. Tamm, memorandum, January 16, 1935 (6:05 PM), FBI File #7-576-3821.

35. Maccabee, *John Dillinger Slept Here*, 106.

36. Karpis, *Alvin Karpis Story*, 82.

37. Karpis, *Alvin Karpis Story*, 91.

38. Hoover, *Persons in Hiding*, 4.

39. Hoover, *Persons in Hiding*, 4.

40. "Kate Barker Brains of Gang," *Capital Journal* (Salem OR) (UP), January 17, 1935.

41. Hoover, *Persons in Hiding*, 9, 22.

42. "The Kidnapping of Edward George Bremer, St. Paul, Minnesota," November 19, 1936, FBI File #7-576, https://vault.fbi.gov/barker-karpis-gang/bremer -investigation-summary/Barker-Karpis%20Gang%20Summary%20Part%201 %20of%201/view.

43. "More Congratulations to the Department of Justice," *New York Daily News*, January 18, 1935.

44. Karpis, *Alvin Karpis Story*, 178.

45. "Bremer Moneychanger Suspect Is Arrested," *Minneapolis Star*, September 27, 1935; "Kidnapping of Edward George Bremer," November 19, 1936.

46. "Kidnapping of Edward George Bremer," November 19, 1936.

47. Karpis, *Alvin Karpis Story*, 182–83. Joe Adams was later indicted for harboring Karpis and went to trial in June 1937. He was acquitted by directed verdict, the presiding judge ruling that the government had failed to prove that he realized it was Karpis he was putting up in the hotel, buying a car for, and helping to get away from Florida after the Ocklawaha shootout. Ash, "The Cross-Eyed Irish Hound Had the Last Laugh"; "Akerman Frees 2 Miamians of Karpis Charges," *Tampa Tribune*, June 11, 1937.

48. E. A. Tamm to Director, memorandum, January 29, 1935, FBI File #7-576-4250.

49. "Two Suspects Seized in Mail Car Robbery," *Pittsburgh Press*, November 8, 1935; "Karpis Gangster Caught in Ohio," *St. Louis Globe-Democrat*, October 2, 1941.

50. "Wed Karpis on Fight Night," *Boston Globe*, May 9, 1936.

51. E. A. Tamm to Director, memorandum, April 30, 1936, FBI File #7-576.

52. Despite Connelley's assurance, Goldstein was tried and convicted of harboring Karpis. Also convicted of harboring with her were Hot Springs' former police chief, chief of detectives, and a police lieutenant. "4 Convicted of Harboring Karpis," *Des Moines Register* (AP), October 30, 1938. Morris (Ruth Hamm Robinson) pleaded guilty to harboring Karpis. "Girl Sentenced as Aide to Public Enemy," *San Francisco Examiner* (AP), June 24, 1938.

53. Memorandum re conversation of Mr. Hoover and Mr. Tamm, April 30, 1936, FBI File #66-4760-62X.

54. Karpis, *Alvin Karpis Story*, 248.

55. "Kidnapping of Edward George Bremer," November 19, 1936.

56. Karpis, *On the Rock*, 285.

57. Memorandum re conversation of Director and Mr. Quinn, May 7, 1936, FBI File #66-4760-75.

58. John D. Rockefeller Jr. to J. Edgar Hoover, letter, June 1, 1936, quoted in Potter, *War on Crime*, 200.

59. "The G-men's Larger Job," *Leader* (Frederick OK), May 11, 1936.

60. Christopher Lydon, "J. Edgar Hoover Made the F.B.I. Formidable with Politics, Publicity and Results," *New York Times*, May 3, 1972.

61. Theoharis, FBI: *A Comprehensive Reference Guide*, 150.

Epilogue

1. Theoharis, FBI: *A Comprehensive Reference Guide*, "Number of FBI Personnel and FBI Appropriations Annually, 1908–97," 4, table 1.1.

2. Lydon, "J. Edgar Hoover Made the F.B.I. Formidable."

3. O'Malley, *Nelly Don*, 65.

4. Hamilton, *Machine Gun Kelly's Last Stand*, 178, 179.

5. Alan Pollock, "Harwich Woman Recalls Kidnapping Ordeal, 77 Years Later," *Cape Cod Chronicle*, October 28, 2010.

6. Alex Kingsbury, "Kidnapped on Old Cape Cod," *Boston Globe*, August 28, 2016.

7. Robert Cantwell, "The Shy Tycoon Who Owns 1/640th of the U.S.," *Sports Illustrated*, August 18, 1969, https://www.si.com/vault/1969/08/18/the-shy-tycoon -who-owns-1640th-of-the-us.

8. Brinkley, *Wheels for the World*, 383, 384.

9. Hamilton, *Machine Gun Kelly's Last Stand*, 153, 154.

10. Hamilton, *Machine Gun Kelly's Last Stand*, 183.

11. Ward, *Alcatraz*, 270, 271.

12. Ward, *Alcatraz*, 377.

13. Maccabee, *John Dillinger Slept Here*, 286.

14. "Murphy Deplores Alcatraz Prison," *San Francisco Examiner*, June 8, 1939.

15. "Calls Alcatraz 'Place of Horror,'" *New York Times*, June 8, 1939.

16. "Public Service," *Baltimore Evening Sun*, July 22, 1948.

17. Sid Boehm, "Faith to Lindy Sealed My Lips—Schwarzkopf," *New York Evening Journal*, February 16, 1935.

18. "Police Are Criticized by Hoffman: Lindbergh Kidnapping Case Most Bungled in Police History, Contends Governor," *Sheboygan Press*, February 29, 1936.

19. C. A. Lindbergh, *Autobiography of Values*, 26.

BIBLIOGRAPHY

Behn, Noel. *Lindbergh: The Crime.* New York: Atlantic Monthly Press, 1994.

Berg, A. Scott. *Lindbergh.* New York: G. P. Putnam's Sons, 1998.

Bergreen, Laurence. *Capone: The Man and the Era.* New York: Touchstone, 1994.

Black, Conrad. *Franklin Delano Roosevelt: Champion of Freedom.* New York: Public Affairs, 2003.

Borne, Ronald F. *Troutmouth: The Two Careers of Hugh Clegg.* Jackson: University Press of Mississippi, 2015.

Breuer, William B. *J. Edgar Hoover and His G-Men.* Westport CT: Praeger, 1995.

Brinkley, Douglas. *Wheels for the World: Henry Ford, His Company, and a Century of Progress.* New York: Viking, 2003.

Burrough, Bryan. *Public Enemies: America's Greatest Crime Wave and the Birth of the FBI, 1933–34.* New York: Penguin, 2004.

Cahill, Richard T., Jr. *Hauptmann's Ladder: A Step-by-Step Analysis of the Lindbergh Kidnapping.* Kent OH: Kent State University Press, 2014.

Chernow, Ron. *The House of Morgan: An American Banking Dynasty and the Rise of Modern Finance.* New York: Grove, 1990.

Cohen, Roger, and Claudio Gatti. *In the Eye of the Storm: The Life of General H. Norman Schwarzkopf.* New York: Farrar, Straus and Giroux, 1991.

Condon, John F. *Jafsie Tells All.* New York: Jonathan Lee, 1936.

Cooper, Courtney Ryley. *Here's to Crime.* Boston: Little, Brown, 1937.

———. *Ten Thousand Public Enemies.* Boston: Little, Brown 1935.

Cromie, Robert, and Joseph Pinkston. *Dillinger: A Short and Violent Life.* Evanston IL: Chicago Historical Bookworks, 1990.

Demaris, Ovid. *The Director: An Oral Biography of J. Edgar Hoover.* New York: Harper's Magazine Press, 1975.

Ellis, George. *A Man Named Jones*. New York: Signet Books, 1963.

Falzini, Mark W. *Their Fifteen Minutes: Biographical Sketches of the Lindbergh Case*. Bloomington IN: iUniverse, 2008.

———. *The Siege at Jutland*. Bloomington IN: iUniverse, 2014.

Falzini, Mark W., and James Davidson. *New Jersey's Lindbergh Kidnapping and Trial*. Charleston SC: Arcadia, 2012.

Farrell, Harry. *Swift Justice: Murder and Vengeance in a California Town*. New York: St. Martin's, 1992.

Fensch, Thomas, ed. *FBI Files on the Lindbergh Baby Kidnapping*. Woodlands TX: New Century Books, 2001.

Fisher, Jim. *The Ghosts of Hopewell: Setting the Record Straight in the Lindbergh Case*. Carbondale: Southern Illinois University Press, 1999.

———. *The Lindbergh Case*. New Brunswick NJ: Rutgers University Press, 1987.

Folsom, Robert G. *The Money Trail: How Elmer Irey and His T-Men Brought Down America's Criminal Elite*. Washington DC: Potomac Books, 2010.

Frates, Kent. *Oklahoma's Most Notorious Cases*. Oklahoma City: RoadRunner, 2014.

Friedman, David M. *The Immortalists: Charles Lindbergh, Dr. Alexis Carrel, and Their Daring Quest to Live Forever*. New York: HarperCollins, 2007.

Gardner, Lloyd C. *The Case That Never Dies: The Lindbergh Kidnapping*. New Brunswick NJ: Rutgers University Press, 2012.

Gentry, Curt. *J. Edgar Hoover: The Man and the Secrets*. New York: Norton, 1991.

Haines, Gerald K., and David A. Langbart. *Unlocking the Files of the FBI: A Guide to Its Records and Classification System*. Wilmington DE: Scholarly Resources, 1993.

Hamilton, Stanley. *Machine Gun Kelly's Last Stand*. Lawrence: University Press of Kansas, 2003.

Hernon, Peter, and Terry Ganey. *Under the Influence: The Unauthorized Story of the Anheuser-Busch Dynasty*. New York: Simon & Schuster, 1991.

Hoover, J. Edgar. *Persons in Hiding*. Boston: Little, Brown, 1938.

Irey, Elmer L., as told to William J. Slocum. *The Tax Dodgers: The Inside Story of the U.S. Treasury's War with America's Political and Underworld Hoodlums*. New York: Greenberg, 1948.

Jennings, Peter, and Todd Brewster. *The Century*. New York: Doubleday, 1998.

Johnston, James A. *Alcatraz Island Prison*. New York: Scribner's, 1949.

Karpis, Alvin, and Robert Livesey. *On the Rock: Twenty-five Years in Alcatraz*. Markham ON: PaperJacks, 1981.

Karpis, Alvin, with Bill Trent. *The Alvin Karpis Story*. New York: Ishi Press International, 2011.

Katz, Leonard. *Uncle Frank: The Biography of Frank Costello*. London: W. H. Allen, 1975.

Kauffman, Sanford B. *Pan Am Pioneer: A Manager's Memoir from Seaplane Clippers to Jumbo Jets*. Lubbock: Texas Tech University Press, 1996.

Kavieff, Paul R. *The Violent Years: Prohibition and the Detroit Mobs*. Fort Lee NJ: Barricade Books, 2001.

Kazanjian, Howard, and Chris Enss. *Ma Barker: America's Most Wanted Mother*. Guilford CT: Rowman & Littlefield, 2017.

Kennedy, Ludovic. *The Airman and the Carpenter: The Lindbergh Kidnapping and the Framing of Richard Hauptmann*. New York: Viking, 1985.

Kessler, Ronald. *The Bureau: The Secret History of the FBI*. New York: St. Martin's, 2002.

Kirkendall, Richard S. *A History of Missouri*. Vol. 5, *1919 to 1953*. Columbia: University of Missouri Press, 1986.

Kirkpatrick, E. E. *Crimes' Paradise: The Authentic Inside Story of the Urschel Kidnapping*. San Antonio TX: Naylor, 1934.

——. *Voices from Alcatraz*. San Antonio TX: Naylor, 1947.

Kirschten, Ernest. *Catfish and Crystal: The Story of St. Louis, U.S.A.* St. Louis: Patrice, 1989.

Larsen, Lawrence H., and Nancy J. Hulston. *Pendergast!* Columbia: University of Missouri Press, 1997.

Lindbergh, Anne Morrow. *Hour of Gold, Hour of Lead: Diaries and Letters of Anne Morrow Lindbergh, 1929–1932*. New York: Harcourt Brace Jovanovich, 1973.

——. *Locked Rooms and Open Doors: Diaries and Letters of Anne Morrow Lindbergh, 1933–1935*. New York: Harcourt Brace, 1974.

Lindbergh, Charles A. *Autobiography of Values*. New York: Harcourt Brace Jovanovich, 1976.

——. *We*. New York: G. P. Putnam's Sons, 1927.

Lowenthal, Max. *The Federal Bureau of Investigation*. New York: William Sloane, 1950.

Maccabee, Paul. *John Dillinger Slept Here: A Crooks' Tour of Crime and Corruption in St. Paul, 1920–1936*. St. Paul: Minnesota Historical Society Press, 1995.

Mahoney, Tim. *Secret Partners: Big Tom Brown and the Barker Gang*. St. Paul: Minnesota Historical Society Press, 2013.

McCullough, David. *Truman*. New York: Simon & Schuster, 1992.

McMillen, Margot Ford, and Heather Roberson. *Called to Courage: Four Women in Missouri History*. Columbia: University of Missouri Press, 2002.

Miles, Ray. *King of the Wildcatters: The Life and Times of Tom Slick, 1883–1930*. College Station: Texas A&M University Press, 1996.

Milton, Joyce. *Loss of Eden: A Biography of Charles and Anne Morrow Lindbergh*. New York: HarperCollins, 1993.

Moley, Raymond. *After Seven Years: A Political Analysis of the New Deal*. New York: Harper & Row, 1939.

Mosley, Leonard. *Lindbergh: A Biography*. Garden City NY: Doubleday, 1976.

Okrent, Daniel. *Last Call: The Rise and Fall of Prohibition*. New York: Scribner, 2010.

O'Malley, Terence Michael. *Nelly Don: A Stitch in Time*. Kansas City: Covington Group, 2006.

Pfaff, Daniel W. *Joseph Pulitzer II and the Post-Dispatch*. University Park: Pennsylvania State University Press, 1991.

Pomerantz, Gary M. *The Devil's Tickets: A Vengeful Wife, a Fatal Hand, and a New American Age*. New York: Broadway Paperbacks, 2009.

Potter, Claire Bond. *War on Crime: Bandits, G-Men, and the Politics of Mass Culture*. New Brunswick NJ: Rutgers University Press, 1998.

Powers, Richard Gid. *G-Men: Hoover's FBI in American Popular Culture*. Carbondale: Southern Illinois University Press, 1983.

―――. *Secrecy and Power: The Life of J. Edgar Hoover*. New York: Free Press, 1987.

Purvis, Alston, and Alex Tresniowski. *The Vendetta:* FBI *Hero Melvin Purvis's War against Crime, and J. Edgar Hoover's War against Him*. New York: Public Affairs, 2005.

Rappleye, Charles. *Herbert Hoover in the White House: The Ordeal of the Presidency*. New York: Simon & Schuster, 2016.

Rudensky, Red. *The Gonif*. Blue Earth MN: Piper, 1970.

Scaduto, Anthony. *Scapegoat: The Lonesome Death of Bruno Richard Hauptmann*. New York: G. P. Putnam's Sons, 1976.

Schrager, Adam J. *The Sixteenth Rail: The Evidence, the Scientist, and the Lindbergh Kidnapping*. Golden CO: Fulcrum, 2013.

Smallwood, James, ed. *Will Rogers' Daily Telegrams*. Vol. 1, *The Coolidge Years, 1926–1929*. Stillwater: Oklahoma State University Press, 1978.

Spiering, Frank. *The Man Who Got Capone*. Indianapolis: Bobbs-Merrill, 1996.

Stevens, Walter. *Centennial History of Missouri (The Center State): One Hundred Years in the Union 1820–1921, Vol. 2*. Chicago: S. J. Clarke, 1921.

St. Johns, Adela Rogers. *The Honeycomb: An Autobiography by the Author of Final Verdict and Tell No Man*. Garden City NY: Doubleday, 1969.

Sullivan, Edward Dean. *The Snatch Racket*. New York: Vanguard, 1932.

Summers, Anthony. *Official and Confidential: The Secret Life of J. Edgar Hoover*. New York: G. P. Putnam's Sons, 1993.

Theoharis, Athan G., ed. *The* FBI: *A Comprehensive Reference Guide*. New York: Checkmark Books, 2000.

Theoharis, Athan G., and John Stuart Cox. *The Boss: J. Edgar Hoover and the Great American Inquisition*. Philadelphia: Temple University Press, 1988.

Toland, John. *The Dillinger Days*. New York: Random House, 1963.

Tomlinson, Gerald. *Murdered in New Jersey*. New Brunswick NJ: Rutgers University Press, 1994.

Touhy, Roger, with Ray Brennan. *The Stolen Years*. Cleveland: Pennington, 1959.

Tuohy, John W. *When Capone's Mob Murdered Roger Touhy*. Fort Lee NJ: Barricade Books, 2001.

Turner, William W. *Hoover's F.B.I.* New York: Thunder's Mouth, 1993.

Turrou, Leon G. *Where My Shadow Falls: Two Decades of Crime Detection*. Garden City NY: Doubleday, 1949.

Ungar, Sanford J. FBI: *An Uncensored Look Behind the Walls*. Boston: Little, Brown, 1975.

Urschel, Joe. *The Year of Fear: Machine Gun Kelly and the Manhunt That Changed the Nation*. New York: Minotaur, 2015.

Vitray, Laura. *The Great Lindbergh Hullabaloo: An Unorthodox Account*. New York: William Faro, 1932.

Waller, George. *Kidnap: The Story of the Lindbergh Case*. New York: Dial, 1961.

Ward, David, with Gene Kassebaum. *Alcatraz: The Gangster Years*. Berkeley: University of California Press, 2009.

Whipple, Sidney B. *The Lindbergh Crime*. New York: Blue Ribbon Books, 1935.

―――, ed. *The Trial of Bruno Richard Hauptmann*. New York: Gryphon Editions, 1989.

Whitehead, Don. *The FBI Story*. New York: Pocket Books, 1956.

Wilson, Frank J., and Beth Day. *Special Agent: 25 Years with the American Secret Service*. London: Frederick Muller, 1966.

Winstead, Charles Batsell. *Memoir of Special Agent Charles Batsell Winstead*. Edited by David G. Edwards. Sherman TX: The Sherman Museum, n.d.

Yagoda, Ben. *Will Rogers*. New York: Knopf, 1993.

Young, John V. *Hot Type & Pony Wire: My Life As a California Reporter From Prohibition to Pearl Harbor*. Santa Cruz CA: Western Tanager, 1980.

Zorn, Robert. *Cemetery John: The Undiscovered Mastermind of the Lindbergh Kidnapping*. New York: Overlook, 2012.

INDEX